THE **BIG** BOOK OF BARBECUEING & GRILLING

HILAIRE WALDEN

THE **BIG** BOOK OF BARBECUEING & GRILLING

365

HEALTHY AND DELICIOUS RECIPES

DUNCAN BAIRD PUBLISHERS

LONDON

THE BIG BOOK OF BARBECUEING & GRILLING
Hilaire Walden

First published in the United Kingdom and Ireland
in 2006 by Duncan Baird Publishers Ltd
Sixth Floor
Castle House
75–76 Wells Street
London W1T 3QH

Conceived, created and designed by Duncan Baird Publishers Ltd

Managing Editor: Grace Cheetham
Editor: Gillian Haslam
Managing Designer: Manisha Patel
Photographic Art Direction: Sailesh Patel
Studio and Locational Photography: William Lingwood
Photography Assistant: Monica Larsen
Stylists: Tessa Evelegh and Helen Trent (props), Sunil Vijayakar and Joss Herd
(home economists)

British Library Cataloguing-in-Publication Data:
A CIP record for this book is available from the British Library

ISBN-10: 1-84483-236-8
ISBN-13: 9-781844-832361

10 9 8 7 6 5 4 3 2 1

Typeset in Monitor
Colour reproduction by Scanhouse, Malaysia
Printed in China by Imago

Publisher's Note: While every care has been taken in compiling the recipes in
this book, Duncan Baird Publishers, or any other persons who have been involved
in working on this publication, cannot accept responsibility for any errors or
omissions, inadvertent or not, that may be found in the recipes or text, nor for
any problems that may arise as a result of preparing one of these recipes.

CONTENTS

INTRODUCTION

The first sign of hot weather makes everyone long to cook over an open fire, so out comes the barbecue. There is no need, though, to restrict your barbecue to summertime use. It can also work well on sunny, still days or in a sheltered spot in spring or autumn, and the 365 recipes in this book will provide you with such a selection of recipes to try that you'll want to barbecue as much as possible.

It is so much easier to barbecue now that the available equipment has improved in both quality and range. There is now a wider choice of fuels, and there are many accessories which make barbecueing easier and extend the types of dishes that can be cooked, from simple, fine-mesh grilling baskets that prevent small pieces of food falling onto the fire, to motorised rotisseries for spit-roasts.

Another factor in barbecueing's favour is that it is not an exact branch of cooking. First, the choice of ingredients in a recipe, and their proportions if there is a combination, can be changed to suit your taste, budget or available ingredients. The same applies to flavourings such as herbs and spices. Second, the cooking times can vary according to a number of factors. What you must do, though, is ensure that meat and poultry are adequately cooked, which is why the optimum temperatures have been quoted on pages 14–15.

It is extremely easy to cook all your barbecued food the way you like it when (as with most things in life) you know how. For example, simply adjusting the height of the grill rack and/or moving the food about on the grill rack can produce far better results. There are many more useful tips for trouble-free, successful barbecues on pages 12–13.

In the following chapters, you will find recipes to suit every occasion, taste and diet. There are simple, traditional dishes, such as Steak with Roasted Garlic and Mushrooms, innovative dishes such as Monkfish, Fennel and Lemon Kebabs and dishes taken from innumerable cuisines such as Moroccan Chicken with Tabouleh. Bacon-wrapped Sausages will be a hit with children and both vegetarians and vegans will find plenty to satisfy them. If you want to make a special meal using your barbecue, you'll even find recipes using ingredients such as scallops, king prawns, lobster, entrecôte steak and guinea fowl.

HOW TO COOK ON A BARBECUE

There are two main cooking methods used in barbecueing; direct and indirect. Direct is when the food is placed directly above the heat source and is usually turned during cooking so that it cooks evenly. This method is suitable for small items that take less than 25 minutes to cook, such as steaks, burgers, chops and vegetables. Indirect is when the foods are covered by the lid of a barbecue, or by aluminium foil, so that they cook by reflected heat, as in a conventional oven. This method is suitable for large pieces of meat or poultry that require long cooking.

COOKING HEATS

Cooking can be done over a high, medium or low heat depending on the type of food.

• The fire is described as hot when the flames have given way to glowing red coals covered with a fine layer of white ash. You should be able to hold your hand 15cm (6in) above it for 2 seconds. This heat is used for cooking thin pieces of food such as fish fillets and chipolata sausages.

• When the coals are covered by a thicker layer of white ash, the fire has reached the medium heat used for most of the cooking. You should be able to hold your hand over it for 4–5 seconds.

• If you can hold your hand over the fire for longer than 5 seconds, it is too cool for cooking, but can be used for keeping cooked food warm.

TYPES OF BARBECUE

There is such a wide range of types and styles available that it is worth spending a few moments identifying your requirements: how often you will use the barbecue; where you will be barbecueing; the number of people you are likely to cook for most often; how sophisticated you want the equipment to be; and how much money you want to spend.

When it comes to deciding on a barbecue, the main points to consider are the sturdiness of the construction not only of the main part of the barbecue but also any shelves, the spacing of the bars on the grill rack, whether the grill rack has a non-stick coating, the position of any air vents, ease of carrying, if it is portable, and how easy it will be to store.

GAS BARBECUES: these are easy to use and heat up within about 10 minutes. They can be regulated, giving good control of the cooking, and do not produce ash. However, they don't burn at as high a temperature as charcoal or wood and do not generally give the food the same 'barbecued' taste, although ceramic beads and chippings which can be used on the barbecue, and modifications such as 'flavouriser' bars, can create the authentic aroma and taste. Portable gas barbecues are also available but the grill height is usually static.

HIBACHI: these cast-iron, trough-like barbecues are heavy but portable. They have short legs and can be used on the ground or on a heat-resistant surface at a comfortable working height. The distance of the cooking rack from the fire is adjustable.

DISPOSABLE BARBECUES: convenient, easy to use and cheap, these barbecues consist of an aluminium foil tray filled with charcoal and a firelighter, covered with a grill. Their limitations are their size, the fact that you cannot adjust the height of the cooking rack or move the food to a cooler part of the grill rack for slightly slower cooking, and a burning time of only about 1 hour.

BRAZIERS: these open barbecues vary in size and can have rotisseries for spit-roasting (powered by electricity, battery or hand), wind shields and hoods. They are usually free-standing with wheels or detachable legs, but make sure the legs are long enough otherwise barbecueing can become back-breaking. They should have several air vents, and the height of the grill rack should be adjustable. Braziers are ideal for single servings of food such as chicken portions, chops, steaks and vegetables.

PEDESTAL BARBECUES: also known as pillar barbecues, these have a fire bed in an open-topped 'chimney' which is filled with newspaper. Simply light the paper with a taper and it quickly ignites the fuel in the fire bed. Cooking temperature is reached in 20–25 minutes.

BARREL BARBECUES: made from cast-iron, these resemble pot-bellied stoves. They are very stable and are used at table height. They have adjustable grill racks and often a stand for a rotisserie, are easy to light (with newspaper or kindling), and can be ready to cook in just 10–15 minutes.

KETTLE BARBECUES: these reliable barbecues come in a range of sizes, from table-top models to free-standing versions up to 60cm (24in) in diameter. They have a domed metal lid that reflects the heat onto the food, cooking it quickly and evenly and allowing large pieces of meat or whole chickens to be cooked by indirect heat. The cover excludes air, thus reducing flare-ups. Smoke is contained within the barbecue, which heightens the flavour of the food. The cover can be left open for conventional barbecueing by direct heat.

HOODED BARBECUES: these are sophisticated, usually large, rectangular barbecues set on a moveable trolley, and with a hinged lid. They come with a temperature gauge, dampers to regulate the airflow, moveable grates and cooking grills. Rotisseries, warming racks and side shelves are also available. They work in the same way as a kettle barbecue.

PERMANENT BARBECUES: choose a sheltered site with easy access to the kitchen but not too near the house. Ordinary house-bricks can be used in the construction, but it is a good idea to line them with firebricks as they withstand the heat better. You will also need a metal container to hold the fuel, and a grill or grid, preferably with provision for adjusting its height, such as pegs, nails or bricks projecting from the walls. Or simply buy a pack containing everything you need from a DIY store.

FUELS

WOOD: hardwoods such as oak, ash, cherry and apple give off a pleasant aroma and burn more slowly than softwoods. These can also produce sparks and smoke. Wood fires take longer to light than charcoal and need careful attention to keep them burning steadily.

CHARCOAL: there are two main types for barbecueing:

Lumpwood charcoal: this is hard wood that has been fired in a kiln without igniting the wood but driving out all the by-products, resulting in a very light, black, combustible form of carbon. Good-quality lumpwood charcoal normally comes in larger pieces, making barbecueing easier. Instant-lighting lumpwood charcoal is impregnated with a lighting agent. It comes in bags of about 1 kg (2¼lb); you simply put one of these in the hearth and light it with a match. Once it is alight, more fuel can be added to the hearth if and when necessary to give a bigger fire.

Charcoal briquettes: these uniformly shaped lumps of fuel are made from particles of waste charcoal combined with a starch binger. Once lit, they tend to burn for longer than lumpwood charcoal. (There are also other cheaper briquettes available which are made from alternative sources of fuel, packed out with products such as sand, sawdust and anthracite and bound with a petroleum-based substance. Needless to say, they do not burn as well or for as long as charcoal briquettes. Recycled briquettes made from wood prunings are also available.)

HEAT BEADS: these generate high temperatures for long periods and can be used on open charcoal and kettle barbecues.

AROMATIC ADDITIVES: woodchips impregnated with mesquite or hickory can be scattered over hot charcoal to give a pleasant wood-smoke aroma and flavour. They can be used dry, but if soaked for 1–2 hours before use they will last longer. You can also use woody herbs (such as rosemary, thyme, sage, bay and juniper) and dried fennel stalks on the coals.

BARBECUEING EQUIPMENT

Equipment can divided into a few essentials which you will need to get you started, and extra items you can buy as the barbecueing bug takes hold.

ESSENTIAL

Long-handled tongs, large spatulas and long-pronged fork: use the fork only towards the end of cooking to test if the food is done. If the food is pierced while it is cooking, it will allow juices to escape and the food will become dry.

Long-handled basting brush: choose a natural bristle one.

Skewers: choose long, flat metal ones for meat, poultry and firm-textured fish kebabs, and for keeping spatchcocked birds and butterflied joints flat during cooking. Metal skewers should be oiled before use to prevent food sticking to them. Long and short bamboo and wooden skewers are best for quicker-cooking, smaller and more delicate items; they should be soaked in water for 30 minutes before use to prevent them burning. Wooden cocktail sticks will secure stuffed foods and hold rolled items in place.

Oven gauntlets or oven gloves

Long matches, if using a charcoal fire

USEFUL BUT NOT ESSENTIAL

Hinged baskets: these are useful for cooking a whole large fish or several small fish, or foods such as sausages, burgers and kebabs. They facilitate the turning of foods and help prevent large or more delicate items breaking up.

Fine, wire-mesh racks: these rest on the bars of the grill rack, and are ideal for cooking smaller items that might otherwise break up or fall through the bars.

Wire brush and scraper: for cleaning the grill rack.

Meat thermometer: for testing the internal temperature of large cuts of meat.

Heavy-duty foil drip tray: place under the food to catch any drips and thus prevent flare-ups.

Kebab rack

Barbecue griddle or frying pan (with holes in the base)

SITING AND LIGHTING THE BARBECUE

Here are a few essential guidelines to help you get the best from your barbecue.

- Always read the manufacturer's instructions for the barbecue and the fuel.
- Choose a place away from overhanging trees or bushes, set free-standing models up where they won't wobble and place portable barbecues on the ground or on a heatproof surface.
- Do not light a fire in high winds or where there is a strong draught.
- Start building a charcoal fire 45–60 minutes before you want to start cooking (30–35 minutes for instant lighting coal briquettes). Open all the air vents or dampers. Arrange a heap of smaller pieces of fuel in the base of the fire basket. Make a well in the centre and put a solid fire lighter in the bottom. Light the firelighter with a taper and, using larger pieces of fuel, build an igloo-shaped dome on top, enclosing the fire but leaving an airspace. Leave the fire undisturbed for 30–40 minutes. Once the flames have subsided and the coals are covered with fine white ash, rake them evenly over the base of the barbecue. The fire is ready.
- 'Chimneys' can be bought (or improvised from a large, thoroughly cleaned metal can) to hasten the initial heating. The fuel is packed inside, lit, then, when ready, the coals are tipped in an even layer into the base of the barbecue.
- To top up the fire, first place extra fuel around the outside to warm up, then move a few pieces at a time into the fire.

FOOD SAFETY

There are a few rules to which you should always adhere.

- Don't leave raw or pre-cooked food lying in the sun.
- Keep cooked food well away from raw food, and use separate equipment for preparing and handling each type.
- Always allow frozen food to thaw completely before cooking.
- Keep food cool before cooking; make use of cool boxes.
- Meat is a poor conductor of heat, so thick pieces will take a surprisingly long time to cook. Meat and poultry are cooked when the juices run clear.
- Use a meat thermometer to check the internal temperature of large pieces of meat to ensure the meat is cooked through.

COOKING SAFETY

To ensure your barbecues are safe and fun, follow these guidelines.

- Never use petrol, paraffin or white spirit on a charcoal fire. When it ignites, the fire can run back to the can and cause an explosion.
- Check the hose and regulator on a gas barbecue.
- Keep matches away from a lit fire.
- Have a water spray or bottle of water handy to douse any small flames.
- If there are more serious flames, smother them with a heat-proof lid or other cover.
- Lift a barbecue cover carefully and away from you, to avoid being burned by the steam and blinded by the smoke.
- Do not wear flowing or very loose clothes (be especially careful with sleeves).
- Wear long barbecue gloves and use long-handled barbecue tools, such as tongs and spatulas, for turning and moving foods (use separate tools for moving coals), and basting brush.
- Never leave a barbecue unattended, and keep children and pets away from the fire.
- When the cooking is complete, push the coals away from the centre to speed the cooling. Charcoal takes a long time to go out; embers that look grey may still be hot.
- Do not move or pack up a charcoal barbecue until the fire is out and the coals are cold.
- Clean the grill rack thoroughly with a stiff wire brush and scraper before putting it away.

HINTS AND TIPS

Before starting to cook always:

- Make sure you have enough fuel for the amount of food you want to cook.
- Have everything you will need.
- Heat the fire in plenty of time according to the fuel being used.
- Position the grill rack about 5cm (2in) above the heat.
- Brush the grill rack or basket with oil and put it over the fire to heat for a few minutes.
- Soak wooden skewers in water for 20–30 minutes (use them for foods that need shorter cooking times). Oil metal skewers (long, flat ones are best for meat, fish and poultry and kebabs that require longer cooking).
- When making kebabs, use foods the take the same amount of time to cook and cut them to the same size so they will cook evenly. Do not pack meat and poultry too tightly onto skewers otherwise they will not cook through properly.
- If food has been left in the fridge to marinate, move it to room temperature about 30–45 minutes before cooking.
- Brush surplus marinade from foods before cooking them (to keep food moist, brush with left-over marinade during cooking).

During cooking:

- Don't put too much food on the grill rack at a time as the food will steam and have a soft surface rather than a crisp, caramelised, tasty one.
- Leave the food to cook for at least 1 minute when you first place it on the barbecue. Don't try to turn or move it until it can be moved easily.

- Place longer-cooking food on the grill rack first, then add quicker-cooking items.
- Sear meat, poultry and thicker pieces of fish over the hottest part of the fire, then move them to a cooler part, or raise the grill rack, to finish cooking.
- The heat from the fire crisps the surface of the food quickly, but the food itself cooks more slowly and steadily. Meat, poultry and fish in particular will cook better on a relatively cool fire that is glowing gently, usually referred to as medium-hot.
- If fat, oil or marinade drips onto the hot fire and flare-ups occur, remove the food, then either sprinkle the flames with water or wait until they die down before continuing.
- Cook thicker pieces of food towards the edge of the fire because this allows plenty of time for the heat to penetrate to the centre before the outside becomes tough.
- If food seems to be cooking too quickly, raise the rack, or move the food to the edge of the grill rack. If the food is cooking too slowly, lower the grill rack, or move the food towards the centre.
- To cool a fire that's too hot, push the hot coals apart. Conversely, to increase the heat, heap the coals together.
- Keep an eye on the cooking and check frequently for doneness. Start checking before the food is due to be ready because once it has become dry and tough it's beyond repair.
- Metal skewers will retain heat for quite a while after being removed from the grill rack, so be sure to warn diners about this.
- Be careful about brushing nearly cooked food with marinade containing raw juices, especially a marinade which has been used for chicken or pork.

COOKING TIMES

These cooking times and those given in the recipes are only a guide: the time depends on the thickness of the food, the temperature of the food and the surroundings; the type of barbecue used, the choice of fuel, the intensity of the heat, the height of the grill rack from the heat source, and whether there are any draughts.

Joints of meat can be tested to see if they are done to your satisfaction by inserting a special meat thermometer into the thickest part of the meat. Meat to be sliced for serving should be removed from the grill rack to a ridged meat plate or a board, covered with foil and left to rest for 5–10 minutes before being carved or cut up.

These timings and those given in the recipes are for foods that are at room temperature before being cooked, then cooked over medium-hot coals using the direct method (see page 8), unless otherwise stated.

POULTRY

Cook chicken and duck breasts with skin on the skin side first until it is crisp, then turn them over to complete the cooking. To check if chicken is cooked through, pierce the thickest part, next to the bone if appropriate, with a skewer or the point of a sharp knife. If the juices run clear, the chicken is ready. If the juices are at all pink, it needs more cooking. The internal temperature should read 82°C/180°F on a meat thermometer.

Breasts on the bone: 275–300g (10–11oz): 25 minutes, turning regularly
Boneless breasts with skin: 7 minutes on skin side, 5 minutes on the other side
Drumsticks/thighs with bone: 225g (8oz): 15–20 minutes, turning regularly
Boneless thigh: 175g (6oz): 4–5 minutes each side
Large wings: 15–20 minutes, turning regularly
Kebabs: 5 minutes each side
Quarters: 250g (9oz): 25–30 minutes, turning regularly
Halves: 700g (1½lb): 35–40 minutes, turning regularly
Poussins, spatchcocked: 25 minutes
Whole chicken: 1.5kg (3lb) cooked over indirect heat: 15 minutes per 450g (1lb) plus 15 minutes
Duck breasts: 5 minutes skin side down, then 8–10 minutes on the other side

PORK

These timings produce pork that is well-done but still juicy. The internal temperature should be 75°C/170°F.

Boneless steaks: 2–2.5cm (¾–1in) thick: 7–8 minutes each side
Chump or loin chops: 2.5cm (1in) thick: 8–10 minutes each side
Kebabs: 12–15 minutes, turning once
Fillets/tenderloin: 450g (1lb): 25 minutes, turning once
Larger joints: cooked over indirect heat: 25–30 minutes per 450g (1lb) plus 25 minutes or to the required temperature

BEEF

Rump or sirloin steaks: 2.5–4cm (1–1½in): rare: 3–4 minutes each side; medium: 5–6 minutes each side; well-done: 7 minutes each side

Fillet steaks: 4–5cm (1½–2in): rare: 3 minutes each side; medium: 4 minutes each side; well-done: 6 minutes each side

Kebabs: 8–10 minutes, turning regularly

Joints: cooked over indirect heat: 18–20 minutes per 450g (1lb) plus 1 hour

Burgers: 2.5cm (1in) thick: rare: 3 minutes each side; medium: 4 minutes each side; well-done: 5 minutes each side

LAMB

These timings are for medium-rare lamb. Decrease the timings slightly for really pink and increase slightly for well-done.

Loin chops with bone: 2.5cm (1in) thick: 6–7 minutes each side

Boneless loin chops: 3 minutes each side

Fillets: 175g (6oz): 4–5 minutes each side

Leg steaks : 4cm (1½in) thick: 5–7 minutes each side

Kebabs: 8–10 minutes, turning regularly

Joints: cooked over indirect heat: 20 minutes per 450g (1lb)

FISH AND SEAFOOD

As a general rule, allow 8–10 minutes for each 2.5cm (1in) thickness (and half the time for half the thickness). Fish is generally considered to be cooked when the flesh in the centre is just changing from translucent to opaque, although there are some exceptions: salmon is often served less well-done, while tuna may be fairly rare.

Steaks: 200–225g (7–8oz), 2.5cm (1in) thick: 4–5 minutes each side

Fillets: 3–4 minutes each side, depending on thickness

Kebabs: 3–4 minutes each side

Whole fish: 275–300g (10–12oz): 6–7 minutes each side; 1.5kg (3lb): 12–15 minutes each side

Large raw prawns: 2–3 minutes each side

Scallops, shucked: 2–3 minutes each side

STARTERS AND SNACKS

In this chapter you will find a huge range of enticing snacks and mouthwatering starters to keep both cooks and guests happy while you are pouring the drinks and waiting for the main course dishes to be cooked.

If you prefer not to eat a heavy meal, though, there is a wonderful choice of recipes here for lighter snacks. Dip into Chicken, Papaya and Rice Noodle Salad, for example, or Scallops with Thai Dipping Sauce. You might even like to make a meal out of a selection chosen from this chapter. Combine Red Pepper, Feta and Olive Wraps with Chicken Bruschettas with Prosciutto and Figs, and Butterflied Prawns with Italian Dip. There are also tempting dishes for children, such as Skewered Potato Crisp Scrolls and Sausage and Cheese Grills.

The recipes are all very quick and simple to cook and many can even be prepared in advance, leaving you to enjoy a lazy afternoon in the sunshine.

001 BUTTERFLIED PRAWNS WITH ITALIAN DIP

PREPARATION TIME *10 minutes, plus 30-60 minutes marinating* **COOKING TIME** *4-6 minutes* **SERVES 3-4**

450g (1lb) raw unpeeled king prawns	5 tbsp extra-virgin olive oil	1 tbsp chopped fresh basil
½ garlic clove, finely chopped	2 tbsp sun-dried tomato paste	sea salt and freshly ground black pepper
juice of 1 lemon	pinch of paprika	basil sprigs, to garnish

1 Remove the heads and fine legs from the prawns. Using sharp scissors, cut the prawns lengthways almost in half, leaving the tail end intact. Lay them in a shallow dish, sprinkle over the garlic and pour over half the lemon juice and 2 tablespoons of the oil. Stir to ensure the prawns are evenly coated. Cover and leave in a cool place for 30-60 minutes.
2 Meanwhile, to make the dip, stir together the remaining lemon juice, oil, tomato paste, paprika and basil in a small bowl. Add a little seasoning.
3 Lift the prawns from the dish. Thread onto skewers for easier turning, if liked. Cook on an oiled grill rack for 2-3 minutes on each side until the prawns turn pink.
4 Remove the prawns from the grill rack, sprinkle with sea salt and black pepper. Either pour the dip over or serve it separately. Garnish the prawns with the basil sprigs.

002 POTATO SKINS WITH CHIVE DIP

PREPARATION TIME *10 minutes* **COOKING TIME** *1½ hours* **SERVES 2-4**

2 large baking potatoes, scrubbed and dried	CHIVE DIP	about 1½ tbsp snipped fresh chives
olive oil, for brushing	2 tbsp Greek yogurt	salt and freshly ground black pepper
sea salt	115g (4oz) cottage cheese, sieved	

1 Preheat the oven to 200ºC/400ºF/Gas 6. Pass a metal skewer through each potato and bake for 1¼ hours, until the potatoes are tender but the skins are still soft..
2 Meanwhile, make the dip by stirring the yogurt into the sieved cottage cheese. Add the chives and seasoning, to taste. Cover and chill until required.
3 Remove the potatoes from the oven, leave until cool enough to handle, then cut each one into quarters lengthways. Using a teaspoon, scoop out most of the flesh, leaving a thin layer next to the skin. (Use the removed flesh in another recipe.)
4 Brush the potatoes with olive oil and sprinkle the skins with sea salt. Cook on an oiled grill rack for 4-6 minutes on each side until golden. Season with black pepper and serve with the dip.

003 CROQUE M'SIEUR

PREPARATION TIME *10 minutes* **COOKING TIME** *4-6 minutes* **MAKES** *6 rounds/12 sandwiches*

12 slices firm bread	wholegrain mustard, for spreading	115g (4oz) Gruyère cheese, grated
unsalted butter, softened, for spreading	6 thin slices good-quality ham	

1 Spread one side of six of the slices of bread with butter, then with mustard. Top with a slice of ham, then some cheese. Cover with the remaining bread and press together.
2 Cook on the oiled grill rack for 2-3 minutes on each side until the bread is browned and the cheese is melting. Press down on the sandwiches with a sturdy spatula during cooking.
3 Remove the crusts and cut the sandwiches into halves. Serve warm.

004 SPINACH-FILLED TOMATOES WITH ROQUEFORT TOPPING

PREPARATION TIME *10 minutes* **COOKING TIME** *15 minutes* **SERVES 4**

4 large plum tomatoes, halved lengthways	1 garlic clove, finely chopped	salt and freshly ground black pepper
2 tsp olive oil	175g (6oz) frozen spinach, thawed and squeezed dry	50-75g (2-3oz) Roquefort cheese, sliced
1 shallot, finely chopped		

1 Carefully scoop the pulp from the tomatoes. Sprinkle the inside of the shells with salt, turn them upside down and leave to drain. Chop the tomato flesh.

2 Heat the oil in a small frying pan, add the shallot and garlic and fry until softened, stirring occasionally. Add the chopped tomato flesh and heat, stirring, until the moisture has evaporated. Stir in the spinach, season and heat through.

3 Stand the tomatoes on a plate, cut-side up. Pack the spinach mixture into the tomato cups and top with a slice of cheese. Season with black pepper.

4 Cook the tomatoes on an oiled grill rack for about 4–6 minutes until the tomatoes are lightly charred and slightly softened. Do not allow them to become too soft otherwise they will be difficult to transfer to a serving plate.

005 COURGETTE TUBES WITH RICOTTA AND SUN-DRIED TOMATOES

PREPARATION TIME *10 minutes* **COOKING TIME** *15 minutes* **SERVES 2-4**

3 large courgettes, 175g (6oz) each, ends trimmed	2 shallots, finely chopped	2 sun-dried tomatoes in oil, drained and chopped
1 tbsp groundnut oil, plus extra for brushing	115g (4oz) ricotta cheese	salt and freshly ground black pepper
1 plump garlic clove, finely chopped	3 tbsp freshly grated Parmesan cheese	
	2 tbsp fresh breadcrumbs	
	½ tbsp snipped fresh chives	
	½ tbsp chopped fresh basil	

1 Cut each courgette crossways into halves. Using an apple corer, carefully remove the centre from each courgette, but keep the courgettes intact. Chop the removed flesh.

2 Heat the oil in a frying pan, add the courgette flesh, garlic and shallots. Cook slowly until the shallots are tender, stirring occasionally. Remove the pan from the heat and stir in the cheeses, breadcrumbs, herbs, sun-dried tomatoes and seasoning.

3 Stand the courgette tubes on end and pack in the filling. Brush the outsides with oil and cook towards the side of an oiled grill rack for 6–8 minutes until softened and lightly charred, turning frequently. Do not allow them to become too soft.

006 GRILLED PIZZA WITH RED PEPPERS, AUBERGINE AND CHORIZO

PREPARATION TIME *20 minutes, plus rising time* **COOKING TIME** *20–30 minutes* **SERVES 4**

350g (12oz) strong
   white flour
2 tsp easy blend
   dried yeast
1 tsp salt
freshly ground black
   pepper
200ml (7fl oz) warm water
2 tbsp olive oil, plus
   extra for brushing

TOMATO SAUCE
2 tbsp olive oil

1 small onion, finely
   chopped
2 garlic cloves, finely
   chopped
1 tsp dried oregano
600g (21oz) can Italian
   chopped tomatoes
about 2 tsp sun-dried
   tomato paste, or to taste
1½–2 tbsp chopped fresh
   herbs such as parsley,
   thyme, oregano,
   tarragon, rosemary

TOPPING
2 large red peppers,
   halved lengthways
1 aubergine, sliced
   into rings
olive oil, for brushing
175g (6oz) piece
   chorizo, chopped
75g (3oz) feta cheese,
   crumbled
75g (3oz) mozzarella
   cheese, grated
small handful of fresh
   basil leaves, torn

1 Stir the flour, yeast, salt and pepper together in a bowl. Make a well in the centre, pour in the water and oil, bringing the flour mixture into the liquids to make a soft dough. Knead on a floured surface for 10–12 minutes until firm and elastic.

2 Turn the dough over in an oiled bowl, cover and leave to rise until doubled in volume.

3 Meanwhile, make the sauce by heating the oil, adding the onion and garlic and frying until softened and translucent. Add the dried oregano. Stir in the tomatoes and simmer until thickened. Add sun-dried tomato paste, fresh herbs and seasoning to taste. Leave to cool.

4 Meanwhile, cook the red peppers on an oiled grill rack, or under a preheated broiler, until charred and blistered. Leave until cool enough to handle, then remove the skins. Slice the peppers. Brush the aubergine slices with oil and cook until tender and lightly charred.

5 Knock the dough back and divide it in half. Roll each piece to an even 25cm (10in) circle. Brush one surface of each pizza with olive oil. Transfer to two flat baking sheets.

6 Carefully slide the pizzas, oil side down, onto an oiled grill rack. Cook for 2–3 minutes until the underside is marked with lines. Transfer the pizzas, cooked side uppermost, back to the baking sheets. Brush the tops of the pizzas with oil. Spread over the tomato sauce, leaving a 1cm (½in) border. Arrange the red pepper and aubergine slices over the top, then scatter with the chorizo and cheeses. Season with plenty of black pepper. Scatter over the basil. Brush the tops of the pizzas again with oil.

7 Slide the pizzas onto the oiled grill rack and cook for a further 3–4 minutes until browned underneath, cooked through and the cheese has melted.

007 CHEESE AND CHIVE BAGUETTES

PREPARATION TIME *10 minutes* **COOKING TIME** *8 minutes* **SERVES 4**

75g (3oz) unsalted butter,
   softened
2 plump garlic cloves,
   crushed

225g (8oz) mature Cheddar
   cheese, finely grated
2½ tbsp snipped fresh
   chives

freshly ground black
   pepper
4 baguette rolls
   (half baguettes)

1 Beat the butter until smooth, then mix in the garlic, cheese, chives and black pepper.

2 Cut the rolls in half lengthways and spread the cut sides with the flavoured butter.

3 Wrap each roll in heavy-duty foil, twisting the edges together tightly. Place on the grill rack for about 8 minutes until the butter has melted and the bread is warm. Serve at once.

008 PRAWN PINWHEELS

PREPARATION TIME *10 minutes, plus 2 hours marinating* **COOKING TIME** *5–6 minutes* **SERVES 6**

24 raw tiger prawns
2 tsp cumin seeds
1 tbsp chilli flakes
1 star anise

1 tbsp fenugreek seeds
3 tbsp groundnut oil
4 shallots, chopped
4 garlic cloves, chopped

2 pinches ground turmeric
sea salt and freshly ground
    black pepper
lemon wedges, to serve

1 Remove the heads from the prawns and peel the bodies, leaving the tails in place. Put in a shallow non-metallic dish.

2 Dry-fry the cumin seeds, chilli flakes and star anise for 1 minute, stirring. Grind finely in a spice grinder, or crush using the end of a rolling pin in a small bowl. Set aside.

3 Fry the fenugreek seeds in 1 tablespoon of the oil until they start to crackle. Add to the spices.

4 Put the shallots, garlic, turmeric and remaining oil into a blender and add the spice mixture, salt and plenty of black pepper. Mix to a coarse paste. Spread evenly over the prawns. Cover and leave in a cool place for 2 hours.

5 Curl each prawn in a tight spiral, then thread onto an oiled skewer, inserting it at the base of the tail end. Cook on an oiled grill rack for 3–4 minutes, turning once, until pink. Squeeze the lemon over the prawns and serve. (If you wish, the lemon wedges can be lightly charred on the barbecue.)

009 HONEY AND HOISIN RIBLETS
PREPARATION TIME *5 minutes, plus 2 hours marinating* **COOKING TIME** *50–55 minutes* **SERVES 6**

1.5–2kg (3½–4½lb) separated pork spare ribs
2 tbsp mild honey
150ml (5fl oz) hoisin sauce

150ml (5fl oz) apple juice
4 tbsp cider vinegar
3 tbsp good-quality tomato ketchup *(see page 184)*

1 tsp English mustard

1   Line a roasting tin with heavy-duty foil. Put the ribs in the tin.
2   Combine the remaining ingredients and spoon evenly over the ribs; don't worry if there seems to be inadequate liquid as the ribs will yield fat during cooking. Cover the tin with clingfilm and leave in a cool place for 2 hours, if possible.
3   Preheat the oven to 200ºC/400ºF/Gas 6. Part-cook the ribs, uncovered, in the oven for 30–35 minutes, turning them over occasionally.
4   Remove from the oven, brush the ribs with the cooking juices and transfer to an oiled grill rack. Cook for 20–25 minutes, turning and brushing occasionally with the cooking juices, until cooked through and dark golden brown.

010 SKEWERED POTATO CRISP SCROLLS
PREPARATION TIME *10 minutes* **COOKING TIME** *10–15 minutes* **SERVES 4-6**

2 baking potatoes, each 225g (8oz), peeled

olive oil, for brushing
freshly ground black pepper

sea salt and paprika, for sprinkling

1   Using a food processor, grater or mandolin, cut the potatoes into wafer-thin slices lengthways. Put immediately into a bowl of salted hot water. Stir to separate the slices, then leave for 3-4 minutes until pliable.
2   Drain and dry the slices thoroughly, then carefully roll up each slice, from the narrowest end. Thread onto oiled long skewers, leaving at least 1cm (½in) between each scroll.
3   Brush the scrolls with oil, sprinkle with black pepper and cook on an oiled grill rack for 10-15 minutes until crisp, turning occasionally.
4   Remove from the grill rack and sprinkle with salt and paprika.

011 ITALIAN BLT
PREPARATION TIME *5 minutes* **COOKING TIME** *8 minutes* **SERVES 4**

1 plump garlic clove, halved lengthways
1 large focaccia loaf, split in half lengthways

virgin olive oil, for brushing
8 slices of pancetta, or very thinly sliced bacon
4 tomatoes, halved lengthways

175g (6½oz) ricotta cheese
fresh basil leaves, to garnish

1   Rub the cut surface of the garlic over the cut surfaces of the focaccia and brush lightly with olive oil. Lightly toast the focaccia on an oiled grill rack.
2   At the same time, cook the pancetta on the grill rack until crisp, and cook the tomatoes towards the side of the grill rack for about 4 minutes on each side until lightly charred and beginning to soften. Remove with a fish slice or spatula.
3   Transfer the focaccia to plates. Top with the pancetta, spread over the ricotta, then add the tomatoes. Scatter over the basil, put on the lids and press lightly together.

012 TANDOORI PRAWN ROLLS

PREPARATION TIME *10 minutes, plus 30–60 minutes marinating* **COOKING TIME** *4–5 minutes* **SERVES 4**

225g (8oz) headless raw tiger prawns, peeled

4 pain rustique rolls or other good-quality rolls or baps

butter, for spreading

Little Gem lettuce leaves

¼ red onion, rinsed and thinly sliced

lemon wedges and fresh coriander, to serve

MARINADE

1 tbsp lemon juice

1 tbsp Greek yogurt

1 small garlic clove, finely chopped

½ tsp grated fresh root ginger

large pinch of paprika

pinch of ground cumin

pinch of garam masala

1½ tsp groundnut oil

1   Make the marinade by mixing all the ingredients together in a non-metallic bowl. Stir in the prawns, ensuring they are evenly coated. Cover and leave in a cool place for 30–60 minutes.

2   Lift the prawns from the marinade and cook on an oiled grill for 2–2½ minutes on each side until they have turned pink.

3   Meanwhile, split the rolls and warm them on the side of the grill rack.

4   Remove the prawns from the grill rack. Squeeze some lemon juice over them.

5   Butter the warm rolls liberally, cover the bottom halves with lettuce leaves, sprinkle over the red onion, top with the prawns, sprinkle over coriander, then cover with the tops. Squeeze together and serve immediately.

013 GRILLED CHEESE, HERB AND TOMATO SANDWICHES

PREPARATION TIME *5 minutes* **COOKING TIME** *4–6 minutes* **MAKES** *4 rounds/8 sandwiches*

8 slices bread

4 slices fontina, taleggio, Gruyère or mature Cheddar cheese, or use them grated

3–4 tomatoes, sliced

olive oil or melted unsalted butter, for brushing

HERB SPREAD

40g (1½oz) wild rocket

15g (½oz) fresh flat-leaf parsley leaves

15g (½oz) fresh basil leaves

½ tsp capers

½ tsp wholegrain mustard

½ tbsp olive oil

salt and freshly ground black pepper

1   Make the herb spread by putting the rocket, parsley and basil in a food processor or blender, pulse 6–7 times until coarsely chopped, then add the remaining ingredients and mix for about 30 seconds to make a coarse paste.

2   Spread one side of each slice of bread with a little of the rocket and herb spread. Lay four slices on the work surface and divide the cheese among them. Top with the tomato slices, then press the other bread slices on top. Brush the outer surfaces of the bread with oil or melted butter.

3   Cook on an oiled grill rack for about 2–3 minutes on each side until browned and the cheese is melting. Press down on the sandwiches with a sturdy spatula during cooking to help them stick together. Remove the crusts and cut the sandwiches into halves. Serve warm.

014 AUBERGINE AND MOZZARELLA ROLLS

PREPARATION TIME *15 minutes, plus 30–60 minutes draining* **COOKING TIME** *6–8 minutes* **SERVES 4–6**

2 aubergines
salt and freshly ground
   black pepper
1 tbsp extra virgin olive oil,
   plus extra for brushing
115g (4oz) Pesto *(see
   page 172)*

12 oil-cured black olives,
   pitted and cut into
   slivers
6 sun-dried tomatoes in oil,
   drained and sliced
3 tbsp shredded fresh basil

150g (5oz) buffalo
   mozzarella, diced
15g (½oz) Parmesan,
   freshly grated

1. Cut each aubergine into six lengthwise slices, 5mm (¼in) thick. Sprinkle salt over the slices and leave to drain for 30–60 minutes. Rinse off the salt and dry the slices thoroughly.
2. Brush the slices with extra virgin olive oil and cook on an oiled grill rack for 2–3 minutes on each side until lightly charred and softened, turning once. Remove from the grill.
3. Using half of the pesto, spread a little over each aubergine slice. Scatter with olives, sun-dried tomatoes, basil and mozzarella. Sprinkle with black pepper.
4. Roll up the aubergines, starting at a short end. Secure with soaked wooden cocktail sticks (see page 10). Sprinkle over the Parmesan and return to the oiled grill rack for about 2 minutes on each side until warmed through and lightly golden.
5. Meanwhile, mix the tablespoon of extra virgin olive oil with the remaining pesto. Transfer the aubergines rolls to plates, spoon over the pesto dressing and serve immediately.

015 MIXED SATAY

PREPARATION TIME *15 minutes, plus 1–8 hours marinating* **COOKING TIME** *20–25 minutes* **SERVES 4**

675g (1½lb) mixed meats and chicken, cut into 2.5cm (1in) wide strips	2 tsp ground coriander	SATAY SAUCE
	2 tsp cumin	75g (3oz) unsalted peanuts
	1 tsp turmeric	1 garlic clove, chopped
	1 tbsp soft dark brown sugar	2 tbsp red Thai curry paste
12 raw large prawns, peeled but with tails left on	4 tbsp coconut milk	400ml (14fl oz) coconut milk
	lemon or lime wedges, to serve	2 tbsp soft dark brown sugar
squeeze of lemon juice		squeeze of lemon juice
1 garlic clove, crushed and chopped		dash of Tabasco sauce

1 Put the meat, chicken and prawns into a shallow, non-metallic dish. Sprinkle with lemon juice.
2 Combine the garlic with the spices, sugar and coconut milk to make a fairly stiff paste. Rub evenly into the meat. Cover and leave in a cool place for at least 1 hour, preferably 8 hours.
3 Meanwhile, make the sauce by toasting the peanuts under a preheated grill, stirring frequently to ensure they brown evenly. Transfer to a blender or food processor. Add the garlic, curry paste and a little of the milk. Mix until smooth, then add the remaining ingredients and mix until evenly blended. Pour into a saucepan. Boil for 2 minutes, then lower the heat and simmer for 10 minutes, stirring occasionally. If the sauce thickens too much, add a little water.
4 Thread the meat, poultry and prawns onto separate skewers. Cook on an oiled grill rack for 5–10 minutes; beef and lamb should still be slightly pink inside, but pork and chicken should be cooked through. Cook prawns for 3 minutes on each side until they just turn pink.
5 Warm the sauce on the side of the grill rack, thinning if necessary with a little water, then pour into a warm serving bowl.
6 Serve the satays with lemon or lime wedges and the sauce.

016 CHICKEN YAKITORI

PREPARATION TIME *10 minutes* **COOKING TIME** *13–15 minutes* **SERVES 6**

6 boneless chicken thighs, cut into 2.5 cm (1in) pieces	YAKITORI SAUCE	1 small garlic clove, finely chopped
	175m (6fl oz) dark soy sauce	1½ tbsp caster sugar
12 baby leeks, outer leaves removed, cut into 2.5 cm (1in) lengths, or 12 fat spring onions, green parts trimmed	90ml (3¼fl oz) sake	freshly ground black pepper
	90ml (3¼fl oz) chicken stock	
	50ml (2fl oz) mirin	

1 Make the sauce by heating the ingredients in a saucepan, stirring until the sugar has dissolved. Bring to the boil, then simmer for 1 minute. Remove from the heat, leave to cool and then strain.
2 Thread the chicken, skin-side out, and the leeks or spring onions alternately onto skewers.
3 Pour about one quarter of the sauce into a small bowl to serve as a dipping sauce.
4 Cook the skewers on an oiled grill rack for 2 minutes, brush with the remaining sauce and continue cooking for 6–8 minutes, basting with the sauce frequently and turning once.
5 Serve the skewers with the dipping sauce.

017 CHICKEN, PAPAYA AND RICE NOODLE SALAD

PREPARATION TIME *15 minutes, plus 1 hour marinating* **COOKING TIME** *4–5 minutes* **SERVES 4**

225g (8oz) skinless chicken breasts, cut into strips
100g (3½oz) rice vermicelli noodles
1 small courgette, cut into thin strips
2½ tbsp fresh coriander leaves, coarsely torn

1 small papaya, peeled, seeded and cut into wedges

MARINADE
1 garlic clove, crushed
1 tbsp Thai fish sauce
1 tsp Thai red curry paste
1 tsp sesame oil
1 tsp clear honey

DRESSING
3 tbsp groundnut oil
3 tbsp lime juice
1½ tbsp Thai fish sauce
few drops of Tabasco sauce
2–3 tsp caster sugar

1   Put the chicken strips in a non-metallic bowl. Make the marinade by combining the ingredients. Stir into the chicken, cover and leave in a cool place for 1 hour, stirring occasionally.
2   Meanwhile, pour boiling water over the noodles and leave to soak for 4–5 minutes or according to packet instructions. Drain, dry well and tip into a large bowl. Add the courgette and coriander.
3   Make the dressing by combining the ingredients. Pour half over the noodles, toss and then chill.
4   Lift the chicken from the marinade and cook on an oiled fine wire mesh, if possible, on the grill rack for about 2 minutes on each side.
5   Cook the papaya wedges on the side of the grill rack for 5 minutes. Remove from the rack and cut into bite-sized pieces.
6   Divide the noodles among four bowls. Mix the chicken and papaya together, pile on top of the noodles and trickle over the remaining dressing.

018 LIME AND HONEY-GLAZED CHICKEN WINGS

PREPARATION TIME *5 minutes, plus 4–8 hours marinating* **COOKING TIME** *20–25 minutes* **SERVES 4**

12 large chicken wings
lime wedges, to serve

MARINADE
2 tbsp olive oil
3 tbsp honey
6 tbsp lime juice
2 tbsp dry white wine

2 tsp chopped fresh marjoram
1 tsp fresh thyme leaves
freshly ground black pepper

1   Place the chicken wings in a shallow non-metallic dish.
2   Make the marinade by mixing all the ingredients together. Pour evenly over the wings, turn them over to ensure they are evenly coated, then cover and leave to marinate in a cool place for 4–8 hours, turning occasionally.
3   To make it easier to turn the chicken wings on the grill rack, cut off the tips of the wings, then thread three wings onto two parallel skewers. Repeat with the remaining wings.
4   Transfer the wings to an oiled grill rack (reserve the marinade) and cook for 20–25 minutes, turning and brushing with the reserved marinade. Serve the wings with lime wedges.

019 VEGETABLE AND PARMA HAM BRUSCHETTAS

PREPARATION TIME *15 minutes* **COOKING TIME** *10–15 minutes* **SERVES 6**

2 chicory heads, quartered	3 plump garlic cloves,	MARINADE
1 red pepper, cut into	halved lengthways	3 tbsp virgin olive oil
6 pieces	6 slices country-style bread	1 plump garlic clove,
6 bottled or canned	6 slices Parma ham, or	crushed
artichokes, halved	coppa*	1 tbsp soy sauce
lengthways	chopped fresh coriander,	1½ tsp harissa
6 mini leeks	to serve	1½ tsp dried marjoram

1   Put all the vegetables, except the garlic, in a large dish.
2   Make the marinade by combining the ingredients. Stir into the vegetables. Lift the vegetables from the marinade (reserve the marinade), and thread onto skewers. Cook on an oiled grill rack for 10–15 minutes until flecked with brown and tender, turning and brushing with the reserved marinade occasionally. When they are cooked, transfer them to a bowl and cover with clingfilm.
3   Meanwhile, spear the garlic halves onto soaked wooden cocktail sticks (see page 10) and cook on the rack, until tender.
4   Toast the bread on the side of the rack, then squash a garlic half over each slice of toast. Lay the ham, or coppa, on top. Top with a mixture of vegetables, sliding them off the skewers. Sprinkle over the chopped coriander.
*   If preferred, instead of or as well as the ham or coppa, the bruschetta slices can be spread with soft goats' cheese or ricotta cheese.

020 PRAWNS WITH LEMON GRASS AND PAPAYA SALSA

PREPARATION TIME *15 minutes, plus 1 hour marinating* **COOKING TIME** *4–6 minutes* **SERVES 4–6**

4 lemon grass stems,	1 red chilli, seeded and	handful of fresh coriander
peeled and finely	chopped	leaves, finely chopped
chopped	28 raw tiger prawns, peeled	salt and freshly ground
1 plump garlic clove,	but tails left on	black pepper
chopped	1 papaya, peeled and	lime wedges, to serve
5 tbsp virgin olive oil	halved	
1½ limes	4 spring onions, chopped	

1   Combine the lemon grass, garlic, 2 tablespoons of the oil, the juice of 1 lime and two-thirds of the chilli in a bowl. Stir in the prawns, cover and leave in a cool place for 1 hour.
2   Meanwhile, scoop the seeds from the papaya and dice the flesh. Mix with the juice of the remaining half lime, the remaining chilli, spring onions, coriander and seasoning.
3   Lift the prawns from the marinade and cook on an oiled grill rack for 2–3 minutes on each side until they turn pink. Serve with the salsa and lime wedges.

021 VEGETABLE WRAPS

PREPARATION TIME *10 minutes* **COOKING TIME** *12-16 minutes* **MAKES 4**

4 slim asparagus spears	1 small aubergine, cut	2 tbsp chopped fresh herbs
8 brown mushrooms	lengthwise into 1cm	such as flat-leaf parsley,
2 courgettes, cut	(½in) slices	coriander, basil
diagonally into 1cm	8 spring onions	4 tbsp Rouille *(see*
(½in) slices	olive oil, for brushing	*page 183)*
3 mini bok choi	4 pitta breads	salt and freshly ground
		black pepper

1 Trim the asparagus spears, then blanch in boiling water for 2 minutes. Rinse under running cold water, drain and dry well.
2 Brush the vegetables with oil and cook on an oiled grill rack. Cook the mushrooms for 6–10 minutes (depending on their size), the courgettes for 6–8 minutes on each side, the bok choi for 4 minutes on each side, the aubergines for 5 minutes and the spring onions for 3 minutes.
3 Meanwhile, split each pitta bread open and separate the two halves.
4 Combine all the vegetables with the herbs and rouille, and season. Divide among the pitta breads, leaving about a 2.5cm (1in) border all around. Fold over 1cm (½in) on opposite sides, then roll up tightly starting at one of the unfolded sides and serve.

022 RED PEPPER, FETA AND OLIVE WRAPS

PREPARATION TIME *10 minutes* **COOKING TIME** *10 minutes* **SERVES 4**

6 red peppers	225g (8oz) feta cheese,	2 tbsp balsamic vinegar
4 tortillas	crumbled	fresh basil leaves, to serve
Basil and Grilled Tomato	12 oil-packed black	
Pesto *(see page 172)*	olives, pitted	

1 Cook the peppers on an oiled grill rack for about 10 minutes until the skin is charred and blistered. Leave until cool enough to handle, then remove the skins. Slice the flesh.
2 Meanwhile, warm the tortillas on the side of the grill rack for 30 seconds.
3 Spread the pesto over the wraps. Divide the peppers, cheese and olives among the wraps, sprinkle with balsamic vinegar and add a few fresh basil leaves, then roll up. Serve immediately.

023 NORTH AFRICAN LAMB BITES

PREPARATION TIME *10 minutes, plus 1 hour marinating* **COOKING TIME** *10-14 minutes* **SERVES 4**

2 tbsp caraway seeds	1½ tsp freshly ground	225g (8oz) boneless leg of
1 tbsp cumin seeds	black pepper	lamb, cut into 16 cubes
1½ tsp coriander seeds	pinch of chilli flakes	small pitta breads and
	salt	yogurt, to serve

1 Heat a small, dry, heavy frying pan, add the seeds and leave over a moderate heat until fragrant. Crush fairly finely, then mix with the black pepper, chilli flakes and salt. Rub into the lamb. Cover and leave in a cool place for 1 hour.
2 Thread the lamb onto four skewers. Cook on an oiled grill rack for 5–7 minutes on each side, turning occasionally, until browned on the outside and cooked to your liking inside.
3 Meanwhile, warm the pitta breads on the side of the grill rack for 30 seconds on each side. Serve the bites with the small pitta breads and yogurt.

024 SCALLOPS WITH THAI DIPPING SAUCE

PREPARATION TIME *10 minutes* **COOKING TIME** *4–6 minutes* **SERVES 4**

20 scallops
sesame oil, for brushing
20 fresh coriander leaves
20 thin slices of pickled
ginger *(see page 167)*

THAI DIPPING SAUCE
2 tbsp Thai fish sauce
1 tbsp lime juice
1 tsp finely chopped garlic
1 tsp finely chopped fresh
red chilli
1 spring onion, thinly sliced

2 tsp finely chopped
peanuts
2½ tsp chopped peeled
cucumber
1½ tbsp palm sugar or
dark brown sugar

1 Make the dipping sauce by stirring the ingredients together until the sugar has dissolved, then pour into a small serving bowl.
2 Brush the scallops lightly with sesame oil. Lay them on the grill rack and cook for 2–3 minutes on each side until they just change colour, turning once. Take care not to overcook.
3 Remove from the rack and pierce each scallop onto a toothpick, adding a coriander leaf and a slice of pickled ginger. Serve with the dipping sauce.

025 CHICKEN BRUSCHETTAS WITH PROSCIUTTO AND FIGS

PREPARATION TIME *10 minutes* **COOKING TIME** *10 minutes* **SERVES 4**

2 large chicken breasts,
   with skin on
2 tbsp balsamic vinegar
1 tsp clear honey
2 tbsp extra virgin olive oil,
   plus extra for trickling

salt and freshly ground
   black pepper
4 large ripe but firm figs,
   halved from top to
   bottom

1 garlic clove, halved
   lengthways
4 large slices of rustic
   bread
4 slices of prosciutto
handful of rocket leaves

1. Make four slashes on each side of each chicken breast.
2. Combine the balsamic vinegar with the honey, oil and seasoning. Brush half of the mixture over the chicken and fig halves; reserve the remaining mixture.
3. Cook the chicken and figs on an oiled grill rack, allowing about 4 minutes on each side for the chicken, until charred and cooked through, and 1–2 minutes for the figs until softened. Remove from the rack and leave the chicken to rest.
4. Meanwhile, rub the cut sides of the garlic over one side of each slice of bread and cook on the oiled grill rack until toasted. Remove from the rack and trickle some oil over. Keep warm.
5. Put the prosciutto on the grill rack until crisp (this can be done at the same time as the bread).
6. Slice the chicken and arrange on the toast with the rocket, prosciutto and figs. Trickle over the remaining dressing.

026 GOATS' CHEESE-FILLED VINE LEAVES

PREPARATION TIME *10 minutes* **COOKING TIME** *5 minutes* **SERVES 3–6**

6 vacuum-packed vine
   leaves*, very well rinsed

6 small goats' cheeses,
   such as St. Marcellin
   crottins, or 3 milder,
   softer cheeses, 115g
   (4oz) each, halved
   crossways

virgin olive oil, for brushing
fresh thyme, for sprinkling
freshly ground black
   pepper
crusty bread, to serve

1. Dry the vine leaves well.
2. Lay each leaf flat on the work surface. Brush each goats' cheese with virgin olive oil and place in the centre of the leaf. Sprinkle lightly with thyme and with plenty of black pepper. Fold the leaf over to enclose the cheese completely and secure with a soaked wooden cocktail stick (see page 10). Brush with more olive oil and sprinkle with black pepper.
3. Cook on an oiled barbecue rack for about 2½ minutes on each side, until the cheese begins to melt. Lift from the rack with a fish slice and eat with crusty bread.
* Use large, fresh tender vine leaves, if available. Blanch them in boiling water for 2 minutes until they become supple, then drain and dry well.

027 CHEESE-FILLED RED PEPPERS

PREPARATION TIME *10 minutes* **COOKING TIME** *10 minutes* **SERVES 4**

75g (3oz) oil-cured black olives, pitted and chopped	4 red peppers, halved lengthways and deseeded	100ml (3½fl oz) herb vinaigrette
2 heaped tbsp chopped fresh basil or flat-leaf parsley leaves	175g (6oz) mixed taleggio and buffalo mozzarella, sliced	freshly ground black pepper
2 tbsp chopped capers		4 slices ciabatta
		virgin olive oil
		rocket leaves, to serve

1 Combine the olives, basil or parsley and capers in a bowl.
2 Cook the pepper halves on an oiled grill rack for about 6 minutes until very lightly charred.
3 Remove from the grill rack and divide the cheeses among the halves. Return to the rack until the cheese has melted. Scatter over the olives, trickle over the dressing and grind over black pepper.
4 Meanwhile, toast the ciabatta slices on the grill rack. Remove from the rack and brush with olive oil. Serve the filled peppers with the ciabatta toasts and rocket leaves.

028 GRILLED TOMATO BRUSCHETTA

PREPARATION TIME *10 minutes* **COOKING TIME** *6 minutes* **SERVES 2-4**

4 ripe sun-ripened tomatoes, halved	1 large ciabatta, halved lengthways	1 peppadew (bottled mild pepper piquante) thinly sliced
salt and freshly ground black pepper	4 tbsp tapenade	small handful (about 10) fresh basil leaves
olive oil, for brushing	1 tbsp extra virgin olive oil	

1 Brush the tomatoes with olive oil, season and cook on the grill rack for 3 minutes on each side.
2 Meanwhile, cut each length of ciabatta in half widthways and toast on the grill rack. Remove from the grill rack and spread the cut sides with tapenade.
3 Squash the tomatoes onto the ciabatta. Trickle over the extra virgin olive oil and sprinkle over the peppadew and basil leaves.

029 SAUSAGE AND CHEESE GRILLS

PREPARATION TIME *15 minutes, plus 30 minutes chilling* **COOKING TIME** *10-15 minutes* **SERVES 4**

8 thin slices bread, crusts removed	225g (8oz) good-quality sausagemeat (or use the meat from sausages)	plain flour
wholegrain mustard, for spreading	4 slices Gruyère cheese, or mature Cheddar cheese	2 eggs, beaten
		50g (2oz) fresh breadcrumbs

1 Spread one side of each bread slice with mustard. Divide the sausagemeat into eight portions and spread a portion over the mustard. Keeping the sausagemeat on the outside, sandwich two slices of bread together, inserting a cheese slice in the centre.
2 Spread plain flour on one plate, put the egg on another and spread the breadcrumbs on a third. Dip the sandwiches lightly in the flour, then in the egg, allow the excess to drain off, then dip into the breadcrumbs to coat evenly. Leave in the fridge for 30 minutes, to firm up.
3 Cook on an oiled grill rack for 5-8 minutes on each side until golden on the outside, the sausagemeat is cooked and the cheese has melted.

030 MARINATED HALLOUMI SALAD

PREPARATION TIME *10 minutes, plus 1–4 hours marinating* **COOKING TIME** *2–3 minutes* **SERVES 4**

350g (12oz) halloumi
cheese, cut into 1cm (½in)
thick slices
1 tbsp salted capers, well
rinsed and dried
12 mixed black and green
olives, pitted
lemon wedges

fresh flat-leaf parsley,
to garnish
sourdough bread or crusty
country bread, to serve

MARINADE
115ml (4fl oz) virgin
olive oil

1 tsp Dijon mustard
2 tsp balsamic vinegar
1 tbsp fresh thyme
pinch of caster sugar
1 red chilli, seeded and
finely chopped

1   Lay the cheese slices in a shallow non-metallic dish.
2   Combine the marinade ingredients and pour over the cheese. Turn the slices over, cover and
leave in a cool place for 1–4 hours, turning the slices occasionally.
3   Lift the cheese from the marinade and cook on an oiled grill rack for 1–1½ minutes on each
side, turning carefully, until golden.
4   Transfer to plates, scatter over the capers and olives. Garnish with the parsley and serve
immediately with the lemon wedges and bread.

031 GLAMORGAN SAUSAGES

PREPARATION TIME *10 minutes, plus 1 hour chilling* **COOKING TIME** *10–15 minutes* **SERVES 4**

175g (6oz) fresh white breadcrumbs	3 spring onions, finely chopped	salt and freshly ground black pepper
115g (4oz) cheese such as Caerphilly, goats', Emmental or mature Cheddar	1 tbsp very finely chopped fresh parsley	about 2 tbsp milk
	½ tsp fresh thyme leaves	plain flour, for dusting
	1 egg, beaten	

1 Mix the breadcrumbs, cheese, spring onions, herbs, egg and seasoning together well, adding enough milk to bind the ingredients and so that the mixture is soft enough to gather into balls, but do not make too soft.
2 Roll into eight sausage shapes. Roll the sausages in the flour to coat evenly, pressing the flour in lightly. Chill, uncovered, for 1 hour.
3 Cook the sausages on the side of an oiled grill rack over a moderately low heat, turning frequently, for 10–15 minutes until browned and cooked through.

032 BREAD, BASIL AND CHEESE KEBABS

PREPARATION TIME *10 minutes, plus 24 hours marinating* **COOKING TIME** *4–5 minutes* **SERVES 4**

225g (8oz) halloumi cheese, cut into 1cm (½in) slices	1 plump garlic clove, crushed and finely chopped	1 French stick, cut into 1cm (½in) slices
4 tbsp virgin olive oil	freshly ground black pepper	about 24 fresh basil leaves
2 tsp lemon juice		

1 Put the halloumi cheese in a shallow, non-metallic dish. Add the olive oil, lemon juice, garlic and plenty of black pepper, stir together, then cover and leave for 24 hours.
2 Drain off and reserve the marinade. Thread the pieces of cheese and bread alternately on skewers, interspersing them with basil leaves and packing them quite tightly.
3 Brush with the reserved marinade and cook on an oiled grill rack over medium-high heat for 4–5 minutes, turning and brushing occasionally with the reserved marinade.

033 SMOKY CHICKEN WINGS

PREPARATION TIME *5 minutes* **COOKING TIME** *20–25 minutes* **SERVES 4**

2 tbsp olive oil	2 tsp sweet chilli sauce	fresh thyme leaves, for sprinkling
1 tbsp sun-dried tomato paste	juice of ½ lemon	salt and freshly ground black pepper
1 garlic clove, finely crushed	1 tsp pimenton (smoked paprika)	
	12 large chicken wings	

1 Combine all the ingredients, except the chicken, thyme and seasoning, to make a thick sauce.
2 To make it easier to turn the chicken wings on the grill rack, cut off the tips of the chicken wings, then thread three wings onto two parallel skewers. Repeat with the remaining wings.
3 Cook on an oiled grill rack for 10 minutes, turning twice. Brush liberally with the sauce and cook for a further 10–15 minutes, until cooked through and a rich golden brown, turning and brushing with the sauce occasionally.
4 Remove from the grill rack, sprinkle with the thyme leaves and seasoning, and serve.

FISH AND SEAFOOD

Cooking on a grill rack over a high heat is ideal for fish as the intense heat improves the flavour by charring the surface. The most suitable fish are firm species such as cod, haddock, monkfish and swordfish, and oily types like tuna, salmon and sardines. Salmon is best served a little translucent, while tuna is best a little on the rare side, but if you prefer them cooked through, remove from the grill just before the inside is opaque so they continue to cook off the heat.

Fish steaks should be more than 2.5cm (1in) thick so that they will not cook too quickly. Cook fish on the highest notch of the grill. The exception is oily fish which should be cooked over a brisk heat close to the fire until the skin is crisp. Allow 10 minutes per 2.5cm (1in) thickness of fish, but do keep an eye on it as it can quickly overcook. Delicate white fish, such as lemon sole and plaice, and thin fillets are difficult to barbecue because they disintegrate when you try to turn them. Large fish are easier to handle if cooked in a double-sided hinged fish grilling basket. They can also be wrapped in foil although they will lose some of the characteristic barbecued flavour.

Shellfish are ideal for barbecueing – it is difficult to make a barbecue too hot for them as by the time you char the exterior they are invariably done to perfection. They are best grilled with the shells on to retain their juices and keep them moist.

CHAPTER 2

034 SALMON BURGERS

PREPARATION TIME *15 minutes, plus 2–3 hours cooling and chilling* **COOKING TIME** *8 minutes* **SERVES 4**

450g (1lb) skinless salmon fillet

salt and freshly ground black pepper

300g (10oz) boiled or steamed potato

small knob of unsalted butter

1–2 tbsp chopped fresh dill*, to taste

zest and juice of ½ large lemon

seasoned plain flour, for coating

2 eggs, beaten

about 50g (2oz) polenta or 115g (4oz) breadcrumbs

Tomato Tartare Sauce *(see page 179)*, to serve

1   Put the salmon in a pan with barely enough water to cover. Season and bring to the boil. Remove the pan from the heat, cover and leave the salmon to cool in the liquid. Drain off the liquid. Skin the salmon and flake the flesh into a bowl.

2   Mash the warm potato with the butter, then combine with the salmon, dill, lemon zest and juice and seasoning. With well-floured hands, form the mixture into four burgers.

3   Tip the beaten eggs onto one plate and the polenta or breadcrumbs onto another. Coat the burgers in the egg, allow the surplus egg to drain off, then coat in the polenta or breadcrumbs, patting them firmly in place. Cover and chill for 1–2 hours.

4   Cook the burgers in an oiled hinged fish basket for 4 minutes on each side until golden and crisp. Alternatively, cook on an oiled grilled rack and turn the burgers carefully with a fish slice.

*   Dill's strength of flavour can vary quite considerably, especially in winter.

035 SEA BASS WITH SAUCE VIERGE

PREPARATION TIME *10 minutes, plus 20 minutes marinating* **COOKING TIME** *6 minutes* **SERVES 4**

4 sea bass fillets with skin on, 175g (6oz) each

olive oil for brushing

salt and freshly ground black pepper

SAUCE VIERGE

6 Italian vine-ripened plum tomatoes, finely diced

2 garlic cloves, finely chopped

3 small shallots, finely chopped

sea salt

150ml (5fl oz) virgin olive oil

1 tsp lemon juice

3 tbsp shredded fresh basil

freshly ground black pepper

1   Make the sauce by putting the tomatoes, garlic and shallots in a bowl, sprinkling with a little sea salt and leaving for 20 minutes until the juices run. Add the virgin olive oil, lemon juice, basil, and black pepper to taste.

2   Brush the sea bass with olive oil and sprinkle with seasoning. Cook the fish in an oiled fish basket or on an oiled grill rack, skin side down first, for 3 minutes, then turn over and cook the other side until the flesh is cooked through.

3   Remove the fish to plates and spoon over the sauce.

036 TERIYAKI TUNA

PREPARATION TIME *5 minutes, plus 1–2 hours marinating* **COOKING TIME** *4 minutes* **SERVES 4**

4 tuna steaks, 175g (6oz) each	MARINADE	**1 garlic clove, crushed through a garlic press**
lightly toasted sesame seeds, lightly crushed, to serve	**2 tbsp mirin**	**½–¾ tsp Sichuan peppercorns, ground**
	2 tbsp soy sauce	
	2 tbsp sake	
	2 tsp grated fresh root ginger	

1 Lay the tuna in a non-metallic dish.
2 Make the marinade by mixing all the ingredients together. Pour over the tuna, turn the steaks over to make sure they are evenly coated, then cover and leave in a cool place for 1–2 hours, turning occasionally.
3 Lift the steaks from the marinade. Reserve the marinade.
4 Cook the tuna on an oiled grill rack for about 2 minutes, brush with the reserved marinade, turn the steaks over, brush again with the marinade and cook for a further 2 minutes, or until cooked to your liking. Serve the tuna with the sesame seeds sprinkled over.

037 ROSEMARY-SKEWERED MONKFISH WITH GARLIC AND LEMON BASTE

PREPARATION TIME *5 minutes* **COOKING TIME** *35–40 minutes* **SERVES 6**

12 rosemary stalks (see
  step 2)
650g (1lb 6oz) monkfish
  fillet, cut into chunks
freshly ground black
  pepper
1 tsp pimenton (smoked
  paprika)

sea salt
6 slices firm white bread,
  cut on the diagonal
lemon wedges, to serve

GARLIC AND LEMON BASTE
225ml (8fl oz) olive oil

2 large garlic bulbs, divided
  into cloves, unpeeled
1 lemon, halved and cut
  into chunks
3 fresh rosemary sprigs
freshly ground black
  pepper

1 To make the baste, cook the ingredients together very gently in a saucepan for 30 minutes; do
   not let the oil become too hot or the garlic will fry. Strain off and reserve the oil and the garlic.
2 Using the rosemary stalks as skewers, carefully pierce a hole through each chunk of fish. Sprinkle
   the fish with black pepper and pimenton, then brush with garlic-flavoured oil. Thread onto the
   rosemary 'skewers'.
3 Cook on the grill rack for about 6–8 minutes, turning occasionally and brushing with garlic oil,
   until browned at the edges. Remove from the grill rack and sprinkle with sea salt.
4 Meanwhile, toast the bread on the side of the grill rack. Using a slotted spoon, lift the garlic from
   the oil and either squash the garlic flesh from the skins onto the toasts, or remove the skins and
   eat the cloves with the fish. Serve the lemon wedges on the side.

038 SEA BREAM WITH FIVE-SPICE POWDER, LIME AND GINGER

PREPARATION TIME *10 minutes, plus 1 hour marinating* **COOKING TIME** *20–25 minutes* **SERVES 4**

2 shallots, chopped
2.5cm (1in) piece of fresh
  root ginger, chopped
1 tbsp Chinese five-spice
  powder
1 tbsp soy sauce

grated zest and juice
  of 2 limes
sea salt
2 sea bream, 675g (1½lb)
  each, cleaned

1 Put the shallots and ginger into a blender and mix to a paste. Add the five spice-powder, soy
   sauce, lime zest and juice and mix briefly.
2 With a sharp knife, cut two slashes in both sides of each fish, going right through to the bone.
3 Brush the five-spice paste over the fish, making sure it goes well into the slashes. Cover and leave
   in a cool place for 1 hour.
4 Cook the sea bream in an oiled fish basket or on an oiled grill rack for 20–25 minutes, turning
   halfway through the cooking time.

039 SEAFOOD KEBABS WITH DILL

PREPARATION TIME *10 minutes, plus 1 hour marinating* **COOKING TIME** *6–8 minutes* **SERVES 4**

450g (1lb) skinned cod fillet, cut into 2.5cm (1in) cubes
16 raw king prawns, peeled but tails left on
1½ limes, sliced
2 small courgettes, sliced diagonally
16 large cherry tomatoes

MARINADE
4 tbsp virgin olive oil
1 tbsp white wine vinegar
juice of ½ lime
2 garlic cloves, crushed
2 tbsp chopped fresh dill
sea salt and freshly ground black pepper

DILL TARTARE DIP
150ml (5fl oz) soured cream
2 tbsp tartare sauce
2 tbsp good-quality mayonnaise *(see page 179)*
1 tsp chopped fresh dill

1 Make the marinade by combining the ingredients.
2 Thread the cod, prawns, lime slices, courgettes and cherry tomatoes alternately onto eight skewers. Lay them in a shallow non-metallic dish and pour over the marinade. Turn the kebabs to coat them in the marinade, cover and leave in a cool place for 1 hour, turning occasionally.
3 Meanwhile make the dip by mixing all the ingredients together. Season to taste. Cover and chill.
4 Lift the kebabs from the marinade (reserve any remaining marinade) and cook on an oiled grill rack for about 6–8 minutes, turning occasionally and brushing with the marinade, until the prawns have turned pink and the fish is cooked. Serve with the dip.

040 RED MULLET WITH FENNEL AND LEMON

PREPARATION TIME *15 minutes* **COOKING TIME** *8-10 minutes* **SERVES 4**

1 fennel bulb	2 tbsp chopped fresh	salt and freshly ground
4 red mullet fillets, 175g	flat-leaf parsley	black pepper
(6oz) each	1 lemon, halved and sliced	1 tbsp olive oil
3 garlic cloves, thinly sliced	1 tsp fennel seeds	

1   Trim the stalks from the fennel bulb, saving the feathery green fronds. Discard the core. Halve and thinly slice the fennel bulb. Blanch in boiling salted water for 2 minutes. Drain very well.
2   Using a sharp knife, cut several slashes in the skin side of each fish.
3   Cut four double-thickness sheets of heavy-duty foil, each large enough to enclose a fillet. Put a quarter of the garlic, sliced fennel and parsley on each sheet of foil, spreading them in an even layer. Lay a fillet on top, skin side uppermost. Insert a lemon slice in each slash and put the rest on top. Sprinkle over the fennel seeds and reserved feathery fronds, and seasoning and trickle over the oil. Fold the foil loosely over the fish and twist the edges together firmly to seal.
4   Cook on an oiled grill rack for 8-10 minutes, turning the packages over halfway through.

041 MONKFISH, FENNEL AND LEMON KEBABS

PREPARATION TIME *10 minutes, plus 30-60 minutes marinating* **COOKING TIME** *6-8 minutes* **SERVES 4**

550g (1¼lb) monkfish, cut	2 tsp finely grated	sea salt and freshly ground
into 2.5cm (1in) cubes	lemon zest	black pepper
2 tsp fennel seeds, crushed	2 tbsp lemon juice	1 lemon, thinly sliced
2 tbsp chopped fresh	3 tbsp olive oil	
fennel herb		

1   Put the monkfish into a non-metallic bowl.
2   Combine the fennel seeds, fennel, lemon zest, lemon juice, oil and seasoning. Stir into the fish, cover and leave in a cool place for 30-60 minutes.
3   Lift the fish from the marinade (reserve any remaining marinade) and thread onto skewers, alternating with folded lemon slices.
4   Cook on an oiled grill rack for about 6-8 minutes until evenly browned, turning once and basting with any remaining marinade.

042 PRAWNS WITH SPANISH TOMATO SAUCE

PREPARATION TIME *10 minutes* **COOKING TIME** *40 minutes* **SERVES 4**

**24 raw unpeeled tiger
prawns
olive oil, for brushing**

SAUCE
**4 tbsp olive oil
1 onion, chopped**

**4 garlic cloves, chopped
2 ripe Italian plum
tomatoes, chopped
1 red pepper, chopped
dash Tabasco sauce
2 tbsp dry sherry
4 tbsp fish stock**

**10 blanched almonds,
toasted
lemon juice, to taste
sea salt and freshly ground
black pepper**

1   Make the sauce by heating half the olive oil, adding the onion and three-quarters of the garlic.
    Fry until softened, stirring frequently. Add the tomatoes, red pepper, Tabasco, sherry and fish
    stock. Bring to the boil, then cover and simmer for 30 minutes, stirring occasionally.
2   Put the almonds into a blender or food processor and grind coarsely. Add the remaining olive oil
    and garlic. Mix until evenly combined. Add the sauce and mix until smooth. Add lemon juice and
    seasoning to taste. Set aside until required.
3   Brush the prawns with oil. Thread onto pairs of parallel skewers and cook on an oiled grill rack for
    3 minutes on each side until the shells turn pink.
4   Meanwhile, heat the sauce on the side of the grill rack. Remove the prawns from the grill rack
    and serve with the sauce.

043 CRAB BURGERS

PREPARATION *10 minutes, plus 1-2 hours chilling* **COOKING TIME** *6-8 minutes* **SERVES 4**

**1 potato, about 225g (8oz),
baked in its skin
small knob unsalted butter
225g (8oz) crab meat**

**1 small red chilli, seeded
and finely chopped
8 plump spring onions,
finely chopped
1 tsp harissa paste**

**2 tsp Thai fish sauce
1 large egg white, lightly
beaten
75-115g (3-4oz) polenta
2 tsp sesame seeds**

1   Scoop the flesh from the baked potato and mash it with the small knob of butter. Leave to cool,
    then mix with the crab meat, chilli, spring onions, harissa, fish sauce and egg white. Divide the
    mixture into eight pieces and form into burgers.
2   Mix the polenta with the sesame seeds, then coat the burgers in the mixture. Chill for 1-2 hours.
3   Cook the burgers in an oiled hinged fish basket for about 3-4 minutes on each side until they
    are golden on the outside and warmed through. Alternatively, cook on an oiled grill rack and turn
    the burgers carefully with a fish slice.

044 SEARED SQUID SALAD

PREPARATION TIME *15 minutes, plus 2–4 hours marinating* **COOKING TIME** *4 minutes* **SERVES 6**

900g (2lb) small squid, cleaned

MARINADE
1 tbsp groundnut oil
1 tsp sesame oil
1 tbsp lemon juice
1 red chilli, seeded and finely chopped

1 garlic clove, crushed
sea salt

TO SERVE
handful of curly endive
12 cherry tomatoes, quartered
1 bunch watercress, trimmed

½ cucumber, peeled, halved, seeded and cut into fine strips
groundnut oil and lime juice, for dressing
salt and freshly ground black pepper
2–3 tbsp fresh coriander leaves

1 Remove the tentacles from the squid and cut the squid bodies lengthways along one side to open them out flat. Using the point of a knife, score diagonal parallel lines on the squid bodies but do not cut right through. Put into a non-metallic bowl. Leave the tentacles whole and add them to the bowl.

2 Make the marinade by combining all the ingredients. Pour over the squid, stir everything together, cover and leave to marinate in a cool place for 2–4 hours.

3 Lift the squid from the marinade and cook on an oiled grill rack for 2 minutes on each side, turning once, until just opaque.

4 Meanwhile, toss the curly endive, tomatoes, watercress and cucumber together. Trickle over about 2 tbsp groundnut oil and 1 tbsp lime juice, to just moisten. Season.

5 Slice the squid into rings and pile onto the salad. Garnish with fresh coriander.

045 THAI FISH BURGERS

PREPARATION TIME *10 minutes, plus 1 hour chilling* **COOKING TIME** *8–10 minutes* **SERVES 4**

1 shallot, coarsely chopped
1 plump garlic clove,
   coarsely chopped
1cm (½in) piece of fresh root
   ginger, coarsely chopped
2 Kaffir lime leaves, or 1 tsp
   lime zest

1 red chilli, seeded and
   coarsely chopped
2 tbsp Thai fish sauce
pinch of caster sugar
450g (1lb) white fish fillets,
   chopped

2 spring onions, coarsely
   chopped
2 tbsp chopped fresh
   coriander
finely chopped fresh
   coriander and lime
   wedges, to serve

1. Combine the shallot, garlic, ginger, lime leaves, chilli, fish sauce and sugar in a food processor. Add the fish and process until reduced to a paste.
2. Add the spring onions and coriander. Pulse a few times until combined but not chopped further.
3. Knead the mixture with your hands until smooth, then form into 2.5cm (1in) thick burgers. Chill for at least 1 hour.
4. Cook the burgers in an oiled hinged fish basket for about 4–5 minutes on each side until they are golden on the outside but still rare to medium in the centre. Alternatively, cook on an oiled grill rack and turn the burgers carefully with a fish slice. Serve with coriander and lime wedges.

046 TIGER PRAWN, BACON AND AVOCADO KEBABS

PREPARATION TIME *10 minutes* **COOKING TIME** *6–8 minutes* **SERVES 4**

8 lean bacon rashers,
   rinds removed
2 large avocados, pitted,
   peeled and cubed
12 raw tiger prawns, peeled
   but tails left intact

8 spring onions, trimmed
   stems only, chopped
1 garlic clove, finely
   chopped
2 tbsp olive oil
1 tbsp soy sauce

freshly ground black
   pepper
chopped fresh coriander
   and lime wedges, to
   serve

1. Stretch the bacon rashers on a chopping board with the back of a knife, then cut each rasher into three pieces. Wrap each bacon piece around an avocado cube. Thread the cubes onto skewers, alternating with the prawns.
2. Stir together the spring onions, garlic, oil, soy sauce and black pepper. Brush over the kebabs and cook on an oiled grill rack for 6–8 minutes, turning regularly and brushing with the oil mixture, until the prawns have turned pink and the bacon is cooked. Serve accompanied by the chopped coriander and lime wedges.

047 BACON-WRAPPED SCALLOP KEBABS

PREPARATION TIME *10 minutes* **COOKING TIME** *4-6 minutes* **SERVES 4**

12 large scallops with roes, shucked	6 rashers of streaky bacon, rinds removed	Worcestershire sauce lemon wedges, to serve

1 Remove the corals from the scallops and set aside.
2 Stretch the bacon rashers on a chopping board with the back of a knife and cut across into halves. Wrap a piece of bacon around each scallop. Thread three wrapped scallops lengthways onto a soaked bamboo skewer (see page 10), putting a coral between each one. Repeat with the remaining scallops and corals.
3 Season the bacon with Worcestershire sauce and cook on an oiled grill rack for 2-3 minutes on each side until the bacon is crisp and the scallops just opaque; take care not to overcook the scallops. Serve immediately, with lemon wedges.

048 COD WITH SPICED ORANGE MARINADE

PREPARATION TIME *10 minutes, plus 2-3 hours marinating* **COOKING TIME** *8-10 minutes* **SERVES 4**

4 cod steaks, 175g (6 oz) each, 2.5cm (1in) thick chopped fresh fennel herb, for garnish lime wedges, to serve	MARINADE 4 tbsp orange juice 4 tbsp dry vermouth 4 tbsp hoisin sauce 4 tbsp soy sauce 1 garlic clove, crushed	½ tsp ground cumin ½ tsp Chinese five spice powder freshly ground black pepper

1 Lay the cod in a shallow non-metallic dish just large enough to hold the steaks.
2 Make the marinade by mixing all the ingredients together. Pour over the cod, turn the steaks to ensure they are evenly coated, then cover the dish and leave in a cool place for 2-3 hours.
3 Lift the cod from the marinade (reserve the marinade) and cook on an oiled grill for 4-5 minutes on each side, brushing occasionally with the marinade. Serve garnished with fennel and accompanied by lime wedges.

049 HERBED FISH BURGERS

PREPARATION TIME *15 minutes* **COOKING TIME** *8-10 minutes* **SERVES 4**

350g (12oz) haddock fillet, skinned 1-2 tbsp lemon juice 1 tbsp Worcestershire sauce 1 tsp creamed horseradish	115ml (4fl oz) milk 1 tbsp snipped fresh chives 1 tbsp chopped fresh parsley	350g (12oz) cooked potatoes, mashed with a little butter 50g (2oz) fresh breadcrumbs

1 Put the fish, lemon juice, Worcestershire sauce, horseradish and milk in a food processor or blender and mix until smooth. Transfer to a bowl and mix in the herbs and mashed potatoes until evenly combined.
2 Shape into four evenly sized burgers. Coat evenly in the breadcrumbs.
3 Cook the fish burgers in an oiled hinged fish basket for 4-5 minutes on each side until golden and crisp. Alternatively, cook the burgers on an oiled grill rack and turn carefully with a fish slice.

050 TROUT WITH TARRAGON

PREPARATION TIME *10 minutes, plus 1–2 hours marinating* **COOKING TIME** *12 minutes* **SERVES 4**

4 trout, 350g (12oz) each, cleaned	2 small shallots, finely chopped	1½ tsp coarsely chopped fresh flat-leaf parsley
	1 garlic clove, finely chopped	1 tsp Dijon mustard
MARINADE		1 tsp anise, such as
75ml (3fl oz) virgin olive oil	1½ tsp coarsely chopped	Pernod or Ricard
1½ tbsp lemon juice	fresh tarragon leaves	1 tsp dark soy sauce

1 Using the point of a sharp knife, cut three slashes in both sides of each trout.
2 Make the marinade by combining all the ingredients. Brush liberally over the inside as well as the skin of the trout, going into the slashes. Cover and leave in a cool place for 1–2 hours.
3 Cook the trout in an oiled fish basket or on an oiled grill rack for about 6 minutes. Turn the fish over (if necessary carefully use a large fish slice), brush liberally with the marinade and cook on the other side for a further 6 minutes or so until the flesh near the head flakes easily when tested with the point of a sharp knife. Move the fish to the side of the grill rack, if necessary, to ensure even cooking.
4 Transfer the trout to plates and pour over any remaining marinade.

051 SPICED PRAWNS WITH TOMATO AND CORIANDER SALSA

PREPARATION TIME *10 minutes, plus 30 minutes marinating* **COOKING TIME** *6 minutes* **SERVES 4**

1 tsp cayenne pepper	½ tsp onion powder	2 tbsp olive oil
1 tsp black pepper	1 tsp sea salt	Tomato and Coriander
1 tsp white pepper	20 raw king prawns,	Salsa *(see page 66)*,
½ tsp garlic granules	unpeeled	to serve

1 Stir together the cayenne, black and white peppers, garlic granules, onion powder and salt.
2 Rub a little of this mixture over the prawns (reserve the rest for another time or discard) and trickle over the oil. Leave in a cool place for 30 minutes.
3 Thread the prawns onto pairs of parallel skewers and cook on an oiled grill rack for about 3 minutes on each side until the shells have turned pink.
4 Meanwhile, taste the salsa for seasoning. Serve the prawns accompanied by the salsa.

052 TROUT WITH BLACK OLIVADE

PREPARATION TIME *10 minutes* **COOKING TIME** *12 minutes* **SERVES 4**

4 trout, 350g (12oz) each, cleaned	BLACK OLIVADE	1 tbsp capers, preferably salt-packed and well-rinsed
olive oil, for brushing	150g (5oz) pitted kalamata olives	
sea salt and freshly ground black pepper	7 anchovy fillets, drained 50g (2oz) sun-dried tomatoes	6 tbsp virgin olive oil about 3 tbsp chopped fresh basil
lemon wedges, to serve		

1   Make the olivade by putting the olives, anchovies, sun-dried tomatoes and capers into a blender. Pulse to chop coarsely. Add the oil and pulse again until just combined. Transfer to a bowl and stir in the basil and season with black pepper. Set aside.

2   Using the point of a sharp knife, cut three slashes in both sides of each trout. Brush the fish with oil, going into the slashes. Season with black pepper.

3   Cook the trout in an oiled fish basket or on an oiled grill rack for about 6 minutes. Turn the fish over (if necessary carefully use a large fish slice) and cook on the other side for a further 6 minutes or so until the flesh near the head flakes easily when tested with the point of a sharp knife. Move the fish to the side of the grill rack, if necessary, to ensure even cooking.

4   Transfer the trout to serving plates, sprinkle with a little sea salt and serve with the olivade and lemon wedges.

053 PRAWN SPIEDINI WITH GREMOLATA

PREPARATION TIME *10 minutes* **COOKING TIME** *3–4 minutes* **SERVES 4**

1 large lemon	sea salt and freshly ground black pepper or chilli powder	virgin olive oil, for brushing
3 garlic cloves, very finely chopped		
4 tbsp chopped fresh flat-leaf parsley	20 raw king prawns, unpeeled	

1   To make the gremolata, peel the zest from the lemon with a sharp potato peeler. Stack the pieces into a pile a few at a time and cut across them to make short, fine strips. Combine with the garlic, parsley and salt and black pepper. Set the gremolata aside.

2   Slice along the underside of the prawns from the thickest part towards the tail, but take care not to cut all the way through. Carefully remove the dark vein. Gently press the prawns to flatten them out, or butterfly them.

3   Brush the prawns with virgin olive oil and then season with salt and either black pepper or chilli powder. Thread lengthways onto pairs of parallel skewers.

4   Cook the prawns on an oiled grill rack for 3–4 minutes, turning once, until the flesh is opaque.

5   Meanwhile, cut the lemon in half and squeeze the juice from one half. Remove the prawns from the rack, trickle over the lemon juice and sprinkle with the gremolata.

054 MUSSELS EN PAPILLOTE WITH COCONUT, GINGER, LEMON AND LIME

PREPARATION TIME *10 minutes* **COOKING TIME** *10 minutes* **SERVES 4**

50g (2oz) chopped fresh root ginger

2 lemon grass stems, crushed and finely chopped

juice and grated zest of 1 lemon

juice and grated zest of 1 lime

4 garlic cloves, finely chopped

leaves from a small sprig of thyme

sea salt and freshly ground black pepper

1.25kg (2lb 12oz) mussels, cleaned

200ml (7fl oz) coconut milk

1   In a large bowl mix together the ginger, lemon grass, lemon and lime zests and juices, garlic, thyme and seasoning. Add the mussels and stir thoroughly.

2   Cut four large pieces of heavy-duty foil and pile a quarter of the mussel mixture onto each one. Trickle the coconut milk evenly over the mussels. Fold the edges of the foil loosely over the mussels and twist the edges firmly together to seal.

3   Cook on the grill rack for about 10 minutes until all the mussels have opened, turning the packages over a couple of times. Discard any mussels that remain closed. Serve the mussels in their parcels.

055 FISH SATAY

PREPARATION TIME *10 minutes, plus 1 hour marinating* **COOKING TIME** *12–15 minutes* **SERVES 4**

2.5 cm (1in) piece fresh root
   ginger, coarsely chopped
1 garlic clove, peeled
2 tsp light soy sauce
1 tbsp lime juice
1 red chilli, seeded and
   finely chopped
salt and freshly ground
   black pepper

550g (1¼lb) mahi mahi, cut
   into 2.5cm (1in) cubes
½ papaya, cubed
fresh coriander leaves,
   shredded

SATAY SAUCE
3 tbsp peanuts, coarsely
   chopped

1 tbsp groundnut oil
1 garlic clove, chopped
1 red chilli, seeded and
   chopped
1 shallot, chopped
115ml (4fl oz) coconut milk
grated zest and juice of
   1 lime

1. Press the ginger in a garlic press to extract the juice into a bowl, then crush the garlic in the press, adding the extract to the bowl. Stir in the soy sauce, lime juice, chilli and seasoning. Add the fish and stir to ensure all the pieces are evenly coated. Cover and leave in a cool place for 1 hour, stirring several times.
2. Meanwhile, make the sauce by frying the peanuts in the oil until lightly browned. Put the garlic, chilli and shallot in a blender or food processor and mix together. Add to the peanuts and fry for 5 minutes, stirring to prevent sticking. Stir in the coconut milk and lime zest and juice. Set aside.
3. Lift the fish from the marinade and thread onto skewers, adding a piece of papaya to the ends of each one. Cook on an oiled grill rack for about 6–8 minutes, turning to brown evenly.
4. Meanwhile, heat the sauce on the side of the grill rack. Serve the fish sprinkled with coriander and accompanied by the satay sauce.

056 MEXICAN WHOLE FISH BURGERS

PREPARATION TIME *10 minutes, plus 30 minutes marinating* **COOKING TIME** *6–8 minutes* **SERVES 6**

850g (1lb 14oz) thick, firm
   white fish fillets, such as
   snapper, haddock or cod
1 bunch fresh coriander,
   coarsely chopped
1 garlic clove, chopped
1 red chilli, seeded and
   chopped

2 tsp paprika
1 tsp ground cumin
zest of 1 lime
5 tbsp olive oil
6 good-quality hamburger
   buns or rolls
baby spinach leaves and
   red onion slices, to serve

LIME MAYO
115ml (4fl oz) mayonnaise
   (see page 179)
2 tbsp lime juice
dash Tabasco sauce
salt and freshly ground
   black pepper

1. Cut the fish into six pieces that are slightly larger than the buns. Put into a non-metallic dish.
2. Mix the coriander, garlic, chilli, paprika, cumin, lime zest and olive oil in a blender. Season to taste. Coat the fish evenly with the paste, cover and leave in a cool place for 30 minutes.
3. Meanwhile, mix all the mayo ingredients together. Adjust the seasoning, if necessary.
4. Cook the fish on an oiled grill rack for 3–4 minutes on each side until the fish is opaque and just cooked through.
5. While the fish is cooking, toast the buns or rolls on the side of the rack. Spread some of the mayo on the cut sides of the buns or rolls, add some spinach leaves and red onion slices to the bases of the buns or rolls, and top with a piece of fish. Cover with the bun or roll tops.

057 FISH WITH HERBS AND LEMON

PREPARATION TIME *10 minutes* **COOKING TIME** *6 minutes* **SERVES 4**

4 white fish fillets with skin
  on, such as monkfish,
  cod, halibut or turbot,
  225g (8oz) each, at least
  2.5cm (1in) thick
1½ tbsp extra virgin oil,
  plus extra for rubbing

2 tbsp chopped mixed fresh
  herbs, such as parsley,
  basil, thyme, chervil
  or fennel
sea salt and freshly ground
  black pepper
1 tbsp lemon juice

lemon wedges, to serve

1 Rub the fish lightly with extra virgin olive oil and sprinkle with seasoning. Mix the 1½ tablespoons of extra virgin olive oil with the herbs to make a paste.
2 Cook the fish in an oiled fish basket or on an oiled grill rack, flesh side down, for about 3 minutes. Turn the fish over, spread with the herb paste and cook for a further 3 minutes or so until the flesh flakes easily when tested with the point of a sharp knife.
3 Remove from the heat and sprinkle over the lemon juice. Serve with extra lemon wedges.

058 OYSTERS WITH PROSCIUTTO AND RED PEPPER

PREPARATION TIME *10 minutes* **COOKING TIME** *3–5 minutes* **SERVES 2-3**

3 slices of prosciutto
½ red pepper, roasted until
  soft *(see page 20)*,
  finely chopped*

2 tsp Tabasco sauce
1 tsp Worcestershire sauce
sea salt and freshly ground
  black pepper

12 oysters, freshly shucked
3-4 tbsp freshly grated
  Parmesan cheese

1 Put the prosciutto on the grill rack until frazzled. Chop finely and mix with the red pepper, Tabasco sauce, Worcestershire sauce and salt and pepper, to taste.
2 Divide among the oysters and sprinkle over the Parmesan. Put on the side of the grill rack for about 3–5 minutes until the oysters are just opaque.
* ½ bottled red pepper could be used instead.

059 SEARED TUNA

PREPARATION TIME *10 minutes, plus 30 minutes marinating* **COOKING TIME** *4 minutes* **SERVES 4**

4 tuna steaks, about 125g
  (4oz) each
1cm (½in) piece fresh root
  ginger, finely chopped
2 tbsp chopped fresh mint

2 tbsp chopped fresh
  coriander
2 tbsp chopped fresh basil
1 red chilli, finely chopped
1 plump garlic clove,
  crushed

50ml (2fl oz) lime juice
1 tbsp sesame oil
1 tbsp Thai fish sauce
sea salt and freshly ground
  black pepper
lime wedges, to serve

1 Lay the tuna in a non-metallic dish.
2 Mix the ginger, herbs, chilli, garlic, lime juice, sesame oil, fish sauce and seasoning together. Pour over the tuna, turn the steaks over, cover and leave in a cool place for 30 minutes, turning once.
3 Lift the steaks from the marinade. Reserve the marinade.
4 Cook the tuna on an oiled grill rack for 2 minutes, brush with the reserved marinade, turn over and cook for a further 2 minutes, or until cooked to your liking. Serve with lime wedges.

060 MOROCCAN SPICED HALIBUT

PREPARATION TIME *10 minutes, plus 30-60 minutes marinating (optional)* **COOKING TIME** *8-10 minutes*
SERVES 4

50ml (2fl oz) olive oil
2 tbsp lemon juice
3 garlic cloves, crushed
2 tbsp chopped fresh
   coriander
1 tbsp chopped fresh
   parsley

1 tbsp chopped fresh mint
1 tsp harissa
1 tsp ground cumin
pinch of saffron threads,
   lightly toasted and
   pounded

4 halibut steaks, 200g (7oz)
   each, 2.5cm (1in) thick
lime wedges, to serve

1   Combine all the ingredients, except the fish and lime wedges.
2   Lay the fish in a single layer in a non-metallic dish, pour over the marinade and turn the fillets
    to ensure they are evenly coated. If liked, cover and leave in a cool place for 30-60 minutes,
    turning occasionally.
3   Lift the fish from the marinade and cook in an oiled fish basket or on an oiled grill rack for
    4-5 minutes on each side, turning halfway, until cooked through. Serve with lime wedges.

061 PRAWNS WITH ASIAN PESTO

PREPARATION TIME *10 minutes, plus 1 hour marinating* **COOKING TIME** *6 minutes* **SERVES 4-6**

700g (1½lb) large raw
   prawns with shells on

ASIAN PESTO
1½-2 tbsp groundnut oil

2 tbsp each finely chopped
   garlic, fresh root ginger
   and fresh basil
1½ tbsp finely chopped
   fresh chilli

2 tsp rice wine
1 tbsp sesame oil
sea salt and freshly ground
   black pepper

1   Make the pesto by mixing the ingredients to a paste in a blender.
2   Remove the legs from the prawns, keeping the shells intact. Using the point of a small sharp
    knife, cut a few slits in the shell of the prawns. Rub the pesto thoroughly over the prawns and
    leave in a cool place for 1 hour.
3   Cook the prawns on an oiled grill rack for about 3 minutes on each side until the shells turn pink.

062 HADDOCK WITH BASIL OIL

PREPARATION TIME *5 minutes* **COOKING TIME:** *8-10 minutes* **SERVES 4**

4 haddock steaks, about
   200g (7oz) each, 2.5cm
   (1in) thick
olive oil, for brushing
Wilted Tomatoes (*see
   page 168*) and lemon
   wedges, to serve

BASIL OIL
100ml (3½fl oz) virgin
   olive oil
1 bunch of basil
1 garlic clove, chopped
juice of ½ lemon

sea salt and freshly ground
   black pepper

1   Make the basil oil by puréeing all the ingredients in a small blender or food processor.
2   Brush the haddock with olive oil and sprinkle with seasoning. Cook in an oiled hinged fish basket
    or on an oiled grill rack, skin side down first, for 4-5 minutes on each side.
3   Remove the fish from the grill rack and serve with some of the basil oil poured over and the rest
    served separately, and accompanied by the wilted tomatoes and lemon wedges.

063 LOBSTER WITH ALMOND, CHEESE AND HERB DRESSING

PREPARATION TIME *15 minutes, plus 20 minutes soaking* **COOKING TIME** *9 minutes* **SERVES 4**

**2 uncooked lobsters, each
750g–1kg (1½–2¼lb)**
olive oil, for brushing
lemon wedges, to serve

DRESSING
25g (1oz) almonds
**6 tbsp fresh flat-leaf
parsley**
**7 tbsp mixed fresh herbs
such as chervil, dill,
fennel, mint and chives**

1 garlic clove, chopped
200ml (7fl oz) mild olive oil
**40g (1½ oz) freshly grated
Parmesan cheese**
about 1 tsp lemon juice
**salt and freshly ground
black pepper**

1   Make the dressing by pouring boiling water over the almonds and leave for 20 minutes. Drain
    the almonds and remove the skins.
2   Put the almonds into a blender or food processor. Add all the herbs and garlic. Process until finely
    chopped. With the motor running, slowly pour in the oil in a thin, steady stream. Add the cheese.
    Mix briefly, then season with lemon juice, salt and pepper. Transfer to a bowl.
3   Put the lobsters on a strong board, stomach down, and, using a large sharp knife, slice them
    in half lengthways. Discard the stomachs and intestines. Crack the claws with the back of the
    knife, or use a hammer.
4   Brush the lobster flesh and shells with olive oil. Lay the lobsters, flesh side down, on a grill rack
    over a medium-hot fire and cook for 30 seconds. Turn them over and cook for a further
    8 minutes or so until the shells have turned bright red and the flesh has become white.
5   Add a little dressing to each lobster half and serve the rest separately with the lemon wedges.

064 SARDINES WITH COURGETTES, LEMON AND DILL

PREPARATION TIME *15 minutes, plus 2 hours chilling* **COOKING TIME** *12–14 minutes* **SERVES 4**

8 large or 12 medium sardines, cleaned	4 courgettes, sliced thinly lengthwise	DRESSING
sea salt and freshly ground black pepper	virgin olive oil, for brushing	2 tbsp lemon juice
	lemon wedges, to serve	2 tbsp extra virgin olive oil
		fine leaves from 3 fresh bushy dill sprigs

1 Bury the sardines in sea salt. Set aside in a cool place for 2 hours.
2 Lift the sardines from the salt and brush them clean.
3 Brush the courgette slices with olive oil and barbecue for about 3 minutes on each side until nicely marked. Remove to a serving dish.
4 Meanwhile, make the dressing by whisking together the lemon juice, oil and seasoning. Add the dill. Trickle over the cooked courgette slices and set aside while cooking the sardines.
5 Brush the sardines with olive oil and sprinkle with black pepper. Put in a hinged fish basket or thread onto pairs of oiled parallel skewers, alternating the heads and tails, and place on an oiled grill rack. Cook lightly on one side for 3–4 minutes, turn them over and cook the other side until the skin is scorched and bubbling. Serve the sardines with the courgettes and lemon wedges.

065 WHOLE CHINESE-STYLE SEA BASS

PREPARATION TIME *10 minutes, plus 2–3 hours marinating* **COOKING TIME** *30–35 minutes* **SERVES 6**

whole sea bass, sea trout or red snapper, 1.35kg (3lb), cleaned	sea salt and freshly ground black pepper	6 spring onions, finely chopped
3 tbsp grated fresh root ginger	4 tbsp rice wine vinegar	several sprigs of fresh coriander
	3 tbsp sesame oil	lime wedges, to serve

1 Cut three or four slashes in both sides of the fish, going right down to the bone. Insert a small amount of the ginger in each slash. Season inside and out and transfer the fish to a large sheet of heavy-duty foil and fold up the sides.
2 Pour over the rice wine vinegar and sesame oil and sprinkle over the spring onions. Lay coriander sprigs on top of and around the fish. Wrap the foil loosely around the fish and twist the edges together tightly to make a secure parcel. Leave in a cool place for 2–3 hours.
3 Cook the parcel on the grill rack for 15 minutes, then turn the parcel over and cook for a further 15–20 minutes until the flesh in the slashes is opaque. Serve the fish with the cooking juices spooned over and accompanied by lime wedges.

066 SALMON WITH LIME, TOMATO AND MUSTARD DRESSING

PREPARATION TIME *10 minutes* **COOKING TIME** *8 minutes* **SERVES 4**

**4 thick salmon steaks with
  skin on, 200g (7oz) each
virgin olive oil, for brushing
sea salt and freshly ground
  black pepper**

**fresh flat-leaf parsley
  leaves, to garnish**

DRESSING
**2 vine-ripened plum
  tomatoes, halved**

**juice of 2 limes
1 heaped tsp wholegrain
  mustard
4 tbsp olive oil
2-3 tsp caster sugar**

1   Make the dressing by slicing the tomatoes into thin strips. Shake the remaining ingredients and
    salt and pepper together in a screw-top jar. Taste and add more sugar, if necessary. Add the
    tomato strips and set aside.
2   Brush the salmon with virgin olive oil and sprinkle with seasoning. Grill, flesh side down, for
    4 minutes, turn over, and cook the other side until the skin is crisp and the flesh barely cooked.
3   Remove from the grill rack, garnish with the parsley and serve with the dressing.

067 GRILLED COD WITH CHERMOULA

PREPARATION TIME *10 minutes, plus 1-2 hours marinating* **COOKING TIME** *6 minutes* **SERVES 4**

**4 cod fillets with skin on,
  about 175-200g (6-7oz)
  each
pitta breads, to serve**

CHERMOULA
2 garlic cloves, chopped

**1 red chilli, seeded and
  chopped
2 tbsp chopped fresh
  coriander
1 tbsp chopped fresh
  flat-leaf parsley
1 tbsp chopped fresh mint**

**1½ tsp roasted cumin seeds
1 tsp saffron threads.
1 tsp paprika
juice of 1 lemon
5 tbsp olive oil
sea salt**

1   Lay the fish in a shallow non-metallic dish.
2   Make the chermoula by mixing all the ingredients in a small blender or food processor until
    smooth. Spoon over the cod and turn the fillets to coat them. Cover and leave in a cool place
    for 1-2 hours, turning occasionally.
3   Lift the fish from the dish and cook in an oiled fish basket or on an oiled grill rack for about
    3 minutes on each side until lightly browned and cooked through.
4   Meanwhile, warm the pitta bread on the side of the grill rack for about 30 seconds on each
    side. Serve the cod with the pitta bread.

068 SPICED SARDINES WITH ORANGE AND OLIVE SALAD

PREPARATION TIME *15 minutes, plus 2–3 hours marinating* **COOKING TIME** *6–8 minutes* **SERVES 4**

4 garlic cloves, crushed
1 tbsp olive oil
1 tbsp lemon juice
1 tsp ground Sichuan
   peppercorns
½ tsp hot paprika
sea salt and freshly ground
   black pepper

12–16 fresh sardines,
   depending on size,
   cleaned

SALAD
5 oranges
1 small red onion, very
   thinly sliced

16 large salt-packed black
   olives, pitted
25g (1 oz) flat-leaf parsley
   leaves, coarsely chopped
extra virgin olive oil, for
   trickling

1   Mix together the garlic, olive oil, lemon juice, peppercorns, paprika and seasoning. Rub thoroughly over the sardines, cover and leave in a cool place for 2–3 hours.

2   Make the salad by peeling and segmenting the oranges, removing all the pith and membranes. Put the segments in a bowl with the red onion, olives and parsley. Season and trickle over some oil.

3   Cook the sardines in an oiled fish basket or thread them onto pairs of oiled parallel skewers, alternating the heads and tails and cook on an oiled grill rack for 3–4 minutes on each side. Serve with the orange and olive salad.

069 SPICED GRILLED SALMON

PREPARATION TIME *10 minutes, plus 2 hours marinating* **COOKING TIME** *8–9 minutes* **SERVES 4**

900g (2lb) salmon fillet with skin on	**seeds from 6 cardamom pods**	**groundnut oil, for brushing**
1 tsp cumin seeds	**½ tsp black peppercorns**	**lime wedges, to serve**
1 tsp coriander seeds	**sea salt**	

1 Using a sharp knife, cut a diamond pattern in the salmon skin.
2 Grind the seeds, peppercorns and salt, or pulverize in a bowl using the end of a rolling pin.
3 Brush the salmon with the oil and press the spice mixture into the skin. Cover and leave in a cool place for 2 hours.
4 Place the fish in an oiled hinged fish basket and cook for 8–9 minutes, turning halfway through, until the flesh is still a little translucent inside. Serve with lime wedges.

070 TROUT WITH PANCETTA

PREPARATION TIME *10 minutes* **COOKING TIME** *12–14 minutes* **SERVES 4**

4 trout, 450g (1lb each), cleaned	**sea salt and freshly ground black pepper**	**6–8 slices pancetta** **Herb Sauce (see page 67)**

1 Sprinkle the trout inside and out with plenty of black pepper but only a little salt.
2 Stretch the pancetta with the back of a knife, then wrap each fish in the pancetta. Secure the loose ends with wooden cocktail sticks that have been soaked in water for 20 minutes.
3 Cook in an oiled hinged fish basket or on an oiled grill rack for about 6–7 minutes, then turn the fish over (use two fish slices and take care if not using a fish basket) and cook on the other side for a further 6–7 minutes until the pancetta is crisp and the fish cooked through. Move the fish to the side of the grill rack, if necessary, to ensure even cooking. Serve with the herb sauce.

071 SALMON WITH ANCHOVIES AND CAPERS

PREPARATION TIME *10 minutes, plus 2–3 hours marinating* **COOKING TIME** *7–8 minutes* **SERVES 4**

900g (2lb) salmon fillet with skin on	**2½ tbsp coarsely chopped fresh parsley**	**freshly ground black pepper**
8 anchovy fillets	**1 tsp grated lemon zest**	**virgin olive oil, for brushing**
1 tbsp salt-packed capers, rinsed	**1½ tbsp lemon juice**	**lemon wedges and rocket salad, to serve**

1 Using the point of a sharp knife, cut several deep slashes through the skin side of the salmon.
2 Chop the anchovy fillets, capers, parsley and lemon zest together finely. Mix with the lemon juice and black pepper. Press well into the slashes in the fish. Season the salmon with black pepper and brush with olive oil. Cover and leave in a cool place for 2–3 hours.
3 Place the fish in an oiled fish basket and cook for 7–8 minutes, turning halfway through. Serve with lemon wedges and a rocket salad.

072 BLACKENED PASTRAMI-STYLE SALMON WITH GRILLED LEMONS

PREPARATION TIME *10 minutes, plus 24 hours marinating* **COOKING TIME** *8 minutes* **SERVES 8**

2 tbsp caster sugar
2 tbsp sea salt
2 tbsp chopped fresh dill
1 tbsp paprika
1 tsp garlic granules
1 tsp onion salt

1 tsp ground allspice
1 tsp freshly ground black
  pepper
1tsp English mustard
  powder

2 salmon fillets with skin
  on, 900g (2lb) each
4 lemons, halved
olive oil, for brushing
rocket leaves dressed with
  virgin olive oil, to serve

1 Combine the sugar, salt, dill, paprika, garlic granules, onion salt, allspice, pepper and mustard powder. Rub over both sides of the salmon fillets. Wrap in a large piece of clingfilm and lay in a long dish or tray. Place a heavy chopping board on top and leave in a cool place for 24 hours.

2 Unwrap the salmon, brush with olive oil and cook, skin side down, near the coals in an oiled hinged fish basket for 5 minutes. Turn carefully and cook on the other side for a further 2½ minutes, or slightly longer if you prefer salmon well-done, but take care not to overcook as it will become dry.

3 Meanwhile, brush the lemon halves with olive oil and cook on the side of the grill rack until they are flecked with brown.

4 Remove the salmon from the grill rack and cut into eight portions. Serve with the lemons and dressed rocket leaves.

073 FRAGRANT WHOLE SALMON

PREPARATION TIME *10 minutes, plus 8 hours marinating* **COOKING TIME** *15-20 minutes* **SERVES 8**

2.5kg (5½lb) whole salmon,
  cleaned
lime wedges, coriander
  leaves and sliced spring
  onions, to garnish

MARINADE
175ml (6fl oz) rice wine
  vinegar
175ml (6fl oz) soy sauce
3 tbsp clear honey
1 red chilli, seeded and
  finely chopped

5 garlic cloves, thinly sliced
  into slivers
4 whole star anise, lightly
  crushed
7.5cm (3in) piece fresh root
  ginger, grated

1 Make the marinade by putting all the ingredients into a blender and mixing to combine well.

2 Cut three or four diagonal slashes in both sides of the salmon, then lay the fish in a non-metallic dish. Pour over some of the marinade, making sure that it goes into the slashes. Turn the fish over and pour over the remaining marinade, again making sure that it goes into the slashes. Cover and leave in a cool place for 8 hours, turning the fish occasionally.

3 Transfer the salmon to a large piece of heavy-duty foil, then fold the foil loosely over the fish and twist the edges together firmly to seal completely. Slash the foil at an angle once or twice down each side but be careful not to cut right round.

4 Cook the fish on the grill rack for 15-20 minutes, turning halfway through, or for longer if the fire begins to cool down.

5 Serve the salmon garnished with the lime wedges, coriander leaves and sliced spring onions.

074 RED SNAPPER WITH BARBECUE SAUCE

PREPARATION TIME *5 minutes* **COOKING TIME** *6 minutes* **SERVES 4**

4 red snapper fillets with skin, 175g (6oz) each	BARBECUE SAUCE	**1 tbsp white wine vinegar**
olive oil, for brushing	**1–2 garlic cloves, crushed**	**1 tsp Dijon mustard**
salt and freshly ground black pepper	**leaves from a sprig of fresh mint, chopped**	**pinch of caster sugar**
	1 tbsp sun-dried tomato paste	**150ml (5fl oz) olive oil**

1   Make the barbecue sauce by putting the garlic, mint, tomato paste, vinegar, mustard and a pinch of sugar into a small blender or food processor. Mix together and then, with the motor running, slowly pour in the oil until completely amalgamated. Season to taste.
2   Brush the red snapper with oil. Cook in an oiled hinged fish basket or on an oiled grill rack for 3 minutes on each side until the flesh is opaque. Transfer to plates and serve with the sauce.

075 SWORDFISH WITH THYME AND ANISE

PREPARATION TIME *10 minutes, plus 1–2 hours marinating* **COOKING TIME** *6 minutes* **SERVES 4**

4 swordfish steaks, about 200g (7oz) each	MARINADE	**1 tsp chilli flakes**
	2 tsp fennel seeds	**4 sun-dried tomato halves, finely chopped**
	3 tbsp Pernod	**sea salt**
	2 tbsp olive oil	
	2 tsp fresh thyme leaves	

1   Lay the swordfish in a shallow non-metallic dish.
2   Make the marinade by heating a small, heavy frying pan. Add the fennel seeds and heat until they begin to darken. Crush lightly, then mix with the remaining ingredients.
3   Pour the marinade over the fish, turn the steaks to coat them evenly, then cover and leave in a cool place for 1–2 hours, turning once or twice.
4   Lift the fish from the marinade and cook on an oiled grill rack for 3 minutes or so on each side so they are still slightly pink in the centre.

076 SICILIAN RED MULLET

PREPARATION TIME *15 minutes* **COOKING TIME** *12–14 minutes* **SERVES 4**

4 red mullet, 350g (12oz) each, cleaned	**½ tsp cumin seeds**	**1 lemon, quartered and thinly sliced**
olive oil, for brushing	**1 tsp dried oregano**	**12 fresh bay leaves**
1 tsp fennel seeds	**½ tsp black peppercorns**	**sea salt**

1   Using a sharp knife, cut three deep slashes on each side of all the fish. Brush them with olive oil.
2   Using a pestle and mortar, crush the fennel, cumin and oregano with the peppercorns.
3   Rub into the fish, making sure the mixture goes into the slashes. Push a lemon slice and bay leaf into each slash. Brush the fish again with oil and sprinkle with sea salt.
4   Cook in an oiled fish basket or on an oiled grill rack for 6–7 minutes on each side until cooked through, turning once.

077 BLACKENED SEA BASS

PREPARATION TIME *10 minutes* **COOKING TIME** *6 minutes* **SERVES 4**

4 sea bass fillets with skin on, 175g (6oz) each	lime wedges, to serve	½ tsp cayenne pepper
50g (2oz) unsalted butter, melted	SPICE RUB	salt and freshly ground black pepper
Avocado, Tomato and Red Pepper Salsa *(see page 174)*, to serve	1½ tbsp paprika	
	2 tsp garlic granules	
	½ tsp dried oregano	
	½ tsp dried thyme	

1   Make the spice rub by mixing all the ingredients together and spread on a plate.
2   Brush the fish with melted butter, then press both sides onto the spice rub, making sure it adheres.
3   Cook the fish, flesh side down first, in an oiled fish basket or on an oiled grill rack for 3 minutes. Turn the fish over and cook for a further 3 minutes until the skin is blistered and browned. Serve with salsa and lime wedges.

078 TUNA WITH TOMATOES, MINT AND BASIL

PREPARATION TIME *10 minutes* **COOKING TIME** *35 minutes* **SERVES 4**

2 very ripe beefsteak tomatoes	1 garlic clove, finely chopped	cracked black pepper
5 tbsp extra virgin olive oil	2 tsp finely chopped fresh mint	4 tuna fillets, 200g (7oz) each
2 tbsp soy sauce	25g (1oz) fresh basil leaves, shredded	olive oil, for brushing
2 tbsp lemon juice		salt and freshly ground black pepper

1   Cut the tomatoes into 5cm (2in) cubes. Mix with the extra virgin olive oil, soy sauce, lemon juice, garlic, mint, basil and black pepper in a small saucepan and warm gently for 30 minutes.
2   Brush the tuna with olive oil and sprinkle with seasoning. Grill, skin side down, on an oiled grill rack for about 2 minutes, then turn over and cook the other side until the flesh is barely cooked, or slightly longer if you don't like the fish too rare. Remove to plates.
3   Stir the sauce and spoon over the tuna.

079 GREEK-STYLE SWORDFISH

PREPARATION TIME *5 minutes, plus 30 minutes marinating* **COOKING TIME** *6 minutes* **SERVES 4**

4 swordfish steaks, 150g (5oz) each	50ml (2fl oz) Greek virgin olive oil	1 tsp dried oregano
	juice of ½ lemon	sea salt and freshly ground black pepper

1   Lay the fish in a single layer in a non-metallic dish.
2   Combine the remaining ingredients. Pour over the fish, turn the steaks over to make sure they are evenly coated, then cover and leave in a cool place for 30 minutes.
3   Lift the steaks from the marinade. Reserve any remaining marinade.
4   Cook the swordfish in an oiled hinged fish basket or on an oiled grill rack for 3 minutes, brush with the reserved marinade, turn the steaks over and cook for a further 3 minutes.

080 RED SNAPPER WITH SESAME, GINGER AND CORIANDER

PREPARATION TIME *10 minutes, plus 1–2 hours marinating* **COOKING TIME** *14 minutes* **SERVES 6**

115ml (4fl oz) groundnut oil
1 tbsp sesame oil
1 tbsp soy sauce
juice of 1 lime
2 tbsp rice wine vinegar
1cm (½in) piece fresh root
ginger, grated

leaves from a small bunch
of fresh coriander,
chopped
sea salt and cracked black
pepper

6 red snapper or other
whole fish, 450g (1lb)
each, cleaned
sesame seeds, to serve

1   Combine the groundnut and sesame oils with the soy sauce, lime juice, vinegar, ginger, coriander, salt and black pepper.
2   Cut two diagonal slashes in each side of the fish and place in a non-metallic dish. Pour the coriander mixture over the fish, turn the snappers to coat them evenly, then cover and leave in a cool place for 1–2 hours, turning occasionally.
3   Cook the snappers in an oiled hinged fish basket for about 7 minutes until the underside is blistered and brown. Turn the fish over and cook on the other side for a further 7 minutes until the flesh near the head flakes easily when tested with the point of a sharp knife. Remove the fish to plates, sprinkle over the sesame seeds and serve.

081 MAHI MAHI WITH CAPERS AND LEMON

PREPARATION TIME *10 minutes, plus 1 hour marinating* **COOKING TIME** *6–8 minutes* **SERVES 4**

4 mahi mahi steaks, or
   other firm fish steaks,
   200g (7oz) each
1 tsp chopped fresh thyme
1 tsp chopped fresh
   tarragon

2 garlic cloves, finely
   chopped
sea salt and freshly ground
   black pepper
2 tbsp olive oil
200ml (7fl oz) dry white
   wine

SAUCE
2 tbsp capers in wine
   vinegar, drained
juice of 2 small lemons
1 tsp grated lemon zest
5 tbsp olive oil

1   Lay the fish in a single layer in a non-metallic dish. Sprinkle over the herbs, garlic and seasoning.
    Pour over the oil and wine, cover and leave in a cool place for 1 hour, turning a couple of times.
2   Meanwhile, make the sauce by briefly mixing the capers, lemon juice and zest in a small blender
    or food processor. With the motor running, slowly pour in the oil. Season to taste.
3   Lift the fish from the dish and cook, skin side down first, in an oiled fish basket or on an oiled grill
    for about 3–4 minutes on each side until the flesh flakes easily when tested with the point of a
    sharp knife. Transfer to plates and pour over the sauce.

082 PIZZA-STYLE FISH PARCELS

PREPARATION TIME *10 minutes* **COOKING TIME** *20–25 minutes* **SERVES 4**

227g (8oz) can chopped
    Italian plum tomatoes
1 garlic clove, finely
    chopped
pinch of crushed chilli
    flakes
2 tbsp coarsely chopped
    fresh basil

4 firm white fish fillets,
    such as Icelandic cod or
    haddock, 175g (6oz)
    each
150g (5oz) mozzarella
    cheese, coarsely grated
1 pepperoni sausage,
    thinly sliced

2 tbsp capers, drained
25g (1oz) freshly grated
    Parmesan cheese
freshly ground black
    pepper

1   Cook the tomatoes, garlic and chilli in a small saucepan over a low heat for 10–12 minutes until most of the liquid has evaporated and the tomatoes are pulpy. Stir in the basil.

2   Cut four pieces of heavy-duty foil large enough to enclose each fish fillet completely. Place a fillet on each piece of foil and spread one quarter of the tomato mixture over each fillet. Top with the mozzarella, sausage, capers and then the Parmesan. Sprinkle with black pepper and fold the foil loosely over the fish, twisting the edges together firmly to seal them.

3   Cook on a grill rack for about 10 minutes, turning over halfway through. Just before the end of the cooking time, carefully open one package to check if the flesh flakes easily when tested with the point of a knife.

083 BASS WRAPPED IN VINE-LEAVES

PREPARATION TIME *10 minutes, plus 2 hours marinating* **COOKING TIME** *20 minutes* **SERVES 4**

1 sea bass or grey mullet,
    2kg (4½lb), gutted, with
    head and tail left on
sea salt and freshly ground
    black pepper
4 garlic cloves, sliced
    lengthways

leaves from 1 large bunch
    fresh herbs, such as
    chervil, fennel, dill,
    oregano and rosemary
100ml (3½fl oz) virgin
    olive oil
2 tbsp white wine vinegar

1 packet vine leaves
    preserved in brine,
    drained and rinsed
lemon wedges, to serve

1   Cut deep slashes in several places in both sides of the fish. Sprinkle seasoning deep into the slashes and insert the garlic slivers and herbs well into the slashes. Put any remaining herbs in the fish cavity. Lay the fish in a non-metallic dish.

2   Whisk together the oil, vinegar, and seasoning. Pour over the fish, cover and leave in a cool place for 2 hours, turning a few times.

3   Meanwhile, pour boiling water over the vine leaves to cover, leave for 5 minutes, then drain.

4   Remove the fish from the dish and wrap in the vine leaves. Place the parcel in an oiled fish basket. Cook for 20 minutes, turning once, until the flesh flakes easily when tested with the point of a knife. Adjust the position on the grill rack to ensure the fish cooks through evenly. Serve with lemon wedges.

084 MONKFISH WITH INDIAN SPICES

PREPARATION TIME *10 minutes, plus 1 hour marinating* **COOKING TIME** *6–8 minutes* **SERVES 4**

2 monkfish fillets, 350g (12 oz) each

MARINADE
2 tsp garam masala
1 tsp ground cumin
½ tsp chilli powder
½ tsp ground turmeric

3 tbsp chopped fresh coriander
1–2 tbsp groundnut oil
salt and freshly ground black pepper

RAITA
½ cucumber, seeded

1 small garlic clove, finely chopped
150ml (5fl oz) Greek yogurt
2 tbsp chopped fresh mint
salt and freshly ground black pepper

1   Put the monkfish into a non-metallic dish.
2   Make the marinade by stirring all the ingredients together. Rub into the monkfish to coat evenly and thoroughly. Cover and leave in a cool place for 1 hour.
3   To make the raita, grate the cucumber on the coarse side of the grater. Drain on kitchen paper. Combine the cucumber with the garlic, yogurt, mint and seasoning.
4   Cook the monkfish in an oiled fish basket or on an oiled grill rack for 6–8 minutes until cooked through, turning once.
5   Remove from the grill rack, cut each fillet in half and serve with the raita.

085 TUNA BURGERS

PREPARATION TIME *10 minutes, plus 1 hour chilling* **COOKING TIME** *4 minutes* **SERVES 4–6**

675g (1½lb) tuna steaks or fillets, skinned
1 tsp grated fresh ginger
1 garlic clove, finely chopped
1 tbsp soy sauce

5 spring onions, very finely chopped
1 tbsp chopped fresh coriander
1 tbsp chopped fresh flat-leaf parsley

dash of chilli sauce
sea salt

1   Chop the tuna evenly by hand until it resembles the texture of coarse mince. Put into a bowl.
2   Combine the remaining ingredients with 1–1½ tablespoons of cold water, then stir carefully into the tuna until just evenly mixed. Divide into four or six equal portions. With wet hands, form into burgers about 2.5 cm (1in) thick. Cover and chill for at least 1 hour to firm up, or for longer to allow the flavours to develop fully.
3   Cook the burgers in an oiled hinged fish basket for about 2 minutes on each side until they are golden on the outside but still rare to medium in the centre. Alternatively, cook the burgers on an oiled grill rack and turn them carefully with a fish slice.

086 MACKEREL WITH SWEET CHILLI AND MINT

PREPARATION TIME *10 minutes, plus 2 hours chilling* **COOKING TIME** *10 minutes* **SERVES 4**

4 mackerel, 325g (11oz) each, cleaned	DRESSING	1 large red chilli, seeded and finely chopped
sea salt	3 tbsp rice wine vinegar	5 cm (2in) piece fresh root ginger, finely chopped
	2 tbsp caster sugar	
	1½ tbsp chopped fresh mint	

1 Bury the mackerel in sea salt. Set aside in a cool place for 2 hours.
2 Lift the mackerel from the salt and brush them clean.
3 To make the dressing, whisk the vinegar with the sugar, then stir in the remaining ingredients.
4 Cut two slashes in each side of all the mackerel, going right through to the bone. Season and cook in an oiled hinged fish basket for about 5 minutes. Turn the fish over and cook on the other side for a further 5 minutes, until the flesh near the head flakes easily when tested with the point of a sharp knife and the skin is very crisp. Remove to plates and serve with the dressing.

087 SEARED SEA BASS WITH TOMATO, AVOCADO AND CAPER RELISH

PREPARATION TIME *10 minutes* **COOKING TIME** *3–5 minutes* **SERVES 4**

4 sea bass fillets with skin on, 150g (5oz) each
virgin olive oil, for brushing
sea salt and freshly ground black pepper
small fresh basil leaves, for garnish
lime wedges, to serve

RELISH
4 tbsp olive oil
1 plump garlic clove, sliced into 8
1 shallot, quartered
bunch of fresh parsley stalks
a few fresh basil stalks

2 tsp salted capers, well rinsed and dried
juice of ½ lime
2 plum tomatoes, seeded and cut into thin strips
1 avocado, peeled, pitted and diced
caster sugar (optional)

1 Make the relish by gently warming the oil, garlic, shallot, parsley and basil stalks, 2 tablespoons water, and salt and pepper in a covered small saucepan for 20 minutes, so the flavours infuse. Strain and leave to cool.

2 Shortly before cooking the sea bass, add the capers, lime juice, tomatoes and avocado to the infused oil. Taste and adjust the seasoning, and add a little caster sugar if necessary.

3 Brush the sea bass with virgin olive oil and sprinkle with seasoning. Cook, skin side down, on an oiled grill rack close to the heat for 1–2 minutes, then turn the fish over, raise the grill rack to about 10–15cm (4–6in) from the heat and cook the other side of the fish for 2–3 minutes until the flesh is barely cooked.

4 Remove from the grill rack. Garnish with basil leaves and serve with the relish and lime wedges.

088 SWEET AND SHARP BROCHETTES

PREPARATION TIME *10 minutes, plus 1 hour chilling* **COOKING TIME** *6–8 minutes* **SERVES 4**

2 swordfish or tuna steaks, 150g (5oz) each, cut into bite-sized chunks
300g (10oz) monkfish fillet, cut into bite-sized chunks

16 raw peeled tiger prawns with tails left on
1 plump garlic clove, crushed
2 tbsp teriyaki sauce

juice of ½ lime
2 tbsp chilli oil
2 limes, cut into 8 wedges
1 lemon, cut into 8 wedges
fresh coriander, to garnish

1 Put the fish and prawns into a bowl.

2 Mix together the garlic, teriyaki sauce, lime juice and chilli oil. Pour over the fish, stir gently to ensure the fish is evenly coated, then cover the bowl and leave in a cool place for 1 hour.

3 Lift the fish and prawns from the bowl and thread alternately on eight skewers, intermingling them with lime and lemon wedges.

4 Cook on an oiled grill for about 3–4 minutes on each side until the prawns have turned pink and the fish is cooked through, turning the brochettes once during cooking. Garnish with coriander.

089 MONKFISH BROCHETTES WITH ROSEMARY AND ANCHOVY SAUCE

PREPARATION TIME *10 minutes* **COOKING TIME** *6–8 minutes* **SERVES 4**

2 monkfish fillets, about 350g (12oz) each, cut into 3cm (1¼in) cubes	**lemon wedges, to serve**	**9 salted anchovy fillets, rinsed and dried**
sea salt and freshly ground black pepper	SAUCE	**100ml (3½fl oz) extra virgin olive oil**
olive oil, for brushing	**1½ tbsp chopped fresh rosemary leaves**	**juice of 1½ lemons**

1 Make the sauce by putting the rosemary into a small blender and chopping finely. Add the anchovy fillets and mix to a thick paste. With the motor running, slowly pour in the oil, then add the lemon juice. Season to taste. Set aside.
2 Thread the monkfish onto skewers. Season them and brush with oil. Cook on an oiled grill rack for about 6–8 minutes until evenly browned, turning once.
3 Serve with the sauce and lemon wedges.

090 SALMON WITH SPICED TEA MARINADE

PREPARATION TIME *10 minutes plus 2½ hours cooling and marinating* **COOKING TIME** *8 minutes*
SERVES 4

2 Assam teabags	**1 tbsp clear honey**	**sesame oil, for brushing**
200ml (7fl oz) boiling water	**1 plump garlic clove, peeled**	**spring onions, sliced on the diagonal, to serve**
6cm (2¼in) piece fresh root ginger	**4 pieces salmon fillet with skin on**	
4 tbsp sweet soy sauce		

1 Put the teabags into a bowl, pour over boiling water, stir once, then leave to infuse for 5 minutes.
2 Lift out and discard the teabags. Press the ginger through a garlic press into the tea, then repeat with the garlic. Stir in the soy sauce and honey. Leave until cold.
3 Put the salmon fillets into a dish in a single layer. Pour over the tea marinade. Turn the salmon over, then cover and leave in a cool place for 2 hours, turning occasionally.
4 Lift the salmon from the marinade and pat dry. Brush with sesame oil, then cook on an oiled grill rack, skin side down first, for about 4 minutes on each side until cooked to your liking. Remove the salmon from the grill rack, scatter over the spring onions and serve.

091 PARMA HAM-WRAPPED MONKFISH

PREPARATION TIME *10 minutes, plus 30–60 minutes marinating* **COOKING TIME** *8 minutes* **SERVES 4**

2 monkfish fillets, 350g (12oz) each	1 lemon, halved	1½ tbsp medium dry white wine
olive oil, for brushing	4-6 slices of Parma ham	2 heaped tsp chopped fresh dill
1 tsp fresh thyme leaves	DRESSING	
1 tbsp chopped fresh flat-leaf parsley	3 tbsp olive oil	2 heaped tsp chopped fresh parsley
freshly ground black pepper	3 tbsp groundnut oil	1½ tsp wholegrain mustard
	1½ tbsp tarragon vinegar	

1 Brush the monkfish with olive oil. Combine the thyme leaves and parsley on a plate. Roll the fillets in the mixture, then season with black pepper. Squeeze lemon juice evenly over the fillets. Wrap each fillet in Parma ham, securing the loose ends with soaked wooden cocktail sticks (see page 10). Brush with olive oil. Place in a single layer in a non-metallic dish, cover and leave in a cool place for 30–60 minutes.

2 Cook the fish on an oiled grill rack for about 4 minutes on each side until the fish is just opaque and the ham is crisp.

3 Meanwhile, make the dressing by whisking the ingredients together in a blender, or using a hand whisk, until a green emulsion is formed.

4 Serve the fish with some dressing trickled over. Serve the remaining dressing separately.

092 FISH TORTILLAS WITH TOMATO AND CORIANDER SALSA

PREPARATION TIME *15 minutes* **COOKING TIME** *6 minutes* **SERVES 4**

1 garlic clove, crushed	4 flounder fillets, with skin on, 175g (6oz) each	1 small red onion, finely chopped
sea salt and freshly ground black pepper	8 tortilla wraps	2 tbsp chopped fresh coriander
½ tsp ground cumin	8 tbsp mayonnaise (see page 179)	1 red chilli, seeded and finely chopped
½ tsp dried oregano		1 tbsp lemon juice
½ tsp hot paprika	SALSA	
1 tbsp lime juice	4 vine-ripened tomatoes, seeded and diced	
2 tbsp olive oil		

1 Make the salsa by combing the ingredients. Cover and set aside.

2 Crush the garlic to a paste and mix with a pinch of salt. Combine with the black pepper, spices, lime juice and olive oil. Brush the fish with the mixture.

3 Cook the fish in an oiled hinged fish basket or on an oiled grill rack for 3 minutes on each side.

4 Meanwhile, warm the tortillas on the side of the grill rack for 30 seconds on each side. (Wrap in a napkin and keep warm, if necessary.)

5 Remove the fish from the grill rack or basket, flake it coarsely with a fork and serve in the tortillas with the salsa and a tablespoonful of mayonnaise.

093 SALMON OLIVES WITH GREEN HERB SAUCE

PREPARATION TIME *15 minutes* **COOKING TIME** *20–25 minutes* **SERVES 6**

3 garlic cloves, unpeeled
olive oil, for brushing
6 pieces salmon tail fillet,
300g (10oz) each,
skinned
50g (2oz) dry breadcrumbs

finely grated zest of
3 limes
3 tbsp chopped fresh dill
sea salt and freshly ground
black pepper
lemon wedges, to serve

SAUCE
6 tbsp virgin olive oil
2 tbsp white wine vinegar
2 tbsp chopped fresh
parsley
2 tbsp chopped fresh dill
1 tsp Dijon mustard

1 Preheat the oven to 200ºC/400ºF/Gas 6. Brush the garlic cloves with olive oil, place in an ovenproof dish and bake for about 10 minutes until soft. Allow to cool a little.

2 Meanwhile, make the herb sauce by mixing all the ingredients with seasoning in a blender until smooth. Set aside.

3 Cut each piece of salmon in half horizontally. Place each piece in turn between two pieces of clingfilm and beat out carefully with a rolling pin until increased in size by about a quarter.

4 Peel the cooked garlic and mash the cloves, then mix with the breadcrumbs, lime zest, dill and seasoning. Divide among the salmon slices and roll up towards the narrow end. Secure with wooden cocktail sticks that have been soaked in water for 5–10 minutes.

5 Brush the salmon rolls with olive oil and cook on an oiled grill rack for about 10–12 minutes, turning occasionally, until just cooked; take care not to overcook. Serve with the herb sauce and lemon wedges.

POULTRY

When selecting poultry, remember that bone and skin add flavour. The skin also protects the flesh from harsh heat, and, when cooked to the proper crispness, adds richness. Take care, though, as fat dripping onto hot coals will cause flare-ups, and bone-in chicken can char on the outside before the flesh near the bone is done. However, boneless, skinless pieces can cook too quickly and dry out. Even if you do not want to eat the skin, it is best to leave it on during cooking.

Move poultry from the fridge 30 minutes before cooking it. Shallow cuts in chicken breasts, and deeper ones through to the bone of thighs and drumsticks, allow flavourings to penetrate and help even cooking. Brush chicken, especially boneless and skinless pieces, frequently during cooking with the marinade or oil.

Cook bone-in pieces bone-side down until no longer pink in the centre. Pieces with skin should be seared skin side down for a couple of minutes (except duck, which should be cooked skin side down for 5 minutes until the skin is crisp), then turned over to continue cooking. All poultry except duck must be well cooked but not dried out. White meat usually takes less time to cook than darker meat such as thighs and drumsticks (see page 14). If you have a lot of chicken to cook, pre-cook bone-in chicken pieces in the oven at 200°C/400°F/Gas 6 for 15 minutes, then finish the cooking immediately on the grill rack, reducing the usual cooking time by about 10 minutes.

CHAPTER 3

094 CHICKEN WITH CORIANDER, LIME AND AVOCADO

PREPARATION TIME *15 minutes, plus 1–2 hours marinating* **COOKING TIME** *15 minutes* **SERVES 4**

8 chicken thighs	2 tsp ground cumin	3 tbsp chopped fresh
2 tbsp olive oil	pinch of caster sugar	coriander
grated zest and juice of	salt and freshly ground	fresh coriander leaves and
1 lime	black pepper	lime wedges, to serve
2 garlic cloves, crushed	2 large avocados	

1 Using the point of a sharp knife, cut three slashes in each chicken thigh. Lay the chicken thighs in a non-metallic dish.
2 Combine the olive oil, lime zest, half the lime juice, garlic, cumin, sugar and seasoning. Brush evenly over the chicken, making sure it also goes into the slashes. Cover and leave in a cool place for 1–2 hours.
3 Lift the chicken from the dish. Cook on an oiled grill rack for 15 minutes, turning every 3 minutes.
4 Meanwhile, halve, pit, peel and chop the avocados, then mix with the remaining lime juice and the chopped coriander. Season.
5 Remove the chicken from the grill rack, garnish with coriander leaves and serve with the avocado and lime wedges.

095 DUCK WITH ORANGE AND MUSTARD DRESSING

PREPARATION TIME *15 minutes* **COOKING TIME** *13–15 minutes* **SERVES 2**

2 Barbary or Gressingham	1 tbsp hazelnut oil	salad leaves, including
duck breasts	1 tbsp olive oil	watercress, to serve
5 oranges	salt and freshly ground	25g (1oz) hazelnuts, lightly
1 tbsp Dijon mustard	black pepper	toasted, skinned and
1 tbsp clear honey		coarsely chopped

1 Using a sharp knife, score diagonal parallel lines 1cm (½in) apart through the skin of the duck breasts to make a criss-cross pattern; do not pierce the flesh.
2 Squeeze the juice from four oranges. Mix 1 tablespoon of the orange juice with the mustard and honey. Spread over the breasts.
3 Cook the breasts, skin side down first, on an oiled grill rack for 5 minutes until the skin is crisp. Turn the breasts over and cook for a further 8–10 minutes, depending how well done you like duck to be.
4 Meanwhile, make the dressing. Whisk together 5 tablespoons of orange juice with the hazelnut oil and olive oil. Season to taste.
5 Transfer the duck to a plate, pour over half the dressing, cover with foil and leave to rest for 5 minutes.
6 Remove the peel and pith from the remaining orange and divide the orange into segments. Divide the salad leaves and orange segments between two serving plates. Slice the duck breasts diagonally, arrange on the salads, sprinkle over the hazelnuts and pour over the remaining dressing.

096 CHICKEN WITH LEMON AND MUSTARD

PREPARATION TIME *10 minutes, plus 2 hours marinating* **COOKING TIME** *16–20 minutes* **SERVES 4**

8 chicken pieces on the bone	MARINADE	3 tbsp Dijon mustard
	2 plump garlic cloves	5 tbsp olive oil
	salt and freshly ground black pepper	5 tbsp lemon juice
		½ tsp dried thyme

1   Cut deep slashes in the chicken, then put in a single layer in a non-metallic bowl.
2   Peel the garlic and crush it to a paste with a pinch of salt. Mix with the remaining ingredients. Spread evenly over the chicken, turn the pieces over to ensure they are evenly coated, then cover and leave in a cool place for 2 hours, turning occasionally.
3   Cook the chicken pieces, skin side down first, on an oiled grill rack for 8–10 minutes on each side, turning occasionally, until the skin is golden and the juices run clear when the thickest part is pierced with a skewer.

097 TANDOORI CHICKEN KEBABS

PREPARATION TIME *10 minutes, plus 2 hours marinating* **COOKING TIME** *10 minutes* **SERVES 4**

8 boneless chicken thighs, cut into approximately 2.5cm (1in) pieces	2 garlic cloves, finely chopped	1 tsp ground cardamom
	2 tsp grated fresh root ginger	1 tsp ground coriander
		1 tsp garam masala
MARINADE	½ red chilli, seeded and finely chopped	1 tsp ground cumin
225ml (8fl oz) yogurt		salt

1   Put the chicken in a shallow, non-metallic dish.
2   Make the marinade by stirring the ingredients together. Pour over the chicken and turn the pieces over to ensure they are coated thoroughly and evenly. Cover and leave in a cool place for 2 hours, turning occasionally.
3   Drain the chicken from the marinade and thread onto skewers. Cook the chicken on an oiled grill rack for 5 minutes on each side, turning occasionally, until browned and the juices run clear when the thickest part is pierced with a skewer.

098 CHICKEN WITH ORANGE AND MINT

PREPARATION TIME *15 minutes, plus 1–2 hours marinating* **COOKING TIME** *12–16 minutes* **SERVES 4**

1 tbsp olive oil	2–3 tbsp chopped fresh mint	500g (1lb 2oz) chicken breasts
1 garlic clove, finely chopped	pinch of caster sugar	fresh mint sprigs, to garnish
5 tbsp orange juice	salt and freshly ground black pepper	
2 tbsp lemon juice		

1   Combine the olive oil, garlic, fruit juices, mint, sugar and plenty of seasoning.
2   Slash the chicken with the point of a sharp knife, lay the pieces in a non-metallic dish and pour over the marinade. Turn the chicken over so the pieces are evenly coated, then cover and leave in a cool place for 1–2 hours, turning occasionally.
3   Lift the chicken from the dish (reserve the remaining marinade) and cook on an oiled grill rack for 6–8 minutes a side, brushing occasionally with the marinade. Serve garnished with mint sprigs.

099 TUSCAN CHICKEN WITH TOMATO AND BLACK OLIVE SALAD

PREPARATION TIME *10 minutes* **COOKING TIME** *10 minutes* **SERVES 4**

4-6 garlic cloves, peeled
2 tsp salt
1 tsp freshly ground black
 pepper
3 tbsp finely chopped fresh
 rosemary
12 boneless chicken thighs,
 skinned

12 thin slices pancetta
olive oil, for brushing

TOMATO AND BLACK OLIVE SALAD
4 vine-ripened tomatoes,
 sliced
1 garlic clove, finely
 chopped

50g (2oz) oil-cured black
 olives, pitted and sliced
salt and freshly ground
 black pepper
3 tbsp extra virgin olive oil
1 tbsp chopped fresh
 flat-leaf parsley

1   Make the salad by putting the tomatoes, garlic and olives into a bowl. Season, then trickle over the oil. Scatter over the parsley. Set aside.
2   Pound the garlic, salt, pepper and rosemary to a paste, using a pestle and mortar, spice grinder or the end of a rolling pin in a small bowl. Rub the paste liberally over the flesh-side of the thighs.
3   Re-shape the thighs and wrap each one in a slice of pancetta. Brush with olive oil. Secure with wooden cocktail sticks that have been soaked in water for 10 minutes.
4   Cook the chicken thighs on an oiled grill rack for 5 minutes on each side until golden, crisp and cooked through. Remove the thighs from the grill rack. Season with black pepper and serve accompanied by the salad.

100 CHICKEN WITH GINGER, GARAM MASALA AND COCONUT

PREPARATION TIME *10 minutes, plus 1-2 hours marinating* **COOKING TIME** *15 minutes* **SERVES 4**

8 chicken drumsticks
salt and freshly ground
 black pepper
fresh coriander leaves, to
 garnish

SPICE MIXTURE
1 onion, chopped
4 garlic cloves, crushed
1 tbsp grated fresh root
 ginger
1 tbsp garam masala

100ml (3½fl oz) coconut
 milk
3 tbsp Thai fish sauce
1 small handful fresh
 coriander

1   Put the chicken thighs in a non-metallic dish. Using a sharp knife, make several slashes in each of the thighs.
2   Put all the spice mixture ingredients in a blender or food processor and pulse until smooth. Pour over the chicken and turn the drumsticks over so they are evenly coated; make sure the mixture goes into the slashes. Cover and leave in a cool place for 1-2 hours, turning occasionally.
3   Lift the chicken from the dish. Cook on an oiled grill rack for 15 minutes, turning every 3 minutes.
4   Remove from the grill rack, sprinkle with salt and pepper and garnish with coriander leaves.

101 CHICKEN STRIPS WITH BASIL AND LIME

PREPARATION TIME *10 minutes, plus 1–2 hours marinating* **COOKING TIME** *10 minutes* **SERVES 4**

450g (1lb) skinless chicken breasts
100ml (3½fl oz) virgin olive oil
grated zest of 1 large lime
55ml (2fl oz) lime juice

2 tbsp shredded fresh basil leaves
salt and freshly ground black pepper

BASIL AND LIME MAYONNAISE
100g (3½oz) mayonnaise
(see page 179)
2 tbsp finely shredded fresh basil leaves
juice of ½ lime, or to taste

1. Cut each chicken breast into three lengthways strips and put into a shallow, non-metallic bowl.
2. Mix the oil with the lime zest and juice, basil leaves and seasoning, using plenty of black pepper. Pour over the chicken, stir to ensure the chicken is well coated, then cover and leave in a cool place for 1–2 hours.
3. Meanwhile, make the basil and lime mayonnaise by mixing the mayonnaise with the basil leaves, and adding lime juice and black pepper to taste.
4. Lift the chicken from the marinade, thread the strips onto skewers, and then cook on an oiled grill rack for about 10 minutes, turning 2–3 times, until golden and cooked through. Serve the skewers accompanied by the mayonnaise.

102 POUSSINS WITH PERSIAN MARINADE

PREPARATION TIME *15 minutes, plus 4–6 hours marinating* **COOKING TIME** *25 minutes* **SERVES 4**

4 poussins, spatchcocked*	1 garlic clove, finely	1 onion, coarsely grated
generous pinch of saffron	chopped	2cm (¾in) piece of fresh root
threads	salt and freshly ground	ginger, grated
pinch of sugar	black pepper	pinch of cayenne pepper
juice of 4 lemons	4 tbsp Greek yogurt	

1 Thread two oiled metal skewers diagonally through each bird to hold them in shape during cooking. Alternatively, thread one skewer through the wings and body and another skewer through the thighs. Place the poussins in a shallow, non-metallic bowl.

2 Grind the saffron and sugar to a powder using a pestle and mortar, or the end of a rolling pin in a small bowl. Stir in the lemon juice.

3 Crush the garlic to a paste with a pinch of salt. Combine with the yogurt, onion, ginger, cayenne pepper and some black pepper. Pour evenly over the poussins, cover and leave in a cool place for 4–6 hours, turning occasionally.

4 Lift the poussins from the marinade (reserve the marinade) and cook bone-side down on an oiled grill rack for 15 minutes. Turn them over and cook for a further 10 minutes, brushing occasionally with the remaining marinade, until the skin is crisp and the juices run clear when the flesh between the legs and the body is pierced with a sharp knife.

* If you are unable to buy spatchcocked birds, do it yourself by placing each one in turn on a board. Cut down either side of the backbone with poultry shears or firm, sharp kitchen scissors. Lift out the backbone. Turn the bird over, open it out and press down firmly to open it out flat.

103 CHICKEN AND LEMON GRASS KEBABS

PREPARATION TIME *10 minutes, plus 8 hours marinating* **COOKING TIME** *10 minutes* **SERVES 4**

4 skinless, boneless	MARINADE	grated zest of 1 lime
chicken breasts, cut into	1 tbsp finely chopped fresh	juice of 2 limes
2.5cm (1in) cubes	root ginger	1 tbsp clear honey
8 stalks of lemon grass,	3 garlic cloves, finely	4 tbsp dark soy sauce
outer layers removed	chopped	4 tbsp rice wine vinegar
	1 red chilli, seeded and	2 tbsp sweet chilli sauce
	finely chopped	

1 Make the marinade by combining the ingredients in a bowl. Stir in the chicken to ensure all the pieces are evenly coated. Cover and leave in a cool place for about 8 hours, stirring occasionally.

2 Lift the chicken from the bowl (reserve the remaining marinade). Pierce a hole through each cube and then thread them onto the lemon grass stalks.

3 Cook on an oiled grill rack for about 10 minutes, turning occasionally and brushing with the reserved marinade.

104 DUCK WITH MANGO DIP

PREPARATION TIME *15 minutes, plus 30–60 minutes marinating* **COOKING TIME** *16–20 minutes* **SERVES 4**

4 Gressingham or Barbary duck breasts	2 pieces of star anise salt and freshly ground black pepper	75g (3oz) finely shredded mango
4 plump garlic cloves, sliced		75g (3oz) finely shredded spring onion
1 tbsp fresh tamarind, or lemon juice	DIP 150g (5oz) caster sugar	75g (3oz) finely shredded cucumber
grated zest and juice of 1 orange	200ml (7fl oz) white wine vinegar	
pinch of dried chilli flakes	pinch dried chilli flakes	

1 Using a sharp knife, score diagonal parallel lines 1cm (½in) apart through the skin of the duck breasts to make a criss-cross pattern; do not pierce the flesh.
2 Put the garlic, tamarind, orange zest and juice, chilli flakes and star anise into a blender and mix to a paste. Brush the spice paste evenly over the duck breasts. Cover and leave in a cool place for 30–60 minutes.
3 Meanwhile, make the dip by gently heating the sugar in the vinegar until it dissolves, then increasing the heat and boiling for 2 minutes. Remove from the heat, add the remaining ingredients and leave to cool.
4 Cook the breasts, skin side down first, on an oiled grill rack for 5 minutes until the skin is crisp. Turn the breasts over and cook for a further 8–10 minutes, depending how well done you like duck to be.
5 Remove the duck from the grill, cover with foil and leave to rest for 5 minutes. Season and serve with the mango dip.

105 GUINEA FOWL WITH RUM, ORANGE AND MAPLE SYRUP

PREPARATION TIME *10 minutes, plus 6 hours marinating* **COOKING TIME** *35 minutes* **SERVES 4**

1 guinea fowl, about 1.3kg (2½lb), spatchcocked*	2 tbsp maple syrup 1 tbsp groundnut oil	1 tbsp finely chopped fresh root ginger
2 tbsp dark rum	large pinch of ground allspice	salt and freshly ground black pepper
2 tbsp fresh orange juice, from a bottle or carton	salt and freshly ground black pepper	

1 Thread two oiled metal skewers diagonally through each bird to hold them in shape during cooking. Alternatively, thread one skewer through the wings and body and another skewer through the thighs. Put the guinea fowl into a non-metallic dish.
2 Combine the remaining ingredients. Brush evenly all over the guinea fowl. Pour any remaining marinade around the bird. Cover and leave in a cool place for 6 hours, basting occasionally.
3 Lift the bird from the marinade (reserve any remaining marinade) and cook, bone-side down, on an oiled grill rack for 20 minutes. Turn the bird over and cook for a further 15 minutes or so, brushing occasionally with the remaining marinade, until the skin is crisp and the juices run clear when the flesh between the legs and the body is pierced with a skewer.
* See note on recipe 102 (above left) regarding spatchcocking.

MOROCCAN CHICKEN WITH TABOULEH

PREPARATION TIME *15 minutes, plus 2–5 hours marinating* **COOKING TIME** *10 minutes* **SERVES 2**

6 boneless chicken thighs, cut into approximately 2.5cm (1in) pieces
2 tbsp olive oil
5 tbsp lemon juice
1 plump garlic clove, finely chopped
small handful fresh coriander, finely chopped

small handful fresh flat-leaf parsley, finely chopped
1 tbsp ground cumin
1 tbsp cinnamon
1 tbsp ground coriander
salt and freshly ground black pepper

TABOULEH
50g (2oz) bulgur

115g (4oz) Italian mixed peppers in oil, drained and chopped
2 tbsp olive oil
2 tbsp lemon juice
handful fresh flat-leaf parsley, finely chopped
4 large sprigs of mint, finely chopped

1 Thread the chicken onto skewers. Lay the thighs in a single layer in a non-metallic dish.
2 Combine the olive oil, lemon juice, garlic, herbs, spices and seasoning. Pour over the chicken, turn the thighs over to ensure they are well-coated, then cover and leave to marinate in a cool place for 2–5 hours.
3 Meanwhile, make the tabouleh by putting the bulgur into a bowl. Pour over 65ml (2½fl oz) boiling water over and leave for 30 minutes until the water has been absorbed. Stir occasionally.
4 Fluff up the bulgur with a fork. Fork through the remaining tabouleh ingredients and season.
5 Lift the chicken from the dish (reserve the marinade) and cook on an oiled grill rack for 5 minutes on each side, brushing with the reserved marinade occasionally. Using a fork, slip the cooked chicken from the skewers onto the tabouleh.

107 POUSSINS WITH GARLIC, LEMON AND THYME

PREPARATION TIME *10 minutes, plus 4 hours marinating* **COOKING TIME** *25 minutes* **SERVES 2**

4 poussins, spatchcocked*	**3 tbsp fresh thyme leaves**	**salt and freshly ground**
	6 tbsp fruity olive oil	**black pepper**
MARINADE	**juice of 1½ large lemons**	
3 garlic cloves, crushed		

1. Thread two metal skewers diagonally through each bird to hold them in shape during cooking. Alternatively, thread a skewer through the wings and body and another skewer through the thighs. Place the poussins in a shallow, non-metallic bowl.
2. Combine the marinade ingredients and pour evenly over the poussins. Cover and leave in a cool place for 4 hours, turning occasionally.
3. Lift the poussins from the marinade (reserve the marinade) and cook bone-side down on an oiled grill rack for 15 minutes. Turn them over and cook for a further 10 minutes, brushing occasionally with the remaining marinade, until the skin is crisp and the juices run clear when the flesh between the legs and the body is pierced with a sharp knife.
* If you are unable to buy spatchcocked birds, do it yourself by placing each one in turn on a board. Cut down either side of the backbone with poultry shears or firm, sharp kitchen scissors. Lift out the backbone. Turn the bird over, open it out and press down firmly to open it out flat.

108 TURKEY MORSELS WITH PEANUT MARINADE

PREPARATION TIME *10 minutes, plus 2 hours marinating* **COOKING TIME** *10 minutes* **SERVES 4**

450g (1lb) turkey cubes	**200ml (7fl oz) yogurt**	**few drops of Tabasco sauce**
115g (4oz) peanut butter	**about 1 tbsp Dijon mustard**	**salt and freshly ground**
1 plump garlic clove, finely	**about 1½ tsp**	**black pepper**
chopped	**Worcestershire sauce**	**bunch of spring onions**

1. Put the turkey cubes into a non-metallic bowl.
2. Mix the peanut butter and garlic with 75ml (3fl oz) of the yogurt, then add the mustard, Worcestershire sauce, and Tabasco and salt to taste. Pour over the turkey and stir gently to ensure it is evenly coated. Cover and leave in a cool place for 2 hours.
3. Meanwhile, slice some of the green parts of the spring onions and reserve for garnish. Finely slice the white parts and mix with the remaining yogurt. Season to taste, cover and chill until required.
4. Lift the turkey from the marinade and thread onto skewers. Cook on an oiled grill rack for about 10 minutes, turning occasionally. Remove from the rack. Sprinkle the sliced green spring onions over the yogurt mixture and serve with the kebabs.

109 POUSSINS GLAZED WITH HONEY AND SPICES

PREPARATION TIME *10 minutes, plus 4–6 hours marinating* **COOKING TIME** *25 minutes* **SERVES 6**

3 large poussins, split down the backbone*	3 tbsp soy sauce	1½ tbsp finely chopped fresh rosemary
	3 garlic cloves, crushed	
	2 tbsp clear honey	2 tbsp light brown sugar
MARINADE	2.5cm (1in) piece fresh root ginger, grated	1 tbsp Dijon mustard
2 tbsp sesame oil		salt and freshly ground black pepper
2 tbsp white wine vinegar		

1 Make the marinade by stirring all the ingredients together until the sugar has dissolved.
2 Put the poussins in a single layer in a non-metallic dish. Pour over the marinade and turn the birds over to ensure they are evenly coated. Cover and leave to marinate in a cool place for 4–6 hours, turning occasionally.
3 Drain the marinade from the poussins into a saucepan and bring to the boil on the grill rack.
4 Cook the poussins, bone-side down, on an oiled grill rack for 15 minutes. Turn them over and cook for a further 10 minutes until the skin is crisp and the juices run clear when the flesh between the legs and the body is pierced with a skewer. Brush occasionally with the marinade.
* If you are unable to buy large poussins, buy medium-sized spatchcocked birds, or spatchcock them yourself by placing each one in turn on a board. Cut down either side of the backbone with poultry shears or firm, sharp kitchen scissors. Lift out the backbone. Turn the bird over, open it out and press down firmly to open it out flat

110 TURKEY STEAKS WITH COCONUT AND CORIANDER

PREPARATION TIME *10 minutes, plus 4–6 hours marinating* **COOKING TIME** *12 minutes* **SERVES 4**

4 turkey steaks	large handful of fresh coriander	1 tbsp garam masala
		100ml (3½fl oz) coconut milk
MARINADE	1 tbsp finely chopped fresh root ginger	freshly ground black pepper
3 garlic cloves, chopped	1 onion, chopped	
½ red chilli, seeded and chopped	3 tbsp Thai fish sauce	

1 Using the point of a sharp knife, make cuts in the surfaces of the turkey steaks. Lay the steaks in a single layer in a non-metallic dish.
2 Make the marinade by putting all the ingredients into a blender or food processor and pulsing until the mixture is smooth.
3 Pour evenly over the steaks, then turn them over to coat thoroughly. Cover and leave in a cool place for 4–6 hours, turning occasionally.
4 Lift the turkey steaks from the dish and cook on an oiled grill rack for about 6 minutes on each side, turning once.

111 GUINEA FOWL WITH MUSTARD AND BALSAMIC VINEGAR

PREPARATION TIME *10 minutes, plus 6–8 hours marinating* **COOKING TIME** *35 minutes* **SERVES 4**

1 guinea fowl, about 1.3kg (2½lb), spatchcocked*	MARINADE 2 garlic cloves, peeled salt and freshly ground black pepper	1 tbsp Dijon mustard 1 tsp herbes de Provence 1 tbsp olive oil 4 tbsp balsamic vinegar

1 Thread two oiled metal skewers diagonally through the bird to hold it in shape during cooking. Alternatively, thread one skewer through the wings and body and another skewer through the thighs. Put the guinea fowl in a non-metallic dish.

2 Make the marinade by crushing the garlic to a paste with a pinch of salt. Combine with the remaining ingredients. Pour evenly over the guinea fowl and turn the bird so that it is well coated. Cover and leave in a cool place for 6–8 hours, turning occasionally.

3 Lift the bird from the marinade (reserve the marinade) and cook, bone-side down, on an oiled grill rack for 20 minutes. Turn the bird over and cook for a further 15 minutes or so until the skin is crisp and the juices run clear when the flesh between the legs and the body is pierced with a skewer. Brush occasionally with the remaining marinade.

* If you are unable to buy a spatchcocked bird, do it yourself by placing it on a board. Cut down either side of the backbone with poultry shears or firm, sharp kitchen scissors. Lift out the backbone. Turn the bird over, open it out and press down firmly to open it out flat.

112 PEPPERED CHICKEN BROCHETTES

PREPARATION TIME *10 minutes, plus 1–2 hours marinating* **COOKING TIME** *10–12 minutes* **SERVES 4**

450g (1lb) skinless chicken breasts, cut into 3.5cm (1¼in) cubes 2 tbsp olive oil 1½ tsp coarsely ground black peppercorns	1 small red chilli, seeded and thinly sliced 1 garlic clove, finely chopped grated zest and juice of 2 small lemons 1½ tbsp clear honey	8 button mushrooms olive oil, for brushing salt and freshly ground black pepper chopped flat-leaf parsley, to garnish

1 Put the chicken pieces in a non-metallic bowl.

2 Mix together the oil,. peppercorns, chilli, garlic, lemon zest and juice, and honey. Pour over the chicken and stir gently to ensure the chicken is evenly coated. Cover and leave to marinate in a cool place for 1–2 hours.

3 Brush the mushrooms with olive oil and sprinkle them with seasoning. Thread one mushroom onto each of four skewers.

4 Lift the chicken from the marinade and thread the cubes onto the skewers, then finish with another mushroom.

5 Cook on an oiled grill rack for 10–12 minutes, turning occasionally. Remove from the rack and sprinkle with parsley.

113 CHICKEN WITH CHILLI JAM

PREPARATION TIME *10 minutes, plus 2 hours marinating* **COOKING TIME** *45 minutes* **SERVES 4**

4 chicken leg portions	**75g (3oz) raisins**	**½ tsp grated fresh root**
	200g (7oz) red chillies,	**ginger**
CHILLI JAM	**seeded and chopped**	**1 tsp soy sauce**
75g (3oz) soft brown sugar	**2 garlic cloves, chopped**	**1 tbsp chopped fresh**
100ml (3½fl oz) rice wine	**2 shallots, chopped**	**coriander leaves**
vinegar		**65ml (2½fl oz) yogurt**

1 Make the jam by gently heating the sugar in the vinegar, stirring, until the sugar has dissolved, then bring to the boil. Add the raisins and cook until the liquid is syrupy and a light caramel colour. Stir in the chillies, garlic, shallots, ginger and soy sauce. Transfer to a blender and pulse until reduced to a coarse purée. Leave to cool. Combine with the coriander leaves and yogurt.

2 Cut deep slashes in the chicken legs and place in a non-metallic bowl. Rub the chilli jam into the legs, making sure it goes well into the slashes. Cover and leave in a cool place for 2 hours.

3 Cook the chicken on an oiled grill rack for 25–30 minutes until cooked through, crisp and slightly charred.

114 CHICKEN, BACON AND SAUSAGE KEBABS

PREPARATION TIME *10 minutes* **COOKING TIME** *10 minutes* **SERVES 4**

450g (1lb) skinless,		**(¾in) cubes**
boneless chicken	**4 good-quality herb**	**16 small fresh sage or bay**
(preferably thighs	**sausages, cut into 2.5cm**	**leaves (optional)**
and/or drumsticks),	**(1in) lengths**	**olive oil, for brushing**
cut into 3.5cm	**115g (4oz) piece bacon or**	**salt and freshly ground**
(1¾in) cubes	**pancetta, cut into 2cm**	**black pepper**

1 Thread the chicken, sausage and bacon onto long skewers, inserting the sage or bay leaves at intervals, if using. Brush with olive oil.

2 Cook the kebabs on an oiled grill rack for about 10 minutes, turning occasionally, until the chicken and sausage are cooked through and browned. Remove the kebabs from the grill rack and sprinkle with seasoning.

115 PERSIAN-STYLE CHICKEN KEBABS

PREPARATION TIME *10 minutes, plus 2 hours marinating* **COOKING TIME** *10 minutes* **SERVES 4**

450g (1lb) boneless chicken	MARINADE	**salt and freshly ground**
thighs, cut into 3.5cm	**200ml (7fl oz) Greek yogurt**	**black pepper**
(1¾in) cubes	**3–4 saffron threads,**	
chopped fresh coriander	**crushed**	
leaves, to garnish	**1 tbsp chopped fresh mint**	
lemon wedges, to serve	**2 tbsp olive oil**	

1 Put the chicken in a non-metallic dish.

2 Make the marinade by combining the ingredients. Stir into the chicken to ensure the chicken is well coated. Cover and leave in a cool place for 2 hours, stirring occasionally.

3 Lift the chicken from the marinade and thread the pieces onto skewers. Cook on an oiled grill rack for about 10 minutes, turning occasionally, until cooked through and browned. Remove from the grill rack, sprinkle with coriander and serve with lemon wedges.

116 DUCK WITH GINGERED PLUMS

PREPARATION TIME *15 minutes* **COOKING TIME** *20–25 minutes* **SERVES 4**

4 Barbary or Gressingham duck breasts	6 purple-skinned plums, pitted and sliced	2 tbsp cider vinegar
clear honey, for brushing	1 small garlic clove, finely chopped	2 tbsp sugar
Chinese five-spice powder, for sprinkling	4 tsp soy sauce	2 tsp grated fresh root ginger

1 Using a sharp knife, score diagonal parallel lines 1cm (½in) apart through the skin of the duck breasts to make a criss-cross pattern; do not pierce the flesh. Brush the breasts with honey, then sprinkle with five-spice powder.

2 Cook the breasts, skin side down first, on an oiled grill rack for 5 minutes until the skin is crisp. Then turn the breasts over and cook for a further 8–10 minutes, depending how well done you like your duck to be.

3 Remove from the grill, cover with foil and leave to rest for 5 minutes.

4 Meanwhile, put the remaining ingredients into a saucepan, bring to the boil on the side of the grill rack and leave to simmer for 5 minutes.

5 Sprinkle the duck with seasoning and serve with the plums and juices.

117 ITALIAN CHICKEN BURGERS

PREPARATION TIME *10 minutes, plus 2–4 hours chilling* **COOKING TIME** *10-12 minutes* **SERVES 4**

450g (1lb) minced chicken	salt and freshly ground	mixed salad leaves
1½ tbsp sun-dried tomatoes	black pepper	mayonnaise *(see page 179)*
in oil, drained and	olive oil, for brushing	sun-dried tomato strips
chopped		fresh basil leaves
1½ tbsp chopped fresh basil	TO SERVE	
3 tbsp freshly grated	4 ciabatta rolls, halved	
Parmesan cheese	horizontally	

1   Combine the minced chicken with the sun-dried tomatoes, basil, Parmesan and seasoning until thoroughly mixed. With wet hands, form the mixture into four burgers, 2cm (¾in) thick. If possible, cover and leave in a cool place for 2–4 hours.
2   Brush the burgers with oil and cook on an oiled grill rack for 5–6 minutes on each side until the juices run clear.
3   Meanwhile, warm the rolls on the side of the grill rack for 20–30 seconds. To serve, put a few salad leaves on the bottom half of each roll. Add a burger, then some mayonnaise and top with sun-dried tomato strips and basil leaves.

118 ASH-BAKED CHICKEN THIGHS

PREPARATION TIME *10 minutes* **COOKING TIME** *35 minutes* **SERVES 3-6**

6 chicken thighs on the	4 tbsp finely chopped	1 lemon, very thinly sliced
bone	fresh parsley	salt and freshly ground
	5 garlic cloves, thinly sliced	black pepper

1   Wrap two chicken thighs with one third of the parsley, garlic, lemon and seasoning in a loose parcel of double-thickness, heavy-duty foil. Twist the edges together to seal tightly. Wrap securely in a third piece of foil. Repeat with the remaining chicken to make two more parcels.
2   Push the hot coals to one side of the fire, add the chicken parcels in a single layer and scatter hot coals in an even layer on the top. Cook for 35 minutes, then carefully remove the parcels and leave to stand for 5–10 minutes before opening.

119 SICHUAN CHICKEN

PREPARATION TIME *10 minutes, plus 1-2 hours marinating* **COOKING TIME** *14-16 minutes* **SERVES 4**

4 chicken breasts	1 tbsp clear honey	1 tsp crushed coriander
with skin on, about	1 tbsp Sichuan	seeds
200g (7oz) each	peppercorns, lightly	1 tbsp garam masala
	toasted and finely	1 tsp ground ginger
MARINADE	crushed	1 tsp sesame oil
2 tbsp sake		1-2 dashes Tabasco sauce

1   Using the point of a sharp knife, score each chicken breast three times on both sides. Place in a non-metallic dish.
2   Make the marinade by mixing all the ingredients together. Pour evenly over the chicken, cover and leave to marinate in a cool place for 1–2 hours.
3   Lift the chicken from the dish and cook on an oiled grill rack for 7–8 minutes on each side.

120 CHICKEN WITH INDIAN SPICES

PREPARATION TIME *10 minutes, plus 1–2 hours marinating* **COOKING TIME** *15 minutes* **SERVES 4**

8 chicken drumsticks
naan bread, to serve
fresh coriander leaves,
  to garnish

SPICE MIXTURE
1 onion, chopped

4 garlic cloves, crushed
1 tbsp grated fresh root
  ginger
3 tbsp Thai fish sauce
100ml (3½fl oz) coconut
  milk
1 tbsp garam masala

1 small handful fresh
  coriander
salt and freshly ground
  black pepper

1   Cut deep slashes in each chicken drumstick and place in a non-metallic dish.
2   Make the spice mixture by putting all the ingredients in a blender or food processor and pulsing until smooth. Pour over the chicken and turn the drumsticks over so the pieces are evenly coated. Cover and leave in a cool place for 1–2 hours, turning occasionally.
3   Lift the chicken from the dish and cook on an oiled grill rack for 15 minutes, turning every 3 minutes, until cooked through.
4   Meanwhile, warm the naan bread on the side of the grill rack for 30 seconds on each side. Remove the chicken from the grill rack, sprinkle with salt and garnish with coriander leaves.

121 CHICKEN WITH PESTO AND LEMON

PREPARATION TIME *10 minutes, plus 2 hours marinating* **COOKING TIME** *14–16 minutes* **SERVES 4**

5 tbsp Pesto (*see page 172*)
juice of 1 small lemon
1½ tbsp extra virgin
  olive oil

freshly ground black
  pepper
4 chicken breasts with skin
  on, about 175g (6oz) each

basil sprigs, for garnish

1   Mix the pesto with the lemon juice, extra virgin olive oil and black pepper.
2   Place the chicken in a non-metallic dish. Spread the pesto mixture evenly over the chicken, cover and leave in a cool place for at least 2 hours.
3   Cook the chicken on an oiled grill rack for 7–8 minutes on each side. Remove from the grill, garnish with basil sprigs and serve.

122 TURKEY KEBABS WITH LEMON AND TERIYAKI SAUCE

PREPARATION TIME *10 minutes, plus 2 hours marinating* **COOKING TIME** *9–10 minutes* **SERVES 4**

550g (1¼lb) cubed turkey

MARINADE
4 tsp lemon juice

1 garlic clove, finely
  chopped
4 tsp teriyaki sauce
1 tbsp clear honey

1½ tbsp chopped fresh
  coriander
4 tbsp groundnut oil
freshly ground black
  pepper

1   Put the turkey into a non-metallic bowl.
2   Make the marinade by combining all the ingredients. Stir into the turkey, making sure all the pieces are evenly coated. Cover and leave in a cool place for 2 hours, stirring occasionally.
3   Lift the turkey from the bowl (reserve any remaining marinade) and thread onto skewers. Cook on an oiled grill rack for 9–10 minutes, turning occasionally, brushing with reserved marinade.

123 INDONESIAN BURGERS

PREPARATION TIME *10 minutes, plus 2 hours marinating* **COOKING TIME** *10–15 minutes* **SERVES 4**

1 tbsp groundnut oil
1 onion, finely chopped
2 plump garlic cloves,
   finely chopped
450g (1lb) minced chicken
1 tsp ground cumin
1 tsp coriander
½ tsp turmeric
salt and freshly ground
   black pepper

8 freshly cut slices of
   firm bread
Fresh Pineapple and Mango
   Salsa *(see page 175)*,
   to serve

PEANUT SAUCE
1 tbsp groundnut oil
1 small onion, finely
   chopped

1 plump garlic clove, finely
   chopped
½ tsp chilli powder
115g (4oz) crunchy peanut
   butter
2 tbsp lime juice
2 tsp dark soy sauce
pinch of dark brown sugar

1   Heat the oil in a frying pan and fry the onion and garlic until softened. Leave to cool.
2   Mix the minced chicken with the cumin, coriander, turmeric, onion and garlic. Season with black
    pepper. With floured hands, form the mixture into four or six burgers, 2cm (¾in) thick. Leave in
    a cool place for at least 2 hours.
3   Meanwhile, make the peanut sauce by heating the oil in a frying pan. Add the onion and fry
    gently until very soft and lightly browned, adding the garlic about halfway through. Stir in
    the chilli powder for 10 seconds, then stir in the peanut butter, lime juice, soy sauce and
    200ml (7fl oz) water. When the sauce is evenly blended and thick, season with salt and sugar.
    Set aside until required.
4   Cook the burgers on an oiled grill rack for 5 minutes on each side until browned and crisp on
    the outside and cooked through. Meanwhile, warm the sauce on the side of the grill rack. Serve
    the burgers in the bread slices with the warm sauce and the salsa.

124 CHICKEN AND TARRAGON BURGERS

PREPARATION TIME *15 minutes, plus 2 hours chilling* **COOKING TIME** *10 minutes* **SERVES 4–6**

1 tbsp olive oil
1 onion, finely chopped
2 garlic cloves, finely
   chopped
675g (1½lb) minced chicken
115g (4oz) prosciutto,
   chopped
2 tbsp chopped fresh
   tarragon leaves

freshly ground black
   pepper
4–6 ciabatta rolls, split
   in half
oakleaf lettuce leaves and
   sliced pitted green
   olives, to serve

TOMATO MAYONNAISE
2–3 tsp sun-dried tomato
   paste, to taste
115ml (4fl oz) mayonnaise
   (see page 179)

1   Heat the oil in a frying pan and fry the onion and garlic until softened. Leave to cool.
2   Mix the minced chicken with the prosciutto, tarragon, onion and garlic. Season with black pepper.
    With floured hands form the mixture into four or six burgers, 2cm (¾in) thick. Leave in a cool
    place for at least 2 hours.
3   Meanwhile, make the mayonnaise by stirring the sun-dried tomato paste into the mayonnaise
    until evenly blended. Season with black pepper, if necessary.
4   Cook the burgers on an oiled grill rack for 5 minutes or so on each side until browned and crisp
    on the outside and cooked through.
5   While the burgers are cooking, toast the cut sides of the rolls on the side of the grill rack.
6   Cover the toasted sides of the bottom halves of the rolls with lettuce leaves, put the burgers on
    top, add a spoonful of the tomato mayonnaise, then finish with green olive slices. Cover with
    the tops of the rolls.

125 TURKISH CHICKEN WRAPS

PREPARATION TIME *10 minutes, plus 1–3 hours marinating* **COOKING TIME** *14–16 minutes* **SERVES 4**

4 skinless, boneless
   chicken breasts
2 garlic cloves, peeled
salt and freshly ground
   black pepper
½ tsp ground cinnamon
½ tsp ground allspice
4 tbsp Greek yogurt

3 tbsp lemon juice
1 tbsp olive oil
4 pitta breads
shredded Iceberg lettuce
   and sliced tomatoes,
   to serve

CORIANDER AÏOLI
3 garlic cloves, chopped

2 egg yolks
juice of 1 lime, or to taste
300ml (10fl oz) groundnut
   oil
salt and freshly ground
   black pepper
small handful of fresh
   coriander leaves,
   chopped

1. Put the chicken into a non-metallic dish.
2. Crush the garlic with a pinch of salt, then mix with the spices, yogurt, lemon juice, oil and black pepper. Coat the chicken evenly with the mixture. Cover and leave to marinate in a cool place for 1–3 hours, turning occasionally.
3. To make the aïoli, put the garlic, egg yolks and lime juice into a blender and mix briefly. With the motor running, slowly pour in the oil until the mixture becomes thick and creamy. Season and transfer to a bowl. Cover and chill, if liked. Stir in the coriander. Serve within 30 minutes.
4. Lift the chicken from the marinade. Cook on an oiled grill rack for 7–8 minutes on each side, turning once. Remove from the grill rack, cover and leave for 5–10 minutes before slicing.
5. Meanwhile, warm the pitta breads on the side of the grill rack for 30 seconds per side. Split each one open and stack the two halves on top of each other, cut side uppermost. Divide the lettuce and tomatoes among the pitta stacks. Lay the chicken on top, then add some coriander aïoli. Roll up the pitta breads around the filling.

126 PEKING-STYLE CHICKEN

PREPARATION TIME *15 minutes, plus 4–6 hours marinating* **COOKING TIME** *30 minutes* **SERVES 4**

	GLAZE	DIPPING SAUCE
1.5kg (3lb 6oz) chicken breasts on the bone	**2 tbsp hoisin sauce**	**2 tsp sesame oil**
1 bunch of spring onions, sliced	**2 tbsp white wine vinegar**	**2.5cm (1in) piece fresh root ginger, grated**
Chinese pancakes, to serve	**2 tbsp clear honey**	**125ml (4fl oz) hoisin sauce**
	2 tbsp mango chutney	
	1 tbsp soy sauce	
	juice of 1 lemon	

1   Make the glaze by stirring the ingredients together. Brush evenly and thoroughly over the chicken, place in a single layer in a shallow, non-metallic dish, cover and leave in a cool place for 4–6 hours, brushing occasionally with any remaining glaze.

2   Meanwhile, make the dipping sauce by heating the sesame oil in a small pan. Add the ginger and cook gently for 5 minutes. Strain the oil into the hoisin sauce and stir to combine. Pour into a small dish.

3   Lift the chicken from the dish (reserve any remaining glaze) and cook on an oiled grill rack for 25 minutes, brushing with any remaining glaze and turning regularly. Remove from the rack, cover and leave to stand for about 5 minutes before slicing the meat.

4   Meanwhile, warm the pancakes. Serve the sliced chicken, spring onions, pancakes and dipping sauce separately so that everyone can assemble their own.

127 BARBECUED CHICKEN DRUMSTICKS

PREPARATION TIME *10 minutes, plus 4–6 hours marinating* **COOKING TIME** *20–25 minutes* **SERVES 4**

8 chicken drumsticks	**8 tbsp good-quality tomato ketchup *(see page 184)***	**2 tbsp dark soft brown sugar**
8 baby onions	**2 tbsp Worcestershire sauce**	
MARINADE	**1 tbsp Dijon mustard**	
1 plump garlic clove, finely chopped		

1   Cut a couple of deep slashes in each chicken drumstick and lay them in a large, shallow, non-metallic dish.

2   Make the marinade by combining the ingredients. Pour evenly over the chicken, then stir the drumsticks around to ensure they are evenly coated. Cover and leave to marinate in a cool place for 4–6 hours, turning occasionally.

3   Meanwhile, blanch the onions for 5 minutes. Drain and dry well. Thread onto skewers.

4   Lift the drumsticks from the marinade (reserving any remaining marinade). Brush the onions with some of the reserved marinade.

5   Cook the drumsticks and onions on an oiled grill rack for 15–20 minutes, turning regularly and brushing occasionally with reserved marinade. Serve the drumsticks with the onion kebabs.

128 CHICKEN WITH CAPER AND ANCHOVY VINAIGRETTE

PREPARATION TIME *10 minutes* **COOKING TIME** *14–16 minutes* **SERVES 4**

1 tbsp small capers, crushed	5 tbsp virgin olive oil, plus extra for brushing	4 boneless chicken breasts, with skin
6 anchovy fillets, pounded	1 tsp freshly ground black pepper	shredded fresh flat-leaf parsley, to garnish
2 tbsp lemon juice		

1 Combine the capers, anchovy fillets, lemon juice, oil and black pepper.
2 Brush the chicken with oil and season with black pepper. Cook on an oiled grill rack for 7–8 minutes on each side.
3 Remove the chicken from the grill rack, cover and leave to rest for 5–10 minutes. Carve the chicken into slices. Stir the vinaigrette and pour over the slices. Sprinkle with the parsley.

129 SPICED GRILLED QUAIL

PREPARATION TIME *15 minutes, plus 1–2 hours marinating* **COOKING TIME** *15 minutes* **SERVES 4–8**

8 quails, spatchcocked	juice of 1½ lemons	salt and freshly ground black pepper
1 tsp fennel seeds, finely crushed	3 tbsp virgin olive oil	
	1½ tsp paprika	

1 Thread a skewer through the wings and body of each quail. Thread another skewer through the thighs. Place the quails in a shallow, non-metallic bowl.
2 Mix the fennel seeds, lemon juice, olive oil, paprika and salt and pepper. Rub thoroughly over the birds, cover and leave in a cool place for 1–2 hours.
3 Cook the quails on an oiled grill rack, bone-side down, for 8 minutes. Turn them over and cook for a further 5–7 minutes until the skin is crisp and browned and the juices run clear when the thickest part is pierced with a fine skewer.

130 JERK CHICKEN

PREPARATION TIME *10 minutes, plus 2 hours marinating* **COOKING TIME** *20–25 minutes* **SERVES 6**

6 whole chicken legs	115ml (4fl oz) dark soy sauce	1–2 red chillies, seeded and finely chopped
JERK SAUCE	50g (2oz) fresh root ginger, coarsely chopped	½ tsp ground allspice
1 onion, coarsely chopped	leaves from small bunch of fresh thyme sprigs	freshly ground black pepper
115ml (4fl oz) white wine vinegar		

1 Put the chicken in a large, shallow non-metallic dish.
2 Make the jerk sauce by combining the ingredients in a blender until smooth. Pour evenly over the chicken, turn the pieces over to ensure they are evenly coated, then cover and leave in a cool place for 2 hours, turning occasionally.
3 Lift the chicken from the marinade (reserve any remaining marinade) and cook, skin side down first, on an oiled grill rack for 20–25 minutes, turning and brushing occasionally with the reserved marinade, until the skin is golden and the juices run clear when the thickest part is pierced with a skewer .

131 CHICKEN, MANGO AND MINT KEBABS

PREPARATION TIME *10 minutes, plus 1–2 hours marinating* **COOKING TIME** *10 minutes* **SERVES 4**

4 skinless, boneless
   chicken breasts cut into
   bite-sized pieces
1 ripe mango
lime wedges and mint
   sprigs, to serve

MARINADE
juice of 2 limes
4 tbsp olive oil
2 tbsp chopped fresh mint
1 tsp soft brown sugar

salt and freshly ground
   black pepper

1   Put the chicken in a non-metallic bowl.
2   Mix together the marinade ingredients. Pour over the chicken and stir gently to ensure that it is
     evenly coated. Cover and leave in a cool place for 1–2 hours.
3   Meanwhile, peel the mango and cut the flesh into the same sized pieces as the chicken.
4   Lift the chicken from the bowl (reserve any remaining marinade) and thread alternately with
     the mango onto four skewers. Brush with the remaining marinade and cook on an oiled grill
     for about 10 minutes until golden and cooked through, turning 2–3 times. Serve the kebabs
     with lime wedges and mint sprigs.

132 CHICKEN WITH EASTERN GREMOLATA

PREPARATION TIME *10 minutes, plus 2 hours marinating* **COOKING TIME** *15–20 minutes* **SERVES 4**

4 chicken thighs
4 chicken drumsticks
salt and freshly ground
   black pepper

GREMOLATA
4 tbsp chopped fresh
   coriander
4 tbsp chopped fresh
   flat-leaf parsley

2 tbsp finely chopped garlic
1 tbsp grated orange zest
50ml (2fl oz) olive oil

1   Make the gremolata by combining the herbs, garlic and zest in a small blender. Add the oil and seasoning and mix to a paste.
2   Cut deep slashes in the chicken and place in a non-metallic bowl. Spread the paste over the chicken thighs and drumsticks, making sure it goes into the slashes. Cover and leave in a cool place for about 2 hours.
3   Cook the chicken on an oiled grill rack for 15–20 minutes, turning frequently.

133 TURKEY STEAKS WITH GARLIC, GINGER AND SESAME

PREPARATION TIME *10 minutes, plus 4–6 hours marinating* **COOKING TIME** *12 minutes* **SERVES 4**

4 turkey steaks

MARINADE
3 garlic cloves, finely
   chopped

2 tbsp grated fresh root
   ginger
115ml (4fl oz) dark soy
   sauce

1 tbsp rice wine or medium
   sherry
1 tbsp sesame oil
2 tsp sesame seeds
2 tbsp dark brown sugar

1   Using the point of a sharp knife, make cuts in the surfaces of the turkey steaks. Lay the steaks in a single layer in a non-metallic dish.
2   Combine the marinade ingredients. Pour evenly over the steaks, then turn them over to coat thoroughly. Cover and leave in a cool place for 4–6 hours, turning occasionally.
3   Lift the turkey steaks from the marinade and cook on an oiled grill rack for about 6 minutes on each side, turning once.

134 BASIL-FLAVOURED CHICKEN

PREPARATION TIME *10 minutes* **COOKING TIME** *14–16 minutes* **SERVES 4**

4 chicken breasts with skin,
   175g (6oz) each
leaves from a 50g (2oz)
   bunch of fresh basil

freshly ground black
   pepper
175ml (6fl oz) virgin olive
   oil, plus extra for
   brushing

4 tsp wholegrain mustard
6 anchovy fillets, drained
2 tbsp red wine vinegar
1 tbsp balsamic vinegar

1   Carefully loosen the chicken skin from the breasts and insert 2–3 basil leaves on each breast, below the skin. Smooth the skin back into place. Season the skin with black pepper. Brush the flesh with oil and season that with black pepper also.
2   Put the remaining basil leaves in a small blender with the mustard, anchovies and vinegars. Mix until smooth. With the motor running, slowly pour in the oil until evenly combined. Transfer to a serving bowl and set aside.
3   Cook the chicken on an oiled grill rack for 7–8 minutes on each side, turning once, until cooked through. Serve with the basil sauce.

135 CHICKEN WITH GINGER, LIME AND YOGURT

PREPARATION TIME *15 minutes, plus 2–3 hours marinating* **COOKING TIME** *14–16 minutes* **SERVES 4**

550g (1¼lb) chicken breasts
naan bread, to serve
chopped fresh coriander,
    to garnish

MARINADE
2 garlic cloves, peeled
salt and freshly ground
    black pepper
115ml (4fl oz) thick yogurt
2.5cm (1in) piece fresh root
    ginger, grated

1 tbsp ground coriander
1 tsp garam masala
pinch of chilli flakes
1 tbsp lime juice
grated zest of 1 lime

1   Put the chicken breasts in a non-metallic dish.
2   Make the marinade by crushing the garlic to a paste with a pinch of salt. Combine the yogurt
    with the garlic paste, the ginger, coriander, garam masala, chilli flakes, lime juice and lime zest.
    Season with black pepper. Pour over the chicken and turn it over so each piece is evenly coated.
    Cover and leave in a cool place for 2–3 hours, turning occasionally.
3   Lift the chicken from the dish (reserve any remaining marinade) and cook on an oiled grill rack
    for 7–8 minutes on each side, turning once and brushing with any remaining marinade.
4   Meanwhile, warm the naan on the side of the grill rack.
5   Remove the cooked chicken from the grill rack, sprinkle over some chopped coriander and serve
    with the warm naan bread.

136 CHICKEN WITH LEMON, MINT AND CHILLI

PREPARATION TIME *10 minutes, plus 1–2 hours marinating* **COOKING TIME** *15 minutes* **SERVES 2**

4 chicken drumsticks
4 tbsp olive oil
handful of mint leaves
    (about 20)

juice of 1 large or 2 small
    lemon(s)
2 garlic cloves, chopped
1 red chilli, seeded and
    chopped

2 pinches of saffron threads
salt and freshly ground
    black pepper
lemon wedges, to serve

1   Cut deep slashes in the drumsticks and put them in a non-metallic dish.
2   Put the oil, most of the mint and most of the lemon juice, the garlic, chilli, saffron and black
    pepper into a blender and mix to a soft purée. Pour over the chicken and turn the chicken over
    so the pieces are evenly coated. Cover and leave in a cool place for 1–2 hours.
3   Lift the chicken from the dish and cook on an oiled grill rack for 15 minutes, turning every
    3 minutes, until cooked through. Remove from the grill rack and sprinkle with salt and the
    remaining lemon juice and mint. Serve with lemon wedges.

137 ITALIAN-STUFFED CHICKEN BREASTS

PREPARATION TIME *15 minutes* **COOKING TIME** *20 minutes* **SERVES 4**

40g (1½oz) pine nuts	**salt and freshly ground**	**olive oil, for brushing**
50g (2oz) unsalted butter,	**black pepper**	
softened	**4 skinless, boneless**	
1 tsp chopped fresh parsley	**chicken breasts**	
1 tsp snipped fresh chives	**12 sun-dried tomatoes,**	
1 tsp chopped fresh	**drained**	
tarragon	**4 large slices of prosciutto**	

1   Toast the pine nuts in a dry heavy-bottomed frying pan, shaking the pan frequently, until lightly and evenly coloured. Reserve 1 tablespoonful. Grind the remaining nuts.

2   Beat the butter with the herbs and seasoning until smooth and then add the ground pine nuts.

3   Cut three slits in the top of each chicken breast, going about halfway through the flesh. Tuck a sun-dried tomato in each slit, then press a teaspoonful of the herb butter into each slit and reform the breasts.

4   Wrap a slice of prosciutto around each chicken breast, overlapping at the ends. Secure with wooden cocktail sticks that have been soaked in water for 20 minutes. Brush with olive oil and season with black pepper.

5   Cook on an oiled grill rack for 20 minutes, turning once, until the chicken juices run clear when the flesh is pierced with a fine skewer.

138 CHICKEN WITH MUSTARD AND HERBS

PREPARATION TIME *10 minutes, plus 2–3 hours marinating* **COOKING TIME** *15 minutes* **SERVES 4**

8 large chicken thighs	1 tbsp dried tarragon	1½ tbsp Dijon mustard
4 tbsp olive oil	1¼ tbsp chopped fresh	salt and freshly ground
2 tbsp red wine vinegar	parsley	black pepper

1. Cut deep slashes in the chicken thighs and lay them in a non-metallic dish.
2. Combine the olive oil, vinegar, tarragon, parsley, mustard and seasoning. Pour over the chicken, making sure it goes into the slashes and that the pieces are evenly coated. Cover and leave in a cool place for 2–3 hours, turning occasionally.
3. Lift the chicken from the dish and cook on an oiled grill rack for 15 minutes or so, turning once and brushing with any remaining marinade.

139 TURKEY TIKKA BURGERS

PREPARATION TIME *10 minutes, plus 4 hours chilling* **COOKING TIME** *12–16 minutes* **SERVES 4**

olive oil, for frying	3 tbsp chopped fresh	salt and freshly ground
1 onion, finely chopped	coriander	black pepper
500g (1lb 2oz) minced	2 tbsp yogurt	4 small naan breads and
turkey	1 tbsp mango chutney	Raita *(see page 62)*,
4 tbsp tikka masala paste		to serve

1. Heat a little oil in a frying pan, add the onion and fry until softened. Remove from the heat and leave to cool.
2. Mix the onion with the remaining ingredients until thoroughly combined. With wet hands, form the mixture into four burgers, 2cm (¾in) thick. If possible, cover and leave in a cool place for 4 hours or overnight to allow the flavours to develop.
3. Cook the burgers on an oiled grill rack for 6–8 minutes on each side until the juices run clear.
4. Meanwhile, warm the naan breads on the side of the grill rack for 20–30 seconds. Serve the burgers with the raita and naan breads.

140 CHICKEN BREASTS WITH GINGER, HONEY AND ORANGE

PREPARATION TIME *10 minutes, plus 1–2 hours marinating* **COOKING TIME** *15–20 minutes* **SERVES 4**

4 part-boned chicken	2 tbsp clear honey	salt and freshly ground
breasts	finely grated zest and juice	black pepper
2.5cm (1in) piece fresh root	of 1 large orange	
ginger, grated		

1. Cut three deep slashes in each chicken breast. Place the chicken in a single layer in a non-metallic dish.
2. Combine the ginger, honey, orange zest and juice and seasoning, then spread over the chicken, working it well into the slashes. Cover and leave in a cool place for 1–2 hours.
3. Lift the chicken from the dish and cook on an oiled grill rack for 15–20 minutes, until cooked through, turning once or twice.

141 JAPANESE CHICKEN KEBABS

PREPARATION TIME *10 minutes, plus 1 hour chilling* **COOKING TIME** *10 minutes* **SERVES 4**

4 tbsp Japanese soy sauce
4 tbsp sake
2 tbsp mirin
1 tbsp caster sugar
8 boneless, skinless
   chicken thighs, cut into
   bite-sized cubes

CUCUMBER SALAD
1 small cucumber
pinch of salt
2 tbsp rice wine vinegar
pinch of caster sugar,
   to taste

2.5cm (1in) piece of
   fresh root ginger

1   Gently heat the soy sauce, sake, mirin and sugar in a small saucepan, stirring frequently, until the sugar has dissolved. Simmer until thickened and syrupy. Leave to cool.
2   Put the chicken in a non-metallic bowl and stir in half the soy sauce mixture. Cover and leave in a cool place for 1 hour, stirring once or twice. Reserve the remaining soy mixture.
3   Make the salad by slicing the cucumber lengthways using a potato peeler. Sprinkle with salt and leave for 30 minutes. Rinse well and dry thoroughly on paper towels. Put into a bowl.
4   Stir the rice wine vinegar and a pinch of sugar together. Using a garlic crusher, squeeze as much ginger juice as possible into the mixture. Pour the dressing over the cucumber and toss together. Set aside.
5   Lift the chicken from the marinade and thread onto skewers. Cook on an oiled grill rack for about 10 minutes, turning occasionally. Remove the kebabs from the grill rack, trickle over the reserved soy mixture and serve with the salad.

142 THAI-STYLE CHICKEN

PREPARATION TIME *10 minutes, plus 2–3 hours marinating* **COOKING TIME** *15 minutes* **SERVES 6**

3 boneless chicken breasts
   with skin on, about 175g
   (6oz) each
6 chicken drumsticks
lime wedges, to serve

MARINADE
2 shallots, finely chopped

2cm (¾in) piece fresh root
   ginger, grated
1 lemon grass stem, peeled
   and finely chopped
2 garlic cloves, finely
   chopped
1 red chilli, seeded and
   finely chopped

3 tbsp chopped fresh
   coriander
75ml (3fl oz) lime juice
1 tsp caster sugar
1 tbsp sesame oil
few drops Thai fish sauce,
   to taste

1   Cut deep slashes in the chicken pieces and put in a single layer in a shallow non-metallic dish.
2   Mix together all the marinade ingredients, pour over the chicken and turn the pieces so they are evenly coated. Cover and leave in a cool place for 2–3 hours, turning occasionally.
3   Lift the chicken from the dish and cook on an oiled grill rack, allowing 6–7 minutes on each side for the breasts and 15 minutes for the drumsticks, turning every 3 minutes, until browned and cooked through. Cut the cooked chicken breasts in half and serve with lime wedges.

143 DEVILLED CHICKEN

PREPARATION TIME *10 minutes, plus 2–4 hours marinating* **COOKING TIME** *15 minutes* **SERVES 6**

12 chicken thighs, with skin on
freshly ground black pepper

SAUCE
1 plump garlic clove, crushed
3 tbsp good-quality tomato ketchup (*see page 184*)
1 tbsp Worcestershire sauce

1½ tbsp apricot jam
1 tsp Bordeaux mustard
pinch of cayenne pepper
1 tbsp Thai fish sauce

1   Cut lengthwise slashes in the chicken thighs with a sharp knife, then place them in a large, shallow non-metallic dish.
2   Make the sauce by stirring the garlic, ketchup, Worcestershire sauce and jam together until smooth, then mix in the remaining ingredients. Spread over the thighs, working it into the slashes. Cover and leave in a cool place for 2–4 hours.
3   Lift the thighs from the dish and grill for 15 minutes, until they are nicely browned and cooked through, turning regularly every 3 minutes. Sprinkle with pepper.

144 CHICKEN WITH GARLIC AND LEMON OIL

PREPARATION TIME *10 minutes* **COOKING TIME** *25 minutes* **SERVES 4**

4 tbsp olive oil
1 small garlic clove, finely chopped
3 tbsp lemon juice

3–4 tbsp chopped mixed fresh herbs, such as flat-leaf parsley, coriander, thyme and oregano

salt and freshly ground black pepper
4 chicken breasts on the bone, with skin on

1   Mix together the olive oil, garlic, lemon juice, herbs and a small pinch of salt. Set aside.
2   Cook the chicken on an oiled grill rack for about 25 minutes until the juices run clear when the thickest part is pierced with a fine skewer, turning once. Remove to plates, spoon over the garlic and lemon oil, and serve.

145 CHICKEN KALAMATA OLIVADE

PREPARATION TIME *10 minutes, plus 2 hours marinating* **COOKING TIME** *25 minutes* **SERVES 4**

4 chicken legs
24 kalamata olives, pitted and finely chopped
4 tbsp oil from the olive jar
2 garlic cloves, finely chopped

2 tbsp sun-dried tomato paste
2 tsp finely chopped fresh oregano leaves
freshly ground black pepper

fresh coriander and lime wedges, to serve

1   Cut four deep slashes in the flesh on both sides of each chicken leg.
2   Mix the olives with the oil, garlic, tomato paste, oregano and black pepper to make a paste. Spread the paste over the chicken, making sure it goes into the slashes. Cover and leave to marinate in a cool place for 2 hours.
3   Cook the chicken on an oiled rack for about 25 minutes, turning once, until the skin is crisp and the juices run clear when the thickest part of the legs is pierced with a skewer. Remove to plates, garnish with coriander and serve with lime wedges.

146 ORIENTAL CHICKEN WITH FRUITED NOODLE SALAD

PREPARATION TIME *15 minutes, plus 4–6 hours marinating* **COOKING TIME** *15 minutes* **SERVES 4**

8 chicken drumsticks
4 tbsp hoisin sauce
2 tbsp clear honey
2 tbsp good-quality tomato
  ketchup *(see page 184)*
1 tbsp Chinese five-spice
  powder
dash Tabasco sauce
1 garlic clove, peeled
salt and freshly ground
  black pepper

FRUITED NOODLE SALAD
6 tbsp virgin olive oil
2 tbsp balsamic vinegar
1 tsp sun-dried tomato
  paste
225g (8oz) fine egg noodles
2 ripe peaches or
  nectarines, pitted
  and chopped
4 ripe purple-skinned
  plums, pitted and sliced

2 tbsp chopped fresh mint
2 tbsp chopped fresh
  coriander
4 tbsp lightly toasted
  cashew nuts

1 Slash each drumstick several times with the point of a sharp knife and lay in a shallow non-metallic dish.
2 Combine the hoisin sauce, honey, ketchup, five-spice powder and Tabasco. Crush the garlic to a paste with a pinch of salt and add to the other ingredients, plus some black pepper. Spoon evenly over the chicken, making sure it goes well into the slashes. Cover and leave in a cool place for 4–6 hours, turning occasionally.
3 Lift the chicken from the dish (reserve any remaining marinade) and cook on an oiled grill rack for 15 minutes until cooked through, turning once and brushing with any remaining marinade.
4 Meanwhile, make the salad by whisking the oil, vinegar, tomato paste and seasoning together. Cook the noodles according to the packet directions. Drain well and toss with the dressing. Leave to cool, then mix with the remaining salad ingredients. Serve the chicken with the salad.

147 CAJUN CHICKEN WITH TOMATO SALSA

PREPARATION TIME *10 minutes, plus 2-3 hours marinating* **COOKING TIME** *15 minutes* **SERVES 6**

2 tsp dried thyme
2 tsp dried oregano
2 tsp paprika
1 tsp ground cumin
1 tsp cayenne pepper
salt and freshly ground
    black pepper

6 boneless chicken breasts,
    with skin on
groundnut oil, for brushing
lime quarters, to serve

TOMATO SALSA
700g (1½lb) firm but ripe
    plum tomatoes, diced

1 red onion, finely chopped
1 small red chilli, seeded
    and finely chopped
1½ tbsp chopped fresh
    coriander
1½ tbsp balsamic vinegar
3 tbsp olive oil

1   Mix together the herbs, spices and seasoning. Brush the chicken lightly with oil, then rub the
    spice mixture into the chicken. Cover and leave in a cool place for 2-3 hours.
2   Meanwhile, make the salsa by combining the ingredients. Add salt to taste. Cover and chill.
3   Thread the lime quarters onto skewers, to grill if preferred.
4   Cook the chicken on an oiled grill rack for about 15 minutes until browned and cooked through,
    turning once. If grilling the limes, cook the skewers alongside until caramelised. Serve the chicken
    with the lime quarters, either fresh or grilled as above, and accompanied by the salsa.

148 BRONZED CHICKEN THIGHS

PREPARATION TIME *5 minutes* **COOKING TIME** *15 minutes* **SERVES 4**

2 tbsp olive oil, plus extra for brushing	1 tbsp sun-dried tomato paste	salt and freshly ground black pepper
1 tsp pimenton (smoked paprika), or sweet paprika	juice of ½ lemon	fresh thyme leaves, to serve
	1 garlic clove, crushed	
	1½ tsp sweet chilli sauce	
	8 chicken thighs	

1 Mix together the olive oil, pimenton, tomato paste, lemon juice, garlic and sweet chilli sauce to form a thick paste.
2 Brush the thighs with oil and cook on an oiled grill rack for 7 minutes, turning once, then brush generously with the paste and cook for a further 7 minutes or so until the juices run clear when the thickest part is pierced with a skewer.
3 Remove from the rack, sprinkle with seasoning and thyme leaves, then serve.

149 CHICKEN SUPREMES WITH TAPENADE

PREPARATION TIME *15 minutes* **COOKING TIME** *25 minutes* **SERVES 4**

4 chicken supremes (chicken breasts on the bone, skin on, and wing bone attached)	4 tbsp black olive tapenade	salt and freshly ground black pepper
	1 tbsp capers, drained and chopped	olive oil, for brushing
75g (3oz) ricotta cheese	4 sun-dried tomatoes in oil, chopped	

1 Loosen the skin covering each chicken breast and cut three or four deep slits in the top of each breast, going about halfway through the flesh.
2 Break up the ricotta with a fork, then beat in the tapenade, capers, sun-dried tomatoes and seasoning. Divide into four and carefully press some of the stuffing into each slit. Smooth the skin back in place to reform the breasts.
3 Brush the skin with olive oil and sprinkle with seasoning. Cook on an oiled grill rack, skin-side up first, for about 25 minutes or until cooked through, turning once.

150 MUSHROOM-STUFFED CHICKEN THIGHS

PREPARATION TIME *10 minutes* **COOKING TIME** *8–10 minutes* **SERVES 4**

50g (2 oz) mushrooms, finely chopped	25g (1oz) full-fat soft cheese	salt and freshly ground black pepper
1 tbsp unsalted butter	1 tbsp chopped fresh parsley	8 boneless chicken thighs
		olive oil, for brushing

1 Fry the mushrooms in the butter until tender. Using a slotted spoon, transfer them onto a piece of kitchen paper to drain.
2 Mix the mushrooms with the cheese, parsley and seasoning and use to stuff the chicken thighs. Secure the thighs closed with cocktail sticks that have been soaked in water for 20 minutes. Brush the thighs with oil and season them.
3 Cook on an oiled grill rack for 8–10 minutes, turning once, until browned and cooked through.

MEAT

When choosing meat for the barbecue, select only lean, tender cuts such as thick sirloin steaks, lamb chops or kebabs made from leg of pork. There is no better treatment for a thick, naturally tender steak than to toss it onto the grill. The high heat delivers a crisp, charred exterior and a juicy interior. Best cuts are sirloin, fillet and T-bone.

Look for steaks at least 2cm (¾in) thick, preferably 5cm (2in), as thinner steaks tend to dry out and toughen. Move cuts thicker than 2.5cm (1in) to a cooler part of the grill once both sides are well seared so that they continue cooking inside. Add or subtract about 1 minute for every 1cm (½in) difference in thickness. Cook over a medium hot fire, with the grill rack 10–15cm (4–6in) above the heat.

Fat dripping onto hot coals can cause flare-ups, so trim any excess (although a little is necessary to give flavour and keep the meat moist) and snip the remainder at 2.5cm (1in) intervals to prevent it curling. Fat dripping from sausages can flare up, and there is a risk of undercooking the centre, so you can pre-cook sausages and simply reheat them over the fire. A simple way of testing meat for readiness is to press it lightly with your finger – rare: the meat will give easily and no juices will appear on the surface; medium: the meat will still be slightly springy but a few juices will appear on the surface; well done: the meat will be very firm to the touch and the surface will be covered with juices.

CHAPTER 4

151 GAMMON WITH PAPRIKA SPICE RUB AND MANGO SALSA

PREPARATION TIME *15 minutes, plus 2 hours marinating* **COOKING TIME** *10-12 minutes* **SERVES 4**

4 gammon steaks, about
   175g (6oz) each
2 tsp ground cumin
2 tsp paprika
4 tsp soft dark brown sugar
4 tbsp olive oil

MANGO SALSA
2 large ripe mangoes
juice of 2 limes
½ red onion, finely chopped
3 tbsp finely chopped fresh
   coriander

pinch of soft dark
   brown sugar
salt and freshly ground
   black pepper

1   Trim any surplus fat from the steaks, leaving enough to keep them moist. Snip the remaining fat at 2.5cm (1in) intervals.
2   Mix the cumin, paprika, sugar and oil together. Rub all over the gammon steaks, then cover and leave to marinate in a cool place for 2 hours.
3   Meanwhile, make the salsa by dicing a quarter of the mango flesh. Purée the remaining mango flesh with the lime juice, then stir in the chopped onion, coriander and diced mango. Add a pinch of sugar, and seasoning to taste.
4   Cook the gammon on an oiled grill rack for 5–6 minutes on each side until the juices run clear when the thickest part is pierced with a fine skewer. Serve with the salsa.

152 LAMB FILLETS WITH CORIANDER, CUMIN AND GARLIC

PREPARATION TIME *10 minutes, plus 4–8 hours marinating* **COOKING TIME** *10-15 minutes* **SERVES 6**

1 tbsp coriander seeds
1 tsp cumin seeds
4 fresh bay leaves, coarsely
   torn
2 plump garlic cloves,
   peeled

leaves from a fresh
   rosemary sprig
2 tbsp balsamic vinegar
2 tbsp olive oil
3 tbsp Greek yogurt

1 tbsp sun-dried tomato
   paste
salt and freshly ground
   black pepper
675-800g (1½-1¾lb) lamb
   neck fillets

1   Heat a small, dry, heavy-based frying pan, add the coriander and cumin seeds and toast them, shaking the pan occasionally, until they become fragrant. Add the bay leaves just before the end. Tip into a spice grinder and grind finely.
2   Chop the garlic and rosemary together finely. Combine with the vinegar, oil, yogurt, tomato paste, ground spices and seasoning. Smear thoroughly and evenly over the lamb, cover and leave to marinate in a cool place for 4–8 hours.
3   Cook the lamb on an oiled grill rack for 8–12 minutes until well-browned on the outside and cooked to your liking in the centre, turning occasionally. Then remove the lamb from the grill rack and allow to stand for about 5 minutes before slicing and serving.

153 PORK, PANCETTA AND PARMESAN BURGERS

PREPARATION TIME *10 minutes, plus 1 hour chilling* **COOKING TIME** *12 minutes* **SERVES 4**

450g (1 lb) minced pork

75g (3oz) pancetta, coarsely chopped

50g (2oz) Parmesan cheese, freshly grated

1½ tbsp finely chopped fresh sage

1 medium egg, beaten

freshly ground black pepper

4 squares of focaccia, halved horizontally

salad leaves, such as rocket, lamb's lettuce, frisée and radicchio, to serve

Roasted Tomato Salsa *(see page 175)* or Red Pepper, Black Olive and Caper Relish *(see page 185)*, to serve

1 Using a fork or your hands, combine the pork, pancetta, Parmesan, sage, egg and black pepper in a large bowl. With damp hands, form into four burgers approximately 2.5cm (1in) thick. Leave in a cool place for at least 1 hour.

2 Cook the burgers on an oiled grill for about 6 minutes on each side, turning once, until the juices run clear.

3 Meanwhile, warm the focaccia on the side of the grill rack. Top the bottom halves of the focaccia with salad leaves, add the burgers and then a spoonful of the salsa or relish.

154 SPANISH BURGERS

PREPARATION TIME *15 minutes, plus 4–8 hours chilling* **COOKING TIME** *15–20 minutes* **SERVES 4**

1 onion, finely chopped

1 tbsp olive oil

500g (1lb 2oz) coarse-ground pork

75g (3oz) chorizo, finely chopped

3 tbsp chopped fresh oregano

salt and freshly ground black pepper

4 rolls, such as ciabatta, split into halves, to serve

mayonnaise *(see page 179)*, lettuce, chopped tomatoes and spring onions, to serve

MARINADE

150ml (5fl oz) olive oil

2 garlic cloves, crushed

1 tbsp sun-dried tomato paste

1 tbsp chopped fresh thyme

2 tsp chopped parsley

1 Fry the onion in the oil until softened. Leave to cool, then mix with the pork, chorizo, oregano and seasoning. With floured hands, form into four burgers 2–2.5cm (¾–1in) thick. Place in a single layer in a shallow dish.

2 Make the marinade by mixing all the ingredients together. Pour over the burgers, turn them over so they are evenly coated, then cover and leave in a cool place for 4–8 hours.

3 Lift the burgers from the marinade and reserve the marinade. Cook the burgers on an oiled grill rack for about 6–7 minutes on each side, brushing occasionally with the marinade.

4 Meanwhile, toast the cut sides of the rolls on the side of the grill rack. Serve the burgers in the rolls with the mayonnaise, lettuce, tomato and spring onions.

155 INDIAN-STYLE LAMB BURGERS

PREPARATION TIME *15 minutes, plus 1 hour chilling* **COOKING TIME**: *10–12 minutes* **SERVES 6**

3 spring onions, finely
chopped
1 peppadew (bottled mild
pepper piquante), finely
chopped
2 garlic cloves, crushed and
finely chopped

1 tsp grated fresh root
ginger
seeds from 6 cardamom
pods, finely crushed
½ tsp ground cumin
leaves from a small bunch
of fresh coriander, finely
chopped

700g (1½lb) lean lamb
salt and freshly ground
black pepper
mini naan bread, and Greek
yogurt mixed with
chopped mint, to serve

1 Combine the spring onions, peppadew, garlic, ginger, spices and coriander, then mix in the lamb and seasoning. With floured hands, form the mixture into four burgers 10cm (4in) in diameter. Chill for at least 1 hour.
2 Cook on an oiled grill rack for 5–6 minutes on each side, turning carefully halfway through, until cooked through and the juices run clear when the burgers are pierced with a fine skewer.
3 Meanwhile, warm the naan on the side of the grill rack for 30 seconds on each side. Serve the burgers with naan bread and Greek yogurt flavoured with chopped mint.

156 KOFTAS

PREPARATION TIME *15 minutes, plus 4 hours marinating* **COOKING TIME** *10–12 minutes* **SERVES 4**

1 small onion, quartered
2 garlic cloves, chopped
2.5cm (1in) piece fresh root
ginger, chopped
1 tsp ground cumin
1 tsp ground coriander
1 tbsp olive oil, plus extra
for brushing

450g (1lb) minced lamb
3 tbsp chopped fresh
coriander
1 large egg, beaten
salt and freshly ground
black pepper
Raita (see page 62), to
serve

cumin seeds, toasted and
crushed, for sprinkling
lemon wedges, to serve

1 Put the onion, garlic and ginger in a small blender or food processor and mix until finely chopped. Add the spices and mix again until evenly combined.
2 Heat the oil in a frying pan, add the onion mix and fry for 2–3 minutes, stirring. Leave to cool.
3 Put the lamb into a bowl and break it up with a fork. Add the cold onion mix, the coriander and seasoning, then mix in enough egg to bind, but don't add so much that the mixture becomes sticky. If time allows, cover and keep in a cool place for up to 4 hours, or overnight in the fridge.
4 Divide the mixture into eight equal portions. With wet hands, mould each portion into a long sausage around a skewer.
5 Brush the koftas with oil and cook on an oiled grill rack for 8–10 minutes, turning occasionally, until nicely browned on the outside and cooked to your liking inside.
6 Serve the koftas with the raita with the cumin sprinkled over and with lemon wedges.

157 BEEF AND MUSHROOM BURGERS WITH ROASTED RED PEPPER DRESSING

PREPARATION TIME *15 minutes, plus 20 minutes soaking and 1 hour chilling*
COOKING TIME *13–15 minutes* **SERVES 4**

2 tbsp dried porcini mushrooms	450g (1lb) lean minced beef	ROASTED RED PEPPER DRESSING
small knob of unsalted butter	4 tsp wholegrain mustard	1 red pepper
	2 tbsp chopped fresh herbs	2 tbsp balsamic vinegar
150g (5oz) chestnut mushrooms, chopped	salt and freshly ground black pepper	1 tsp fresh thyme
	4 rolls, split horizontally,	1 tsp chopped garlic
1 garlic clove, finely chopped	and salad leaves, to serve	6 tbsp olive oil
		salt and freshly ground black pepper

1 Place the dried porcini in a bowl and just cover with boiling water. Soak for 20 minutes, then drain, pat dry and chop finely.

2 Heat the butter in a frying pan, add the chestnut mushrooms and garlic and fry until the liquid has been given off and the mushrooms are tender. Stir in the soaked porcini just before the end of cooking. Leave to cool.

3 Mix the beef with the mushroom mixture, mustard, herbs (such as marjoram, tarragon, parsley, sage or thyme) and seasoning until thoroughly combined. Divide the mixture into four equal portions. With wet hands, form each portion into a burger approximately 2.5cm (1in) thick. If time allows, cover and leave in a cool place for 1 hour, or more, to allow the flavours to develop.

4 To make the dressing, roast the red pepper whole (see page 20). Leave until cool enough to handle, then peel off the skin and discard, along with the seeds. Put into a blender with the vinegar, thyme and garlic. Pulse to mix, then, with the motor running, slowly pour in the olive oil until smooth. Season to taste.

5 Cook the burgers on an oiled grill, turning once, for 4–5 minutes on each side for medium-rare, or for longer if you prefer them more well-done.

6 Meanwhile, toast the rolls on the grill. Mix the salad leaves with a little dressing, then put them on the bottom half of each roll. Top with the burgers and spoon a little more dressing over them. Cover with the top halves of the rolls and serve.

158 STEAK AND MUSHROOM KEBABS

PREPARATION TIME *15 minutes, plus 8 hours marinating* **COOKING TIME** *6–8 minutes* **SERVES 6-8**

900g (2lb) rump steak, cut
   into 3cm (1¼in) cubes
225g (8oz) smoked streaky
   bacon, rind removed
4 button chestnut
   mushrooms

MARINADE
5 tbsp soft red wine
2½ tbsp olive oil, plus extra
   for brushing
2 shallots, finely chopped
2 garlic cloves, crushed

1 tbsp tomato purée
2 tbsp chopped fresh
   parsley
sprig of fresh thyme
salt and freshly ground
   black pepper

1 Put the steak into a non-metallic dish.
2 Make the marinade by combining the ingredients. Stir into the steak to ensure all the pieces are evenly coated, cover and leave in a cool place for 8 hours, stirring occasionally.
3 Lay the bacon rashers on a board and stretch with the back of a knife. Cut each rasher in half crossways. Roll up tightly.
4 Brush the mushrooms with oil and season with black pepper.
5 Lift the steak from the marinade and thread onto skewers, alternating with the mushrooms and bacon rolls. Cook over medium-hot coals on an oiled grill rack for 6–8 minutes, turning occasionally, until cooked to your liking.

159 GREEK LAMB BROCHETTES

PREPARATION TIME *10 minutes, plus 2 hours marinating* **COOKING TIME** *6–8 minutes* **SERVES 4**

450g (1lb) lean lamb, cut
   into 3cm (1¼in) cubes
4 small pitta or naan
   breads, to serve

MARINADE
1 tbsp chopped fresh mint
3-4 saffron strands,
   crushed
2 tbsp olive oil

salt and freshly ground
   black pepper
200ml (7fl oz) Greek yogurt

1 Put the lamb into a non-metallic bowl.
2 Stir the mint, saffron, oil and seasoning into the yogurt until evenly mixed. Pour over the lamb, stir to ensure it is evenly coated, then cover and leave to marinate in a cool place for 2 hours, stirring occasionally.
3 Lift the lamb from the bowl and thread the cubes onto skewers. Cook on an oiled grill rack for 6–8 minutes, turning regularly so that the lamb cooks, until well browned on the outside and still juicy inside.
4 Meanwhile, warm the pitta or naan breads on the side of the grill rack for 30 seconds on each side. Remove the brochettes from the grill rack, sprinkle with salt and serve with the breads.

160 LAMB KEBABS WITH FIGS AND APRICOTS

PREPARATION TIME *10 minutes, plus 8 hours marinating* **COOKING TIME** *8–10 minutes* **SERVES 4**

350g (12oz) boned leg of lamb, cut into 3cm (1¼in) cubes	MARINADE	1 tsp ground cumin
	2½ tbsp smooth peanut butter	1 tsp coriander seeds
1 large orange, sliced	1½ tbsp olive oil	½ tsp ground fenugreek
65g (2½oz) ready-to-eat dried figs	3 tbsp Greek yogurt	pinch of chilli powder
	juice of 1 lemon	salt and freshly ground black pepper
40g (1½oz) ready-to-eat dried apricots	1 garlic clove, finely chopped	
1 onion, quartered	2 spring onions, chopped	

1   Put the lamb into a non-metallic bowl.
2   Mix together the peanut butter, olive oil, yogurt, lemon juice, garlic, spring onions, spices and seasoning. Pour over the lamb. Stir to ensure all the cubes are evenly coated, then cover and leave in a cool place for 8 hours, stirring occasionally.
3   Cut the orange slices in half. Separate the onion quarters into leaves. Lift the lamb from the bowl and thread onto skewers, alternating with the halved orange slices, apricots, figs and onions.
4   Cook on an oiled grill rack for 8–10 minutes, turning regularly, until the lamb is browned on the outside but still pink in the centre.

161 PORK BROCHETTES WITH LEMON AND GINGER

PREPARATION TIME *10 minutes, plus 2½ hours marinating* **COOKING TIME** *12–15 minutes* **SERVES 4**

550g (1¼lb) pork, cut into 3cm (1¼in) cubes	3 garlic cloves, peeled	½ tsp ground cumin
	4 tbsp Greek yogurt	½ tsp grated nutmeg
juice of 1 lemon	1 tbsp grated fresh root ginger	½ dash Tabasco sauce
salt and freshly ground black pepper		1½ lemons
	1 tsp ground cardamom	

1   Put the pork into a non-metallic bowl. Stir in the lemon juice and plenty of black pepper. Cover and leave to marinate in a cool place for 30 minutes.
2   Meanwhile, crush the garlic with a pinch of salt and combine with the yogurt, ginger, cardamom, cumin, nutmeg and Tabasco.
3   Drain the lemon juice from the pork. Stir in the ginger mixture to coat the cubes evenly and thoroughly. Cover and leave in a cool place for 2 hours.
4   Meanwhile, cut the lemons into thick slices, then cut the slices in half.
5   Lift the pork from the ginger mixture, shaking off the excess, and thread onto skewers with the lemon pieces. Cook on an oiled grill rack for 12–15 minutes, turning regularly, until well browned on the outside and cooked through.

162 PEPPERED STEAKS WITH AÏOLI

PREPARATION TIME *15 minutes, plus 3–4 hours marinating* **COOKING TIME** *6–8 minutes* **SERVES 4**

4 sirloin steaks, 175–200g
  (6–7oz) each
2 plump garlic cloves,
  halved lengthwise
olive oil, for brushing
2 tbsp mixed black and
  white peppercorns,
  lightly crushed

AÏOLI
6 plump garlic cloves,
  crushed
2 egg yolks, at room
  temperature
juice of 1 small lemon, plus
  extra, to taste
425ml (15 fl oz) olive oil

3 tbsp wholegrain mustard
freshly ground black
  pepper

1 Rub the steaks with the cut sides of the garlic, then brush the steaks with the oil.
2 Spread the peppercorns close together on a plate. Press one side of each steak firmly onto the peppercorns, turn the steaks over and repeat with the other side. Cover the steaks and leave to marinate in a cool place for 3–4 hours.
3 Meanwhile, make the aïoli by putting the garlic, egg yolks and lemon juice in a blender and mixing briefly. With the motor running, slowly pour in the olive oil in a thin, steady stream until the mixture becomes the consistency of thick cream. Transfer to a bowl, stir in the mustard and season to taste; add more lemon juice, if necessary.
4 Cook the steaks on a lightly oiled grill rack, turning once, for about 3 minutes each side for rare, 4 minutes each side for medium, or until cooked to your liking. Serve the steaks with the aïoli.

163 LAMB BROCHETTES WITH APRICOT AND MINT SALSA

PREPARATION TIME *15 minutes, plus 4 hours marinating* **COOKING TIME** *8–10 minutes* **SERVES 4**

550g (1¼lb) lean lamb, cut
  into 3cm (1¼in) cubes
2 tbsp orange marmalade
2 tbsp soy sauce
1 tsp wholegrain mustard

SALSA
115g (4oz) ready-to-eat
  dried apricots, finely
  chopped
1 red pepper, seeded and
  finely chopped

4 tbsp chopped fresh mint
juice of 2 limes
1 red onion, finely chopped
salt and freshly ground
  black pepper

1 Put the lamb into a non-metallic bowl.
2 Mix together the marmalade, soy sauce, mustard and seasoning. Pour over the lamb. Stir to ensure all the cubes are evenly coated, then cover and leave to marinate in a cool place for 4 hours, stirring occasionally.
3 Make the salsa by combining all the ingredients.
4 Lift the lamb from the bowl (reserve any remaining glaze) and thread onto skewers. Cook on an oiled grill rack for 8–10 minutes, turning regularly and brushing with any remaining glaze, until the lamb is nicely browned on the outside and cooked to your liking inside. Serve with the salsa.

164 PORK AND APPLE SKEWERS

PREPARATION TIME *10 minutes, plus 3–4 hours marinating* **COOKING TIME** *12–15 minutes* **SERVES 4**

**450g (1lb) pork tenderloin,
  cut into 3cm (1¼in)
  cubes**
**1 tbsp finely chopped
  sage leaves**

**50ml (2 fl oz) sharp apple
  juice**
**grated zest and juice of
  ½ lemon**
2 tbsp wholegrain mustard
4 tbsp grapeseed oil

**salt and freshly ground
  black pepper**
2 crisp red apples
few sprigs of sage

1. Put the pork into a non-metallic bowl.
2. Mix the chopped sage leaves with the apple juice, lemon zest and juice, mustard, oil and salt and black pepper. Stir into the pork to ensure the cubes are evenly coated, then cover and leave to marinate in a cool place for 3–4 hours.
3. Meanwhile, core the apples and cut into wedges.
4. Lift the pork from the bowl, reserving the marinade. Thread the pork and apple alternately onto skewers, interspersing the pieces with sage leaves.
5. Cook on an oiled grill rack for about 12–15 minutes, turning regularly and brushing with the remaining marinade, until the pork is cooked through.

165 PORK WITH CORIANDER AND LIME

PREPARATION TIME *10 minutes, plus 1–2 hours marinating* **COOKING TIME** *14–16 minutes* **SERVES 4**

4 pork steaks, 2–2.5cm (¾–1in) thick	MARINADE	grated rind and juice of 2 limes
small bunch of fresh chives, finely snipped	2 tbsp dry white vermouth	1 tsp caster sugar
2 tbsp chopped fresh coriander	3½ tbsp olive oil	salt and freshly ground black pepper
lime quarters, to serve	2 garlic cloves, finely chopped	
	3 tbsp chopped fresh coriander	

1 Lay the pork in a shallow non-metallic dish.
2 Combine the vermouth, oil, garlic, 3 tbsp of coriander, lime zest and juice, sugar and seasoning. Pour over the pork, turn the steaks to ensure they are evenly coated, then cover and leave in a cool place for 1–2 hours, turning once or twice.
3 Lift the pork from the marinade (reserve the marinade) and cook on an oiled grill rack over medium-hot coals for 7–8 minutes on each side, turning occasionally and basting with the remaining marinade, until the juices run clear when the thickest parts of the steaks are pierced with a fine skewer.
4 Meanwhile, combine the remaining coriander with the chives.
5 Remove from the rack, sprinkle over the herbs and serve with lime quarters.

166 LAMB KEBABS WITH SUN-DRIED TOMATOES AND THYME

PREPARATION TIME *10 minutes, plus 2 hours marinating* **COOKING TIME** *8–10 minutes* **SERVES 4**

450g (1lb) boneless leg of lamb, cut into 3cm (1¼in) cubes	MARINADE	2 tbsp olive oil
	150ml (5fl oz) yogurt	2 tbsp sun-dried tomato paste
	3 garlic cloves, finely chopped	1 tsp dried thyme
	4 tbsp red wine	

1 Put the lamb into a non-metallic bowl.
2 Make the marinade by combining the ingredients. Stir into the lamb to coat the pieces evenly. Cover and leave in a cool place for 2 hours.
3 Lift the lamb from the bowl (reserve any remaining marinade) and thread onto skewers. Cook on an oiled grill rack, turning regularly and brushing with the reserved marinade, for 8–10 minutes until well browned on the outside and still juicy inside.

167 BEEF AND RED PEPPER KEBABS

PREPARATION TIME *15 minutes, plus 4 hours marinating* **COOKING TIME** *5–10 minutes* **SERVES 6**

**900g (2lb) steak, cut into
  3cm (1¼in) cubes**
**1 small onion, cut
  lengthways into
  9 wedges, keeping the
  root end intact**
**1 red pepper, cut into
  2.5cm (1in) pieces**

MARINADE
3 tbsp olive oil
**1 garlic clove, finely
  chopped**
1½ tbsp lemon juice
**1½ tsp pimenton (smoked
  paprika)**

1 tsp harissa
1 tsp ground coriander
1 tsp ground cumin
**salt and freshly ground
  black pepper**

1 Place the steak in a non-metallic bowl.
2 Make the marinade by combing the ingredients. Pour over the steak and stir to ensure all the pieces are evenly coated, then cover and leave in a cool place for 4 hours, stirring occasionally.
3 Lift the meat from the marinade and thread onto skewers, alternating with the onion wedges and pepper pieces. Cook on an oiled grill rack for 5–10 minutes until well browned on the outside and cooked to your liking inside.

168 SOUVLAKIA

PREPARATION TIME *10 minutes, plus 3–4 hours marinating* **COOKING TIME** *8–10 minutes* **SERVES 6**

**700g (1½lb) lean lamb, cut
  into 3cm (1¼in) cubes**
1 large onion
75ml (3fl oz) olive oil
**4 garlic cloves, coarsely
  chopped**

½ tsp ground cumin
**1½ tsp ground cayenne
  pepper**
**freshly ground black
  pepper**
sea salt

TO SERVE
pitta breads
lemon wedges
**seasoned Greek yogurt
  with chopped fresh
  coriander stirred in**

1 Put the lamb into a non-metallic bowl.
2 Put the olive oil, onion, garlic, cumin, cayenne and plenty of black pepper into a food processor or blender and mix until mushy. Tip over the lamb, stir to coat the cubes evenly, then cover and leave in a cool place for 3–4 hours, stirring occasionally.
3 Lift the lamb from the bowl (reserve the remaining marinade) and thread onto skewers. Cook on an oiled grill rack for 8–10 minutes, turning regularly and brushing with the remaining marinade, until the lamb is nicely browned on the outside and cooked to your liking inside.
4 Meanwhile, warm the pitta breads on the side of the grill rack for 30 seconds on each side. Remove the kebabs from the grill rack, sprinkle over some sea salt and a little lemon juice, then tuck into pitta breads with a spoonful of the yogurt.

169 BACON-WRAPPED SAUSAGES WITH MUSTARD DIP

PREPARATION TIME *10 minutes* **COOKING TIME** *12–14 minutes* **SERVES 4-6**

12 pork sausages
12 rashers smoked streaky
bacon, rinds removed

2 tbsp fresh thyme leaves
(optional)

MUSTARD DIP

4 tbsp wholegrain mustard
115ml (4fl oz) mayonnaise
(see page 179)

1   Make the mustard dip by beating the mustard into the mayonnaise.
2   Add the sausages to a pan of boiling water, quickly return to the boil and then simmer gently for 3 minutes. Drain and rinse under cold running water to speed cooling. Pat dry.
3   Stretch each bacon rasher with the back of a knife. Sprinkle the thyme, if using, over one side of each rasher. Place a sausage diagonally across one end of each rasher and roll up to enclose the sausage completely. Secure with soaked wooden cocktail sticks (see page 10).
4   Cook the wrapped sausages on an oiled grill rack for 7–8 minutes until well browned and cooked through, turning regularly.

170 HONEY AND MUSTARD GLAZED SAUSAGES

PREPARATION TIME *5 minutes* **COOKING TIME** *13–15 minutes* **SERVES 4**

2 tbsp clear honey
2 tbsp wholegrain mustard
juice of 1 small lemon

2 garlic cloves, finely
    chopped (optional)

salt and freshly ground
    black pepper
8 pork sausages

1 Mix the honey, mustard, lemon juice and garlic (if using), and season lightly.
2 Add the sausages to a pan of boiling water, quickly return to the boil and then simmer gently for 3 minutes. Drain and rinse under cold running water to speed cooling. Pat dry.
3 Brush the sausages with some of the honey mixture, then cook on an oiled grill rack for 8–10 minutes, turning occasionally and brushing with the glaze, until evenly browned and cooked through.

171 LAMB WITH YOGURT, MINT AND LIME

PREPARATION TIME *10 minutes, plus 2 hours marinating* **COOKING TIME** *8–10 minutes* **SERVES 6**

675g (1½lb) boneless lamb,
    cut into 3cm (1¼in)
    cubes

MARINADE
250ml (9fl oz) Greek yogurt
2 tbsp virgin olive oil
1 garlic clove, finely
    chopped
4 saffron strands, crushed

1 tbsp chopped fresh mint
grated zest and juice of
    ½ lime
salt and freshly ground
    black pepper

1 Put the lamb into a non-metallic bowl.
2 Make the marinade by combining the ingredients together. Add to the lamb and stir to coat evenly. Cover and leave in a cool place for 2 hours.
3 Thread the lamb onto skewers. Cook on an oiled grill rack for 8–10 minutes, turning regularly, until well browned on the outside and still juicy inside.

172 FRAGRANT LAMB KEBABS

PREPARATION TIME *10 minutes, plus 4–6 hours marinating* **COOKING TIME** *8–10 minutes* **SERVES 6–8**

900g (2lb) lean lamb, cut
    into 4cm (1½in) cubes
1 lemon, cut into 12
    wedges
12 fresh bay leaves

MARINADE
4 tbsp olive oil
2½ tsp dried oregano
1 tsp paprika
1 tsp ground cumin

grated rind and juice of
    ½ large lemon
salt and freshly ground
    black pepper

1 Put the lamb into a non-metallic dish.
2 Combine the oil, oregano, paprika, cumin, lemon rind and juice, and black pepper. Mix with the lamb so the cubes are evenly coated, then cover and leave in cool place for 4–6 hours.
3 Thread the lamb onto skewers alternating with the lemon wedges and bay leaves. Cook the kebabs on an oiled grill rack for 8–10 minutes, turning regularly, until well browned on the outside and still juicy inside.

173 SURPRISE BEEFBURGERS

PREPARATION TIME *10 minutes, plus 2 hours chilling* **COOKING TIME** *10-15 minutes* **SERVES 4**

1 onion, finely chopped
1 tbsp olive oil
1 plump garlic clove, finely
  chopped
450g (1lb) lean minced beef

2 tsp chopped fresh parsley
salt and freshly ground
  black pepper
50g (2oz) feta cheese
4 sesame buns

salad leaves and tomato
  ketchup *(see page 184)*,
  to serve

1 Cook the onion in the oil until softened and lightly coloured. Stir in the garlic towards the end.
   Remove from the heat and leave to cool.
2 Mix the onion and garlic with the beef, parsley and seasoning. Divide the mixture into four equal
   portions and form into burgers about 10cm (4in) in diameter, enclosing a quarter of the cheese
   in each one. Leave in a cool place for 2 hours.
3 Cook the burgers on an oiled grill rack for 3-4 minutes on each side for medium-rare, or longer
   if you prefer the burgers more well-done.
4 Meanwhile, warm the sesame buns on the side of the rack. Split in half, place salad leaves on the
   bottom, top with a burger and ketchup, and close with the top of the bun.

174 VENISON SAUSAGES WITH RED ONION MARMALADE

PREPARATION TIME *5 minutes* **COOKING TIME** *35-40 minutes* **SERVES 4**

8 venison sausages

RED ONION MARMALADE
2 tbsp olive oil

350g (12oz) red onions,
  thinly sliced
pinch of brown sugar
1 tsp fresh thyme leaves
225ml (8fl oz) red wine

55ml (2fl oz) red wine
  vinegar
salt and freshly ground
  black pepper

1 Make the marmalade by heating the oil in a pan, adding the onions and sugar and cooking
   gently for about 10 minutes until the onions are golden and softened. Add the thyme, pour in
   the wine and vinegar, bring to a simmer, then season and leave to simmer gently, uncovered,
   until the liquid has almost evaporated. Season to taste and adjust the sweetness/sharpness with
   more sugar or vinegar, as necessary.
2 Cook the sausages on an oiled grill rack for 8-10 minutes, turning occasionally, until cooked
   through. Serve with the marmalade.

175 SAVOURY STUDDED LEG OF LAMB

PREPARATION TIME *10 minutes, plus 1 hour marinating* **COOKING TIME** *30–40 minutes* **SERVES 6**

1 leg of lamb, about 2–2.5kg (4–4½lb), boned and butterflied	handful of mixed fresh mint and parsley	freshly ground black pepper
3 plump garlic cloves, cut into thin slivers	6 anchovy fillets	small handful of rosemary sprigs, for cooking
	50g (2oz) pancetta	lemon wedges, to serve
	1 tbsp lemon juice	

1 Lay the lamb skin side down. With a sharp knife, cut approximately 1cm (½in) deep slashes across the lamb at 5cm (2in) intervals.

2 Put the garlic, herbs, anchovy fillets, pancetta, lemon juice and black pepper into a food processor or blender; pulse until mixed to a smooth paste. Push well into the incisions in the lamb. Season the outside of the lamb with black pepper.

3 Push skewers diagonally from opposite corners of the lamb to hold it in place. Cover the lamb and leave in a cool place for 1 hour.

4 Just before cooking the lamb, scatter the rosemary sprigs over the barbecue coals. Cook the lamb on an oiled grill rack for 15 minutes on each side for medium rare, or for 20 minutes on each side for well done.

5 Remove the lamb from the grill rack, cover and leave for about 10 minutes before carving.

176 INDONESIAN PORK BURGERS

PREPARATION TIME *10 minutes, plus 10 minutes soaking and 1 hour chilling* **COOKING TIME** *12 minutes* **SERVES 4**

50ml (2fl oz) coconut milk	2 tbsp Thai red curry paste	1 tbsp lime juice
50g (2oz) fresh bread crumbs	2 tbsp chopped fresh basil	pinch of caster sugar
450g (1lb) minced pork	1 tbsp chopped fresh coriander	groundnut oil, for brushing
1 garlic clove, finely chopped	1 tbsp Thai fish sauce	
	grated zest of 1 lime	

1 Pour the coconut milk over the breadcrumbs and leave to soak for 10 minutes.

2 Combine the soaked breadcrumbs with the remaining ingredients, mixing thoroughly until well combined. With wet hands, form the mixture into eight equal burgers, 2–2.5cm (¾–1in) thick. Chill for an hour or more.

3 Brush the burgers with groundnut oil and cook on an oiled grill rack, turning once, for about 6 minutes on each side until golden and the juices run clear.

177 RACK OF LAMB WITH SESAME AND MUSTARD

PREPARATION TIME *10 minutes, plus 2 hours marinating* **COOKING TIME** *15-25 minutes* **SERVES 4**

2 racks of lamb, 700g (1½lb) each, trimmed of excess fat	MARINADE	1½ tbsp sugar
	3 tbsp soy sauce	1 plump garlic clove, finely chopped
	2 tbsp Dijon mustard	
large sprigs of sage, for cooking	2 tbsp lightly toasted sesame seeds	1 tbsp sea salt
		2 tsp freshly ground black pepper
	1½ tbsp sesame oil	

1 Make the marinade by stirring all the ingredients together. Rub over the lamb and leave to marinate in a cool place for 2 hours.
2 Just before cooking the lamb, scatter the sage over the coals.
3 Cover the lamb bones with foil to prevent them burning. Cook on an oiled grill rack, turning once, for 15 minutes for rare lamb, 20 minutes for medium rare and 25 minutes for well done.
4 Remove from the grill rack and leave to rest, covered, for 10 minutes before dividing into cutlets.

178 AROMATIC LAMB FILLET

PREPARATION TIME *10 minutes, plus 4-8 hours marinating* **COOKING TIME** *8-12 minutes* **SERVES 6**

675-800g (1½-1¾lb) lamb neck fillets	2 plump garlic cloves, crushed	2 tsp ground cinnamon
		pinch of cayenne pepper, to taste
	1½ tbsp sun-dried tomato paste	
MARINADE		handful of fresh mint leaves, finely chopped
2 tbsp olive oil	juice of 1 lemon	
	2 tsp ground cardamom	

1 Lay the lamb in a non-metallic dish.
2 Make the marinade by combining the ingredients. Rub thoroughly over the lamb, cover and leave to marinate in cool place for about 4-8 hours.
3 Cook the lamb on an oiled grill rack for 8-12 minutes, turning regularly, until well browned on the outside and cooked to your liking inside.
4 Remove from the grill rack and leave to rest, covered, for about 5 minutes before carving.

179 GAMMON STEAKS WITH APRICOT GLAZE

PREPARATION TIME *10 minutes* **COOKING TIME** *10-12 minutes* **SERVES 4**

4 gammon steaks	1 tbsp Dijon mustard
	2 tsp Worcestershire sauce
APRICOT GLAZE	freshly ground black pepper
3 tbsp good-quality apricot jam, warmed slightly	

1 Trim any surplus fat from the steaks, leaving enough to keep them moist. Snip the remaining fat at 2.5cm (1in) intervals.
2 Make the glaze by combining all the ingredients.
3 Brush the glaze over the gammon steaks and cook on an oiled grill rack for 5-6 minutes on each side, turning once.

180 SPICED LAMB CHOPS

PREPARATION TIME *15 minutes, plus 4 hours marinating* **COOKING TIME** *12-18 minutes* **SERVES 4**

olive oil, for frying	1 tbsp mustard seeds,	salt and freshly ground
1 large onion, finely	lightly crushed	black pepper
chopped	2 tsp cumin seeds,	8 lamb loin chops
1 plump garlic clove, finely	lightly crushed	chopped fresh coriander
chopped	1 tsp paprika	Pineapple and Macadamia
1 tbsp coriander seeds,	150ml (5 fl oz) Greek yogurt	Nut Salsa *(see page 178)*,
lightly crushed		to serve

1 Heat the oil in a frying pan, add the onion and cook until softened and lightly coloured; stir in the garlic towards the end of cooking. Add all the seeds and cook, stirring, for 1–2 minutes. Transfer the onion mixture to a bowl and stir in the paprika, yogurt and seasoning. Leave to cool.

2 Coil the 'tail' end of the chops round the eye of the meat and secure with wooden cocktail sticks. Put the chops in a single layer in a shallow non-metallic dish. Pour over the yogurt mixture, turn the chops over, cover and leave in a cool place for about 4 hours, turning occasionally.

3 Lift the lamb from the dish. Cook on an oiled grill rack, turning once, for 3 minutes on each side for medium rare or for 5 minutes on each side for well done.

4 Remove the chops from the grill rack and sprinkle with chopped coriander. Serve with the salsa.

181 PORK WITH PLUM SAUCE

PREPARATION TIME *15 minutes* **COOKING TIME** *30-35 minutes* **SERVES 4**

6 chump chops, 2.5cm (1in)
  thick
groundnut oil, for brushing
salt and freshly ground
  black pepper

PLUM SAUCE
1 tbsp groundnut oil
2 shallots, finely chopped
1 tbsp finely chopped fresh
  root ginger
½ tbsp Sichuan
  peppercorns, finely
  crushed

225g (8oz) plums,
  quartered and pitted
1 tbsp light soy sauce
5 tbsp sweet sherry
½ tbsp clear honey
lime juice, to taste

1   Make the plum sauce by heating the oil in a frying pan, adding the shallots and frying until softened. Add the ginger and peppercorns towards the end and continue cooking until they smell fragrant. Add the plums, soy sauce, sherry and honey. Bring to the boil, cover and simmer until the plums are tender. Add lime juice to taste. Set aside.

2   Trim any excess fat from the chops and snip the remaining fat at 2.5cm (1in) intervals. Brush the chops with groundnut oil and season them.

3   Cook the chops on an oiled grill rack for 8-10 minutes on each side until lightly charred and the juices run clear when the thickest part is pierced with a skewer. Meanwhile, warm the sauce on the side of the grill rack. Serve the chops with the warm sauce.

182 THAI-STYLE LAMB BURGERS

PREPARATION TIME *15 minutes, plus 4 hours chilling* **COOKING TIME** *15-18 minutes* **SERVES 4**

olive oil, for frying
1 small onion, finely
  chopped
2 garlic cloves, finely
  chopped
500g (1lb 2oz) minced lamb
1 tbsp red Thai curry paste

1 tbsp fish sauce
1 tbsp lime juice
1 tbsp chopped fresh mint
1 tsp lime zest
1 tsp finely chopped
  lemon grass

TO SERVE
4 small pitta breads
lightly dressed mixed salad
  leaves with coriander
lime slices

1   Heat a little oil in a frying pan, add the onion and fry until softened, adding the garlic towards the end of the cooking. Remove with a slotted spoon and drain on paper towels. Leave to cool.

2   Mix the onion with the remaining ingredients until thoroughly combined. With wet hands, shape the mixture into eight burgers, 2.5cm (1in) thick. If time allows, cover and leave in a cool place for at least 4 hours or overnight.

3   Cook on an oiled grill rack for 5-6 minutes on each side, turning once, until cooked through and the juices run clear when the burgers are pierced with a fine skewer.

4   Meanwhile, warm the pitta breads on the side of the grill rack for 30 seconds on each side. Split the pittas open to form a pocket and fill with salad. Add two burgers to each pitta bread, and serve with lime slices.

183 VEAL CHOPS WITH GREEN HERB SAUCE

PREPARATION TIME *10 minutes, plus 2 hours marinating* **COOKING TIME** *12-15 minutes* **SERVES 4**

4 veal rib chops, 2.5-4cm (1-1½in) thick	GREEN HERB SAUCE	**3 tbsp chopped fresh basil**
2 tbsp virgin olive oil	**1 tsp Dijon mustard**	**1-2 garlic cloves, crushed**
1 tbsp lemon juice	**115ml (4fl oz) extra virgin olive oil**	**2 tsp small salted capers, well rinsed and dried**
sea salt and freshly ground black pepper	**1½ tsp lemon juice**	
	3 tbsp chopped fresh flat-leaf parsley	

1   Put the veal into a non-metallic dish.
2   Stir the oil, lemon juice and black pepper together. Pour over the veal and turn the chops over to ensure they are coated thoroughly and evenly. Cover and leave to marinate in a cool place for 2 hours, turning occasionally.
3   Meanwhile, make the green herb sauce by whisking the mustard, olive oil and lemon juice together until emulsified. Stir in the herbs, garlic and capers, and season to taste. Add more lemon juice, if necessary.
4   Lift the veal from the dish and cook on an oiled grill rack, turning once, for 12-15 minutes until browned on the outside but still moist and slightly pink inside. Remove from the grill rack, sprinkle with sea salt and serve with the sauce.

184 STEAK SANDWICHES WITH ONION RELISH

PREPARATION TIME *10 minutes* **COOKING TIME** *45-50 minutes* **SERVES 4**

4 sirloin steaks	ONION RELISH	**pinch of brown sugar**
olive oil, for brushing	**2 tbsp olive oil**	**salt and freshly ground black pepper**
4 small baguettes, about 20cm (8in) long	**450g (1lb) large onions, sliced thinly into rings**	
butter, for spreading	**1 tbsp balsamic vinegar**	
Dijon or wholegrain mustard, for spreading	**1 tbsp Worcestershire sauce**	

1   Make the onion relish by heating the oil in a large, heavy frying pan. Add the onions and cook very gently, stirring occasionally, until they are soft and tinged with brown. Stir in the vinegar, Worcestershire sauce, sugar and seasoning. Continue to cook until the liquid has evaporated. Check the sweetness and seasoning. Set aside to cool.
2   Brush the steaks with olive oil and cook on an oiled grill rack for about 3 minutes on each side for rare, 4 minutes for medium, or until cooked to your liking.
3   Meanwhile, split the baguettes lengthways and warm them on the side of the grill rack. Spread the inside of each bottom half with butter and just a little mustard. Lay a steak in each baguette and top with onion relish. Close the baguettes and eat immediately.

185 CARIBBEAN PORK AND PINEAPPLE KEBABS

PREPARATION TIME *10 minutes, plus 3-4 hours marinating* **COOKING TIME** *12-15 minutes* **SERVES 4-6**

675g (1½lb) pork, cut into 3cm (1¼in) cubes	MARINADE	1½ tbsp groundnut oil
½ small fresh pineapple, peeled, cored and cubed	2 garlic cloves, crushed	2 tbsp pineapple juice from a carton
	2.5cm (1in) piece of fresh root ginger, grated	2 tbsp dark rum
	¼ tsp ground allspice	salt and freshly ground black pepper
	2 tbsp dark brown sugar	

1 Put the pork into a non-metallic bowl.
2 Make the marinade by combining the ingredients. Stir into the pork, ensuring the cubes are evenly coated, then cover and leave in a cool place for 3-4 hours.
3 Lift the pork from the bowl, reserving the marinade. Thread the pork and pineapple cubes alternately onto skewers. Cook on an oiled grill rack, turning regularly and brushing with the remaining marinade, for about 12-15 minutes until the pork is cooked through and browned.

186 STEAKS WITH MUSTARD AND SOY

PREPARATION TIME *10 minutes, plus 4 hours marinating* **COOKING TIME** *6-12 minutes* **SERVES 4**

3 tbsp Dijon mustard	1 tbsp olive oil	4 rump or sirloin steaks, 2.5cm (1in) thick
1 tbsp soy sauce	3 tbsp chopped fresh coriander	
1 tbsp grated fresh root ginger		

1 Mix together the mustard, soy sauce, ginger, olive oil and coriander. Smooth over the steaks, cover and leave in a cool place for about 4 hours.
2 Cook the steaks on an oiled grill rack, turning once, for about 3-4 minutes on each side for rare steaks, 5-6 minutes on each side for medium steaks, or until cooked to your liking.

187 RIB OF BEEF WITH MUSTARD AÏOLI

PREPARATION TIME *10 minutes* **COOKING TIME** *8 minutes* **SERVES 8**

1.8kg (4lb) rib of beef, cut into individual ribs	MUSTARD AÏOLI	juice of 1 small lemon, plus extra, to taste (optional)
sea salt and freshly ground black pepper	6 plump garlic cloves, crushed	425ml (15 fl oz) olive oil
	2 egg yolks, at room temperature	3 tbsp wholegrain mustard

1 Make the mustard aïoli by putting the garlic, egg yolks and lemon juice in a blender and mixing briefly. With the motor running, slowly pour in the olive oil in a thin steady stream until the mixture becomes the consistency of thick cream. Transfer to a bowl, stir in the mustard and season to taste; add more lemon juice, if necessary.
2 Meanwhile, lay the ribs on an oiled grill rack and cook for about 4 minutes, turning the ribs through 90 degrees halfway through cooking, to create a criss-cross pattern. Turn them over and repeat on the other side. Cook for longer if you prefer well-done ribs.
3 Move the ribs from the grill rack, sprinkle with seasoning, cover with foil and leave to rest for 5-10 minutes.
4 Cut the bones from the ribs, then cut the meat into thick slices. Serve the beef with the aïoli.

188 MEXICAN TORTILLA WRAPS

PREPARATION TIME *10 minutes, plus 8–24 hours marinating* **COOKING TIME** *20 minutes* **SERVES 6–8**

900g (2lb) thick piece of skirt, flank or rump steak

MARINADE
2 tbsp olive oil
3 garlic cloves, finely chopped

juice of 1½ limes
½–1 tsp chilli flakes
1 tbsp paprika
1 tsp dried oregano
1 tsp ground cumin
salt and freshly ground black pepper

TO SERVE
12–16 tortillas
Roasted Tomato Salsa
 (*see page 175*)
1 small Iceberg lettuce, finely shredded
300ml (10fl oz) soured cream

1 Lay the steak in a non-metallic dish.
2 Make the marinade by mixing all the ingredients in a blender. Pour over the beef, then cover and leave in a cool place for 8–24 hours, turning occasionally.
3 Lift the beef from the marinade (reserve the marinade) and cook on an oiled grill rack, basting frequently with the remaining marinade, for about 20 minutes for medium rare. Remove the beef from the rack, cover and leave for about 5 minutes.
4 Meanwhile, wrap the tortillas in foil and put on the side of the grill rack to warm for 5 minutes.
5 To serve, slice the beef thinly and serve with the salsa, lettuce, soured cream and tortillas separately so that each person can assemble and roll their own wraps.

189 LAMB CHOPS WITH SAFFRON AND LEMON

PREPARATION TIME *10 minutes, plus 2 hours marinating* **COOKING TIME** *8-10 minutes* **SERVES 6**

6 lamb chump chops, 2.5cm (1in) thick	2 tbsp virgin olive oil	1½ tsp lemon zest
	1 garlic clove, finely chopped	1½ tsp lemon juice
		salt and freshly ground black pepper
MARINADE	4 saffron strands, crushed	
250ml (9fl oz) Greek yogurt	1 tbsp chopped fresh mint	

1   Put the lamb into a non-metallic bowl.
2   Make the marinade by combining the ingredients together. Add to the lamb and stir to coat evenly. Cover and leave to marinate in a cool place for 2 hours.
3   Cook the chops on an oiled grill rack, turning regularly, for 8-10 minutes until well browned on the outside and still juicy inside.

190 TURKISH LAMB BROCHETTES

PREPARATION TIME *10 minutes, plus 3-4 hours marinating* **COOKING TIME** *10 minutes* **SERVES 4**

500g (1lb 2oz) lean lamb, cut into bite-sized cubes	2 tbsp olive oil, plus extra for brushing	salt and freshly ground black pepper
4 tbsp lemon juice	1 tsp ground cumin	12 cubes of aubergine
1 garlic clove, finely chopped	1 tsp ground cardamom	8 bay leaves

1   Put the lamb into a non-metallic bowl.
2   Combine the lemon juice, garlic, olive oil, cumin, cardamom and salt and pepper. Stir into the lamb to coat the pieces evenly, cover and leave in a cool place for 3-4 hours.
3   Brush the aubergine cubes with olive oil, and season them.
4   Lift the lamb from the marinade (reserve any remaining marinade) and thread onto skewers, alternating with the aubergines and inserting the bay leaves at intervals.
5   Cook on an oiled grill rack, turning frequently and brushing with the reserved marinade, for about 10 minutes until browned and cooked to your liking.

191 BUTTERFLIED CHINESE LAMB

PREPARATION TIME *15 minutes, plus 8 hours marinating* **COOKING TIME** *30-35 minutes* **SERVES 8**

1.1kg (2½lb) shoulder of lamb	MARINADE	1 tbsp clear honey
4 garlic cloves, cut into thin slivers	150ml (5fl oz) soy sauce	3 star anise
	150ml (5fl oz) Madeira or medium dry sherry	3 tbsp chopped fresh coriander
	2.5cm (1in) piece fresh root ginger, grated	freshly ground black pepper

1   Make the marinade by mixing all the ingredients in a blender.
2   Open out the lamb and cut a few slits all over the surface. Insert the garlic slivers into the slits. Put the lamb into a non-metallic dish, pour over the marinade, cover and leave in a cool place for 8 hours or overnight, turning occasionally.
3   Lift the lamb from the marinade (reserving the marinade) and cook on an oiled grill rack, basting frequently with the remaining marinade, over a medium heat for 30-35 minutes for medium rare.

192 STEAK WITH ROASTED GARLIC AND MUSHROOMS

PREPARATION TIME *10 minutes* **COOKING TIME** *35-40 minutes* **SERVES 6-8**

**6-8 small whole garlic
   bulbs, papery skins
   removed**
**olive oil, for sprinkling
   and brushing**
1.5kg (3lb) entrecote steak
**sea salt and freshly ground
   black pepper**

**12-16 medium-sized field
   mushrooms**

TO SERVE (OPTIONAL)
**Tomatoes with Tapenade
   and Parsley Topping** *(see
   page 160)*

Herb Damper Breads *(see
   page 161)*
**bottled or home-made
   béarnaise or hollandaise
   sauce**

1   Place each garlic bulb on a piece of heavy-duty foil and sprinkle with a little oil. Fold the foil
    loosely round the bulbs, then twist the edges together tightly to seal. Cook on the grill rack for
    20 minutes, turning frequently.
2   Season the beef generously with black pepper and brush with oil. Brush the mushrooms with oil
    and season them.
3   Cook the beef on an oiled grill rack, turning frequently, for 10-15-minutes until well-browned on
    the outside and medium rare inside.
4   Remove the beef from the grill rack, cover and leave to stand for 5-10 minutes before sprinkling
    with sea salt and slicing thickly.
5   Meanwhile, cook the mushrooms on the grill rack, gill side uppermost, for 4-6 minutes.
6   Unwrap the garlic and spread either on the steak or the damper bread. Serve with tomatoes with
    tapenade and parsley topping, and with béarnaise or hollandaise sauce.
*   Put some hickory chips on the barbecue coals (soak first according to the manufacturer's
    instructions) for a characteristic flavour.

193 KENTUCKY GRILLED BEEF

PREPARATION TIME *10 minutes, plus 4 hours marinating* **COOKING TIME** *10-14 minutes* **SERVES 6**

**2 beef fillets, about 350g
   (12oz) each**
**6 slices sourdough bread,
   or country bread**
Aïoli *(see page 106)*, **lettuce
   & 4-6 tomatoes, to serve**

KENTUCKY RUB
1 tbsp paprika
**1½ tsp freshly ground
   black pepper**
**½ tsp English mustard
   powder**

½ tsp garlic granules
½ tsp dried sage
½ tsp dried oregano
½ tsp ground chillies
salt

1   Using a large, sharp knife held parallel, cut through one side of each fillet going almost but not
    quite through to the opposite side. Open out flat, like a book.
2   Make the Kentucky rub by combining all the ingredients. Rub thoroughly into all the surfaces of
    the beef. Cover and leave in a cool place for about 4 hours.
3   Reform each piece of beef and cook on an oiled grill rack for about 5-7 minutes on each side,
    until nicely browned on the outside but still pink in the centre.
4   Remove the beef from the rack, cover with foil and leave to rest for 5-10 minutes.
5   Shred a few lettuce leaves and slice the tomatoes. Carve the beef into thin slices and serve with
    the bread, aïoli, lettuce and tomatoes.

194 SPICED BEEF KEBABS

PREPARATION TIME *15 minutes, plus 8 hours marinating* **COOKING TIME** *6–8 minutes* **SERVES 4**

550g (1¼lb) rump steak, cut
   into 3cm (1¼in) cubes
1 red pepper
1 yellow pepper
16 cherry tomatoes
olive oil, for brushing

salt and freshly ground
   black pepper

MARINADE
8 tbsp good-quality tomato
   ketchup *(see page 184)*

4 tbsp red wine
2 tbsp soy sauce
1 tbsp chilli sauce
2 tsp Jamaican Jerk
   Seasoning *(see
   page 189)*

1   Put the beef into a non-metallic bowl.
2   Make the marinade by combining all the ingredients. Stir into the beef to cover the cubes evenly
     and thoroughly. Cover and leave in a cool place for 8 hours, stirring occasionally.
3   Meanwhile, cut the peppers into 2.5cm (1in) squares. Stack in pairs of one of each colour. Brush
     the pepper stacks and the tomatoes with oil and season them.
4   Lift the beef from the marinade (reserve any remaining marinade) and thread onto skewers,
     alternating with the pepper stacks and tomatoes.
5   Cook on an oiled grill rack for 6–8 minutes, turning regularly and brushing with any remaining
     marinade, until cooked to your liking.

195 GREEK LAMB STEAKS WITH AUBERGINE SALSA

PREPARATION TIME *10 minutes, plus 3 hours marinating* **COOKING TIME** *18–25 minutes* **SERVES 4**

4 lamb steaks
2 garlic cloves, finely
  chopped
2 tbsp chopped fresh mint
2 tsp lemon juice
3 tbsp olive oil

salt and freshly ground
  black pepper

AUBERGINE SALSA
450g (1lb) aubergine, diced
1 small onion, chopped
1 garlic clove, crushed and
  chopped

olive oil, for frying
2 tbsp chopped fresh
  flat-leaf parsley
2 tbsp chopped fresh mint
2 tbsp lemon juice
115g (4oz) feta cheese,
  crumbled

1   Score the lamb on each side and place in a non-metallic dish.
2   Combine the garlic, mint, lemon juice, olive oil and seasoning. Pour over the lamb, turn to coat
    the steaks, then cover and leave in a cool place for 3 hours, turning occasionally.
3   Meanwhile, make the salsa by frying the aubergine, onion and garlic in a little olive oil, stirring
    occasionally, for about 10 minutes until the aubergine is a good golden brown. Remove from the
    heat and stir in the herbs, lemon juice, cheese and seasoning. Set aside.
4   Lift the lamb from the dish and cook on an oiled grill rack for 4–5 minutes on each side for
    medium, 6–7 minutes for well done. Remove from the grill rack and serve with the salsa.

196 LAMB WITH MEDITERRANEAN FLAVOURS

PREPARATION TIME *10 minutes, plus 8 hours marinating* **COOKING TIME** *15 minutes* **SERVES 6**

1.6kg (3½lb) shoulder of
  lamb, with bone, cut
  into large pieces

MARINADE
4 tbsp olive oil
3 garlic cloves, finely
  chopped

3 tbsp chopped fresh
  coriander
2 tbsp sun-dried tomato
  paste
1 tbsp clear honey
2 tsp Dijon mustard
2 tsp paprika
2 tsp ground cumin

½ tsp saffron threads,
  lightly toasted and
  pounded
salt and freshly ground
  black pepper

1   Put the lamb into a non-metallic bowl.
2   Combine the marinade ingredients. Pour over the lamb. Stir to ensure all the pieces are evenly
    coated then cover and leave in a cool place for 8 hours, stirring occasionally.
3   Lift the lamb from the bowl. Cook on an oiled grill rack for about 15 minutes, turning regularly,
    until the lamb is nicely browned and cooked through.

197 LAMB STEAKS WITH ROSEMARY AND LEMON

PREPARATION TIME *5 minutes, plus 3 hours marinating* **COOKING TIME** *8–12 minutes* **SERVES 4**

4 lamb leg steaks, 150g (5oz) each	3 tbsp virgin olive oil	leaves from 3 rosemary sprigs, finely chopped
juice and zest of 1 lemon	2 garlic cloves, crushed	2 lemons, halved

1 Lay the lamb in a single layer in a shallow non-metallic dish.
2 Combine the lemon juice and zest, virgin olive oil, garlic and rosemary. Pour over the lamb, turn the steaks over, cover and leave in a cool place for 3 hours, turning a couple of times.
3 Lift the lamb from the dish (reserve the marinade) and cook on an oiled grill rack, turning once, for 4 minutes on each side for medium lamb, 6 minutes on each side for well-done.
4 Meanwhile, brush the halved lemons with the remaining marinade and cook, cut side down, on the grill rack for 4–5 minutes on each side. Serve the lamb with the caramelised lemon juice squeezed over.

198 PASTRAMI-STYLE LAMB

PREPARATION TIME *10 minutes, plus 8 hours marinating* **COOKING TIME** *10–12 minutes* **SERVES 6**

2 fillets of lamb, each 350g (12oz)	RUB	1½ tsp English mustard powder
light rye bread, sliced tomatoes and red onions, to serve	1 plump garlic clove	1½ tsp dried thyme
	1 tbsp sea salt	1½ tsp ground sage
	1½ tsp freshly ground black pepper	½ tsp ground allspice

1 Make the rub by mashing the garlic it to a paste with the salt. Combine with the remaining ingredients. Rub thoroughly over the lamb, then cover and leave in a cool place for 8 hours.
2 Cook the lamb on an oiled grill rack, turning regularly, for 10–12 minutes until medium rare and nicely browned.
3 Remove the lamb from the grill rack, leave to stand for 5–10 minutes, then slice thinly. Serve on light rye bread with sliced tomatoes and red onions.

199 SPICED PORK STEAKS

PREPARATION TIME *10 minutes, plus 4 hours marinating* **COOKING TIME** *15 minutes* **SERVES 4**

4 pork steaks	½ tsp ground coriander	pinch of caster sugar
	2 tbsp sun-dried tomato paste	salt and freshly ground black pepper
MARINADE	1 tbsp olive oil	
1 tsp ground cumin	4 garlic cloves, crushed	
1 tsp dried oregano	grated zest 1 lime	
½ tsp ground cardamom	3 tbsp lime juice	
½ tsp harissa		

1 Using the point of a sharp knife, cut three or four slashes in each pork steak. Place in a shallow, non-metallic bowl.
2 Combine all the marinade ingredients and spread evenly and thoroughly over the pork. Cover and leave to marinate in a cool place for 4 hours.
3 Cook on an oiled grill rack over medium-hot coals for 7–8 minutes on each side, turning once.

200 ORIENTAL PORK

PREPARATION TIME *10 minutes, plus 4–6 hours marinating* **COOKING TIME** *25 minutes* **SERVES 6**

2 pork tenderloins, 450g (1lb) each	**1 red chilli, seeded and chopped**	**1 tsp Chinese five-spice powder**
2 plump garlic cloves, cut into thin slivers	**150ml (5 fl oz) Chinese plum sauce**	**fine strips of spring onion and thinly sliced cucumber, to serve**
2.5cm (1in) piece fresh root ginger, grated	**2 tbsp groundnut oil**	
	1 tbsp dark soy sauce	

1   Using the point of a thin, sharp knife, make cuts in the pork. Insert the garlic slivers in the cuts. Place in a non-metallic dish.

2   Mix together the ginger, chilli, plum sauce, groundnut oil, soy sauce and Chinese five-spice powder. Pour over the pork, turn the tenderloins to ensure they are evenly coated, then cover and leave in a cool place for 4–6 hours.

3   Lift the pork from the marinade and cook on an oiled grill rack over medium-hot coals for about 25 minutes, turning occasionally and basting with the remaining marinade, until the juices run clear when the thickest parts of the tenderloins are pierced with a skewer. Serve with spring onions and cucumber.

201 KOREAN SPICED PORK

PREPARATION TIME *10 minutes, plus 4–6 hours marinating* **COOKING TIME** *18 minutes* **SERVES 4**

2 pork fillets, 350g (12oz) each	MARINADE	**2 garlic cloves, crushed**
1 tbsp lime juice	**150ml (5fl oz) soy sauce**	**2.5cm (1in) piece of fresh root ginger, grated**
50g (2oz) fresh coriander leaves	**75ml (3fl oz) medium-dry sherry**	**pinch of dried chilli flakes**
	1 tbsp sesame oil	
	1 tbsp light brown sugar	

1   Put the marinade ingredients in a small saucepan and bring to the boil. Remove from the heat and leave to cool.

2   Lay the pork in a shallow non-metallic dish. Pour over the marinade, turn the pork to ensure it is completely coated, then cover and leave to marinate in a cool place for at least 4–6 hours, turning occasionally.

3   Lift the pork from the marinade (reserve the remaining marinade) and cook on an oiled grill rack for about 18 minutes, turning regularly and basting with the marinade, until the juices run clear when the thickest part of the fillet is pierced with a skewer, and the surface is caramelised.

4   Meanwhile, pour the remaining marinade into a pan, put on the grill rack and bring to the boil. Add the lime juice and cook for 2 minutes. Remove from the heat and add the coriander. Slice the pork and serve accompanied by the sauce.

202 CHAR SUI PORK

PREPARATION TIME *10 minutes, plus 4–6 hours marinating* **COOKING TIME** *14–16 minutes* **SERVES 4**

4 pork shoulder steaks

MARINADE
1 tbsp sunflower oil
1 tbsp sesame oil
2 tbsp hoisin sauce
2 tbsp clear honey
2 tbsp soy sauce

1 tsp Chinese five-spice
   powder
freshly ground black
   pepper
2 garlic cloves, finely
   chopped
5cm (2in) piece fresh
   root ginger, grated

TO SERVE
6 spring onions, sliced
   lengthways into thin
   shreds
½ cucumber, seeded and
   cut into long, thin strips
Chinese plum sauce
lime wedges

1   Lay the pork steaks in a single layer in a shallow non-metallic dish.
2   Make the marinade by stirring together all the ingredients except the ginger. Using a garlic press, squeeze the ginger juice into the other ingredients, then stir in. Pour over the pork, turn the steaks to ensure they are completely coated, then cover and leave to marinate in a cool place for at least 4–6 hours, turning occasionally.
3   Lift the pork from the marinade (reserve the remaining marinade) and cook for 7–8 minutes on each side, turning once and basting with any remaining marinade, until the juices run clear when the thickest part of the steak is pierced with a skewer. Serve the steaks with the spring onions, cucumber, plum sauce and lime wedges.

203 BARBECUED SHREDDED PORK SANDWICH

PREPARATION TIME *10 minutes, plus up to 24 hours marinating* **COOKING TIME** *2½–3 hours* **SERVES 8**

**2kg (4½lb) boneless pork
    shoulder**

SOUTHERN SPICE RUB
**1 tbsp cumin seeds
1½ tsp black peppercorns**

**3 tbsp mixed caster and
    light soft brown sugar
2 tbsp paprika
2 tsp chilli powder
salt**

TO SERVE
**16 crisp buns or rolls
Barbecue Sauce (see
    page 179)
coleslaw**

1   Make the spice rub by heating a small, dry, heavy frying pan. Add the cumin seeds and heat over a moderate heat until fragrant. Grind the cumin seeds. Add the peppercorns to the pan and heat until fragrant, then coarsely grind. Mix the ground cumin and peppercorns with the remaining rub ingredients.
2   Rub the spice mixture thoroughly into the pork. Re-roll the joint and tie tightly with string at regular intervals. Cover and leave in a cool place for up to 24 hours.
3   Cook the pork on an oiled grill rack over indirect medium heat (see page 9) for 2½–3 hours, turning regularly, until very tender.
4   Remove from the rack, cover and leave to rest for about 10 minutes.
5   Using two forks, pull or shred the pork into pieces. Mix with the barbecue sauce and serve in the buns or rolls, with coleslaw.

204 PORK WITH GINGER AND CHILLI

PREPARATION TIME *10 minutes, plus 4 hours marinating* **COOKING TIME** *20 minutes* **SERVES 4**

**2 pork fillets, 350g (12oz)
    each**

MARINADE
**3 garlic cloves, finely
    chopped
½ small red chilli, seeded
    and thinly sliced**

**5cm (2in) piece of fresh
    root ginger, grated
1½ tbsp lemon juice
3 tbsp soy sauce
2 tbsp clear honey
1½ tsp sesame oil
1½ tsp groundnut oil**

**freshly ground black
    pepper**

DIPPING SAUCE
**4 tbsp Thai sweet chilli
    sauce
2 tbsp lime or lemon juice**

1   Make the marinade by pounding the garlic, chilli and ginger together in a bowl using the end of a rolling pin. Stir in the remaining ingredients.
2   Prick the pork all over with a fork, then rub in the marinade. Lay in a non-metallic dish and pour over any remaining marinade. Cover and leave in a cool place for 4 hours, turning occasionally.
3   Make the dipping sauce by mixing the chilli sauce with the lime or lemon juice in a small bowl.
4   Lift the pork from the marinade (reserve any remaining marinade) and cook on an oiled grill rack for about 20 minutes, turning twice and brushing with the reserved marinade.
5   Remove the pork from the grill rack, cover and leave to rest for 5–10 minutes, before slicing and serving with the dipping sauce.

205 SWEET AND STICKY SPARE RIBS

PREPARATION TIME *5 minutes* **COOKING TIME** *45–55 minutes* **SERVES 4**

1.4kg (3lb) meaty pork
spare ribs
5 garlic cloves, crushed and
finely chopped

7.5cm (3in) piece of fresh
root ginger, grated
6 tbsp soy sauce
6 tbsp dry sherry

6 tbsp clear honey
2 tsp chilli sauce
lemon wedges, to serve

1 Preheat the oven to 190°C/375°F/Gas 5. Lay the ribs in a large foil-lined roasting tin and cook in the oven for about 35–40 minutes until tender.
2 Combine the garlic, ginger, soy sauce, sherry, honey and chilli sauce to make the baste.
3 When cooked, brush the ribs liberally and evenly with the baste. Reserve the remaining baste.
4 Continue cooking the ribs on an oiled grill rack for 10–15 minutes, turning occasionally and brushing with the baste, until the meat is browned and comes off the bone easily. Brush once more and remove from the grill rack.
5 Transfer to a board and divide into individual ribs. Serve with the lemon wedges.

206 VENISON WITH FRESH FIG CHUTNEY

PREPARATION TIME *15 minutes, plus 2 hours marinating* **COOKING TIME** *12–15 minutes* **SERVES 4**

4 venison steaks, 175g
(6oz) each
freshly ground black
pepper
½ tsp Chinese five-spice
powder

2 tbsp balsamic vinegar
1½ tsp clear honey

FRESH FIG CHUTNEY
2 tsp olive oil
4 shallots, quartered

pinch of cayenne pepper
2 tbsp port
1 tbsp redcurrant jelly
6 ripe figs, quartered
salt and freshly ground
black pepper

1 Season the venison liberally with black pepper, then rub in the five-spice powder. Mix the balsamic vinegar with the honey and brush liberally over the steaks. Cover and leave in a cool place for 2 hours.
2 Meanwhile, make the chutney by heating the oil in a pan, adding the shallots and cooking gently until softened but not coloured. Stir in the cayenne, then add the port and redcurrant jelly. Bring to the boil, then simmer gently until syrupy. Add the figs and season to taste. Heat through, then remove from the heat and leave to cool.
3 Cook the venison on an oiled grill rack for about 4 minutes on each side or until cooked to your liking. Serve with the fig chutney.

207 WARM BEEF SALAD

PREPARATION TIME *15 minutes, plus 6–8 hours marinating* **COOKING TIME** *12–20 minutes* **SERVES 6**

**5cm (2in) piece of fresh
  root ginger**
2 garlic cloves, chopped
**150ml (5fl oz) rice wine
  or dry sherry**
**2 tbsp Chinese fermented
  black beans, crushed**

**450g (1lb) tail end of
  fillet of beef**
**2 tbsp finely chopped
  fresh coriander leaves**
**1 tbsp rice vinegar or
  sherry vinegar**
1 tbsp groundnut oil
1 tbsp sesame oil

**4 handfuls of small spinach
  leaves, coarsely torn**
**1 bunch of watercress,
  coarsely torn**
**1 small head radicchio,
  coarsely torn**
**lightly toasted sesame
  seeds, to serve**

1 Thinly slice half of the ginger and grate the rest. Cut the slices into shreds and set aside.
2 Combine the grated ginger with the garlic, rice wine and black beans.
3 Put the beef into a non-metallic bowl, pour over the ginger mixture, cover and leave in a cool
   place for 6–8 hours, turning occasionally.
4 Lift the beef from the marinade (reserve the marinade) and dry it thoroughly. Flatten the thicker
   end with a rolling pin. Pour the marinade into a pan and bring to the boil on the side of the grill
   rack until slightly reduced.
5 Cook the beef on an oiled grill rack, turning and brushing with the marinade occasionally, for
   4–8 minutes on each side until done to your liking.
6 Remove the beef from the grill rack, cover and leave to rest for 5–8 minutes while you strain the
   marinade into a jug and stir in the coriander, rice vinegar, oils and shredded ginger.
7 Mix the salad leaves in a serving bowl or deep plate. Slice the beef thinly, mix with the sauce
   and toss with the salad. Scatter over the sesame seeds.

208 CHINESE-STYLE RIBS

PREPARATION TIME *10 minutes* **COOKING TIME** *1 hour* **SERVES 4-6**

2kg (4lb) meaty pork
   spare ribs
1½ tsp Sichuan peppercorns
150ml (5fl oz) clear honey
3 garlic cloves, crushed
2 tbsp rice wine or dry
   sherry

2 tbsp plum sauce
2 tbsp ginger juice
   (produced by squeezing
   ginger through a garlic
   press)
2-3 tsp chilli sauce

1 tbsp Chinese five-spice
   powder
lime wedges, to serve

1   Preheat the oven to 190°C/375°F/Gas 5. Lay the ribs in a large foil-lined roasting tin and cook
    in the oven for about 45 minutes until tender.
2   Meanwhile, heat a dry, heavy-based frying pan. Add the Sichuan peppercorns and heat until
    they smell fragrant. Grind in a spice grinder or in a small bowl using the end of a rolling pin.
    Combine with the remaining ingredients (except the lime wedges).
3   Brush this mixture liberally over the cooked ribs, making sure they are evenly coated. Reserve
    the remaining mixture.
4   Continue cooking the ribs on an oiled grill rack for 10-15 minutes until the meat is browned
    and comes off the bone easily, turning occasionally and brushing with the remaining mixture.
    Brush once more and remove from the grill rack.
5   Transfer to a board and divide into individual ribs. Serve with the lime wedges.

209 ITALIAN BEEFBURGERS

PREPARATION TIME *15 minutes, plus 4 hours chilling* **COOKING TIME** *10-15 minutes* **SERVES 4**

1 small onion, finely
   chopped
olive oil, for cooking
1 garlic clove, finely
   chopped
500g (1lb 2oz) minced beef

4 tbsp Pesto *(see page 172)*
2 tbsp black olives,
   chopped
115g (4oz) mozzarella,
   coarsely chopped

salt and freshly ground
   black pepper
4 ciabatta rolls
sliced tomato, lightly
   dressed rocket, to serve

1   Fry the onion in a little oil until softened, adding the garlic towards the end of the cooking.
    Remove with a slotted spoon and drain on paper towels. Leave to cool.
2   Mix the beef with the onion, garlic and pesto, using your hands. Then knead in the olives,
    mozzarella and seasoning.
3   Divide the mixture into four equal portions. With wet hands, form each portion into a burger
    shape approximately 2.5cm (1in) thick. If time allows, cover and leave the burgers in a cool
    place for at least 4 hours.
4   Cook on an oiled grill for 4-5 minutes on each side, turning once, until the burgers are cooked
    through and the juices run clear when they are pierced with a fine skewer.
5   Meanwhile, toast the rolls on the side of grill. Serve the burgers in the rolls with the sliced tomato
    and rocket.

210 STEAK WITH SAVOURY TOMATO SAUCE

PREPARATION TIME *10 minutes* **COOKING TIME** *20-25 minutes* **SERVES 4**

4 sirloin steaks
salt and freshly ground
    black pepper

SAVOURY TOMATO SAUCE
100g (3½oz) can anchovy
    fillets in oil
3 tbsp extra virgin olive oil

3 garlic cloves, finely
    chopped
3 sage leaves, finely
    shredded
1 fresh red chilli, seeded
    and finely chopped
450g (1lb) vine-ripened
    tomatoes, chopped

115g (4oz) good-quality
    black olives, pitted and
    chopped
50g (2oz) capers, drained
1 tbsp chopped fresh
    oregano
2 tbsp chopped fresh
    flat-leaf parsley

1   Drain and reserve the oil from the anchovies. Chop the anchovies finely. Brush the steaks with some of the anchovy oil, then season them. Set aside in a cool place while preparing the sauce.

2   Heat the extra virgin olive oil in a pan, add the garlic and sage and cook until the garlic begins to colour. Stir in the chilli, cook briefly, then add the tomatoes, olives, capers, anchovies and oregano. Simmer for 10 minutes and season with black pepper.

3   Cook the steaks on a lightly oiled grill rack for about 3-4 minutes each side for rare steaks, 5-6 minutes for medium, or until cooked to your liking.

4   Meanwhile, add the parsley to the sauce and warm through on the side of the grill rack. Serve the steaks accompanied by the sauce.

211 SAUSAGES WITH PLUM SAUCE

PREPARATION TIME *10 minutes* **COOKING TIME** *25-30 minutes* **SERVES 6**

12 good-quality pork
    sausages

PLUM SAUCE
1 tbsp groundnut oil
2 shallots, finely chopped

1 tbsp finely chopped
    fresh root ginger
½ tbsp Sichuan
    peppercorns,
    finely crushed

225g (8oz) plums,
    quartered and pitted
1 tbsp light soy sauce
5 tbsp sweet sherry
½ tbsp clear honey
lime juice, to taste

1   Make the plum sauce by heating the oil in a frying pan, adding the shallots and frying until softened. Add the ginger and peppercorns towards the end and continue cooking until they smell fragrant. Add the plums, soy sauce, sherry and honey. Bring to the boil, cover and simmer until the plums are tender. Add lime juice to taste. Set aside while preparing the sausages.

2   Add the sausages to a pan of boiling water, quickly return to the boil and then simmer gently for 3 minutes. Drain and rinse under cold running water to speed cooling. Pat dry.

3   Cook the sausages on an oiled grill rack for 8-10 minutes, turning occasionally, until well browned and cooked through. Serve the sausages with the plum sauce either poured over or as a dipping sauce.

VEGETARIAN DISHES

A selection of grilled vegetable dishes works well as a main course for a barbecue. Add an interesting dressing or sauce, some cheese, and bread, cooked or warmed on the grill rack, and a barbecued potato dish to make a delicious spread.

Many vegetables respond well to being barbecued, but some take a surprisingly long time to cook. Pre-cook firm veg such as carrots, cauliflower, baby onions and broccoli in boiling water to reduce the cooking time and to prevent the outside becoming overdone before the inside is tender. Drain and dry them well before cooking on the grill rack. Coat cut surfaces with oil or dressing to prevent them drying and to promote browning. Sweet potatoes and baby squash can be cooked in the embers of the fire. Wrapping them in double-thickness foil keeps them clean and helps them to cook evenly.

When choosing vegetables, bear in mind cooking times. This is particularly important when making kebabs as all the items must cook in the same time, (after any initial cooking for items such as new potatoes and mini fennel bulbs). If cooking vegetables loose, put those that require the longest cooking on first. Use an oiled hinged grill basket because it will make turning and lifting vegetables easier, or try an oiled fine mesh grill rack which will prevent small items, such as button mushrooms and shallots, falling onto the coals. Vegetables can also be enclosed in foil parcels and cooked on the grill rack for maximum flavour.

CHAPTER 5

212 VEGETABLE SATAY

PREPARATION TIME *15 minutes* **COOKING TIME** *30 minutes* **SERVES 4**

1 small squash, peeled and cut into chunks
2 leeks, cut into chunks
1 courgette, cut into chunks
100g (3½oz) mushrooms, halved
3 tbsp dark soy sauce
2 tsp sesame oil

8-12 fresh bay leaves

SATAY SAUCE
1 tbsp groundnut oil
1 shallot, finely chopped
2 garlic cloves, crushed
2.5cm (1in) piece fresh root ginger, grated
1 stalk lemon grass

1 red chilli, seeded and finely chopped
1 tsp curry powder
150g (5oz) crunchy peanut butter
3 tbsp chopped fresh coriander
sugar, salt and freshly ground black pepper

1 To make the sauce, heat the oil and fry the shallot, garlic, ginger and lemon grass until softened. Stir in the chilli and curry powder for a couple of minutes. Then stir in the peanut butter and 250ml (8fl oz) boiling water. Bring to the boil, add the coriander and season with sugar, salt and pepper. Remove from the heat.

2 Meanwhile, cook the squash in a pan of boiling water for 5 minutes. Add the leeks and cook for a further 3 minutes. Drain and cool under running cold water. Put into a bowl with the courgette and mushrooms.

3 Combine the soy sauce, sesame oil and black pepper. Trickle over the vegetables and stir gently to coat all the vegetables.

4 Thread the vegetables alternately onto skewers, adding bay leaves along the way. Cook on an oiled grill rack for about 8 minutes, turning occasionally.

5 Meanwhile, warm the satay sauce on the side of the grill rack and serve with the vegetables.

213 MUSHROOM AND MOZZARELLA BROCHETTES

PREPARATION TIME *10 minutes, plus 1-2 hours marinating* **COOKING TIME** *8 minutes* **SERVES 4**

350g (12oz) mozzarella cheese, cut into 2.5 cm (1in) cubes
8 medium-cup chestnut mushrooms, halved lengthways

1 red pepper, cut into 2.5cm (1in) pieces
175g (6oz) courgettes, cut diagonally into 8 chunks

MARINADE
8 tbsp virgin olive oil
1 tbsp balsamic vinegar
2 tbsp fresh thyme leaves
salt and freshly ground black pepper

1 Put the cheese and vegetables into a non-metallic dish.

2 Make the marinade by combining the ingredients. Pour over the vegetables and cheese and stir gently so everything is evenly coated. Cover and leave in a cool place for 1-2 hours.

3 Lift the cheese and vegetables from the marinade (reserve any remaining marinade) and thread alternately on eight skewers.

4 Cook on an oiled grill rack for about 8 minutes until the cheese is golden, turning occasionally and brushing with the remaining marinade.

214 STUFFED ONIONS

PREPARATION TIME *15 minutes* **COOKING TIME** *20–25 minutes* **SERVES 4**

4 large onions, about 300g (10oz) each, peeled
small knob of unsalted butter
1 large leek, chopped
leaves from 4 fresh thyme sprigs

2 tbsp chopped fresh parsley
115g (4oz) feta cheese, crumbled
8 sun-dried tomato halves in oil, drained and sliced

6 oil-cured black olives, pitted and chopped
2 egg yolks
freshly ground black pepper

1 Trim the root ends of the onions but do not cut them off completely because they hold the layers together. Cut each onion in half from top to bottom. Remove the inner layers of each onion half, leaving a shell two layers thick. Chop the removed layers.

2 Add the onion shells to a saucepan of boiling water, lower the heat and simmer for 10 minutes. Lift from the water with a slotted spoon and leave upside down to drain.

3 Meanwhile, melt the butter in a heavy frying pan. Add the chopped onion and cook over a very low heat until very soft and golden. Add the leek about three-quarters of the way through. Stir in the thyme and parsley, leave to cool slightly, then add the cheese, sun-dried tomatoes, olives and egg yolks. Season with plenty of black pepper.

4 Place each onion shell upright and pile the filling into the shells.

5 Cook the stuffed onions towards the side of the grill rack for 10–15 minutes until the shells are tender and the filling is warmed through.

215 HALLOUMI, SQUASH AND CHERRY TOMATO SKEWERS

PREPARATION TIME *5 minutes, plus 2–24 hours marinating* **COOKING TIME** *10 minutes* **SERVES 4**

350g (12oz) halloumi cheese, cut into 2.5cm (1in) cubes
16 small patty pan squash
16 cherry tomatoes, preferably plum

MARINADE
6 tbsp extra virgin olive oil
2 tbsp mixed chopped fresh oregano, thyme, mint, rosemary and parsley
juice of 1 lemon

freshly ground black pepper

1 Put the cheese and vegetables into a shallow non-metallic dish.

2 Make the marinade by mixing all the ingredients together. Pour over the cheese and vegetable mixture, then stir to make sure everything is coated. Cover and leave in a cool place for at least 2 hours and up to 24 hours.

3 Lift the cheese and vegetables from the marinade (reserve any remaining marinade) and thread alternately onto skewers, beginning and ending with a patty pan squash and pushing all the ingredients quite closely together.

4 Cook on an oiled grill rack for about 10 minutes, turning frequently and brushing with any remaining marinade, until flecked with brown at the edges.

216 MEDITERRANEAN VEGETABLES WITH GARLIC TOASTS

PREPARATION TIME *15 minutes, plus 1 hour marinating* **COOKING TIME** *10–16 minutes* **SERVES 4**

3 baby aubergines, halved lengthways, or 2 small aubergines, sliced lengthways into 1cm (½in) slices

1 red pepper and 1 yellow pepper, cut into wedges

4 mini courgettes

1 small fennel bulb, thinly sliced with the root end intact

4 spring onions

4 flat mushrooms

6–7 tbsp virgin olive oil

2 tbsp chopped mixed fresh herbs such as thyme, oregano and rosemary

salt and freshly ground black pepper

6 ripe but not soft plum tomatoes, halved

1 garlic clove, crushed

1 French stick, sliced diagonally

balsamic vinegar, for sprinkling

10 black olives, halved and pitted

1 Put the aubergines, peppers, courgettes, fennel, spring onions and mushrooms into a large dish. Mix 4–5 tablespoonfuls of the oil with the herbs and seasoning. Brush the tomatoes with some of the mixture and carefully stir the rest into the vegetables in the dish. Cover and leave in a cool place for 1 hour.

2 Mix the garlic with the remaining oil and brush over one side of each slice of bread. Sprinkle with salt. Cook on the side of an oiled grill rack until golden.

3 Meanwhile, lift the vegetables from the dish and cook on an oiled grill rack for 5–8 minutes on each side until tender and lightly charred. Add the tomatoes and cook for 3 minutes on each side until lightly charred but still firm.

4 Transfer the toasted bread to a large platter. Put the vegetables as they are done onto the toasts. Sprinkle over a little balsamic vinegar and scatter over the olives.

217 FENNEL WEDGES WITH PARMESAN DRESSING

PREPARATION TIME *10 minutes* **COOKING TIME** *8–10 minutes* **SERVES 4**

4 small fennel bulbs

salt and freshly ground black pepper

olive oil for brushing

PARMESAN DRESSING

1 tbsp lemon juice

1 tbsp lemon zest

1 tbsp white wine vinegar

1 tsp Dijon mustard

115ml (4fl oz) virgin olive oil

2 tbsp freshly grated Parmesan cheese

1 Trim the fennel bulbs (reserve the feathery leaves), then cut into thick wedges, each with some of the core. Brush with olive oil and thread onto oiled skewers. Sprinkle with seasoning.

2 Cook on an oiled grill rack for 8–10 minutes, turning occasionally, until the fennel is slightly soft and lightly charred. For softer fennel, cook for a little longer, further from the heat.

3 Meanwhile, make the dressing by whisking all the ingredients together. Season to taste.

4 Serve the fennel with the dressing poured over and sprinkled with the reserved feathery tops. (If the fennel bulbs don't have their feathery tops, substitute herb fennel.)

218 VEGETABLE BROCHETTES

PREPARATION TIME *20 minutes, plus 1 hour marinating* **COOKING TIME** *10 minutes* **SERVES 6**

1 large aubergine, cut
    into 12 slices
3 red peppers, quartered
24 large button mushrooms
3 courgettes, scored
    lengthways with a fork,
    cut diagonally into 2cm
    (¾in) pieces

175g (6oz) halloumi cheese,
    cut into 2.5 x 1cm
    (1 x ½in) pieces
2 tbsp extra virgin olive oil
juice of 1 lime
leaves from a small bunch
    of fresh coriander,
    chopped

MARINADE
3 tbsp soy sauce
1½ tbsp olive oil
2 garlic cloves, crushed
1 tbsp paprika
1 tbsp ground cumin
dash of Tabasco sauce

1 Make the marinade by combining the ingredients with 3 tablespoons of water. Brush the aubergine slices with some of the marinade.

2 Put the remaining vegetables in a dish and stir in the remaining marinade. Cover and leave in a cool place for an hour or so.

3 Meanwhile, cook the aubergine slices on an oiled grill rack, or under a preheated grill, for 3–4 minutes until browned, turning once. Grill the halloumi for 2 minutes until golden but not melting. Wrap the aubergine slices round the pieces of halloumi.

4 Remove the vegetables from the marinade. Beginning and ending with a mushroom, thread the vegetables, including the aubergines, alternately onto oiled skewers.

5 Cook on an oiled grill rack for about 4 minutes, turning to ensure even cooking and browning.

6 Meanwhile, combine the olive oil, lime juice, coriander and seasoning. Remove the brochettes from the grill rack and trickle over the dressing.

219 MINIATURE BOK CHOI WITH BALSAMIC DRESSING

PREPARATION TIME *5 minutes* **COOKING TIME** *8 minutes* **SERVES 4**

8 miniature bok choi
1 tbsp groundnut oil, plus
   extra for brushing

1 tbsp balsamic vinegar,
   plus extra for sprinkling

sea salt and freshly ground
   black pepper

1   Brush the bok choi with groundnut oil and sprinkle with balsamic vinegar. Cook on an oiled grill rack for about 4 minutes on each side until softened and marked with charred lines.
2   Meanwhile, make the dressing by combining 1 tablespoon of groundnut oil with 1 tablespoon of balsamic vinegar and seasoning.
3   Remove the bok choi from the grill rack and trickle over the dressing. Serve immediately.

220 AUBERGINE SLICES WITH MINT DRESSING

PREPARATION TIME *10 minutes, plus 15–30 minutes marinating* **COOKING TIME** *10 minutes* **SERVES 4**

2 aubergines, cut into
   1cm (½in) thick slices
olive oil, for brushing
salt and freshly ground
   black pepper

MINT DRESSING
1 garlic clove, chopped
5 tbsp extra virgin olive oil
juice of 1 lemon

3–4 tbsp chopped
   fresh mint
sea salt and freshly ground
   black pepper

1   Make the dressing by mixing the garlic, olive oil and lemon juice in a blender. Pour into a bowl and add the mint and seasoning. Set aside.
2   Brush both sides of the aubergine slices with oil. Cook on an oiled grill rack for 5 minutes on each side until softened and lightly charred.
3   Transfer to a plate, season and pour over the dressing. Leave to marinate for 15–30 minutes.

221 SPICED SWEET POTATO WEDGES

PREPARATION TIME *15 minutes* **COOKING TIME** *20–30 minutes* **SERVES 4**

2 large sweet potatoes,
   550g (1¼lb) total weight
2 tsp mustard seeds

2 tsp cumin seeds
1 tsp coriander seeds
1 tsp black peppercorns

2 tbsp olive oil
salt

1   Simmer the whole, unpeeled potatoes in a covered pan of water for 15–20 minutes until just tender. Drain, leave until cool enough to handle, then cut into large wedges.
2   Heat a small, dry, heavy frying pan, add the seeds and peppercorns and toast over a low heat for 3 minutes. Tip into a spice grinder and grind.
3   Pour the oil into a large bowl, stir in the spices, add the sweet potatoes and toss to coat.
4   Cook on an oiled grill rack for 4–5 minutes on each side until softened and marked with charred lines. Remove from the grill rack, sprinkle with salt, and serve.

222 HONEY-GLAZED SQUASH WEDGES WITH SESAME SEEDS

PREPARATION TIME *10 minutes* **COOKING TIME** *20–30 minutes* **SERVES 4**

1 large butternut squash, cut into wedges
100ml (3½fl oz) clear honey

2 tbsp pumpkin seed oil
2 tbsp sesame seeds

salt and freshly ground black pepper

1 Place the squash wedges on a double layer of foil and drizzle over the honey and oil. Sprinkle over the sesame seeds and season generously. Fold over the sides of the foil and twist the edges together to seal tightly.

2 Cook the parcels on the edge of the grill rack for 20–30 minutes, turning them over a couple of times so that the squash cooks evenly.

223 SQUASH WEDGES WITH THYME AND GARLIC

PREPARATION TIME *10 minutes* **COOKING TIME** *15–18 minutes* **SERVES 4**

900g (2lb) seeded squash, cut into wedges
2 tbsp olive oil
2 plump garlic cloves, finely chopped

leaves from 2 fresh sprigs of thyme
salt and freshly ground black pepper

Tomato Tartare Sauce *(see page 179)*, to serve

1 Par-boil the squash wedges for 5 minutes. Drain, pat dry, and, while still warm, toss with the olive oil, garlic, thyme and seasoning.

2 Cook on an oiled grill rack for 5–6 minutes on each side until softened and charred. Serve with tomato tartare sauce.

224 GRILLED LEEKS NIÇOISE

PREPARATION TIME *10 minutes* **COOKING TIME** *5 minutes* **SERVES 2**

200g (7oz) mini leeks
150ml (5fl oz) virgin olive oil, plus extra for brushing
grated zest and juice of 1 lemon

salt and freshly ground black pepper
4 vine-ripened tomatoes, seeded and chopped
1 tbsp capers
6 black olives, halved and pitted

2-4 salted anchovy fillets, rinsed, dried and chopped
handful of chopped fresh parsley and basil

1 Brush the leeks with oil and cook on an oiled grill rack for 5 minutes, turning once, until softened and marked with charred lines.

2 Meanwhile, whisk the oil with the lemon juice and seasoning until emulsified, or shake them together in a screw-topped jar.

3 Transfer the leeks to a plate, or plates, and pour over the dressing. Scatter over the remaining ingredients. Serve warm or at room temperature.

225 ARTICHOKES WITH PARSLEY AND LEMON BUTTER

PREPARATION TIME *20 minutes, plus 1 hour marinating* **COOKING TIME** *25–30 minutes* **SERVES 4**

4 globe artichokes
lemon juice
5 tbsp olive oil
salt and freshly ground
    black pepper

PARSLEY AND LEMON BUTTER
1 garlic clove, peeled
50g (2oz) unsalted butter
1 tbsp finely chopped fresh
    flat-leaf parsley

1–1½ tbsp lemon juice

1   Make the butter by blanching the garlic in simmering water for 5 minutes. Drain well, then mash to a paste. Beat the butter with a fork or wooden spoon until softened. Gradually work in the garlic paste, then the parsley, lemon juice and seasoning. Leave in a cool place for several hours for the flavours to infuse.

2   Snap off the artichoke stems near the base. Boil the artichokes in water acidulated with the juice of half a lemon for 10 minutes. Drain, leave until cool enough to handle, then trim off the outer layer of leaves.

3   Cut the artichokes into quarters and brush the cut surfaces with lemon juice. Scrape out the hairy choke and halve the quarters.

4   Lay the artichokes in a single layer in a shallow, non-metallic dish. Whisk together the olive oil, 2 tablespoons of lemon juice and seasoning. Pour over the artichokes, turn them over to make sure they are evenly coated, then cover and leave for an hour or so, or until needed.

5   Lift the artichokes from the dish and cook, straight side down, on an oiled grill for 5–8 minutes until well patched with brown (don't worry if the leaves start to char). Turn the artichokes over and cook for a further 5–8 minutes until just tender.

6   Meanwhile, warm the butter gently on the side of the grill rack. Serve the artichokes immediately with the butter for dipping.

226 SWEET AND SPICY AUBERGINE AND RED ONION KEBABS

PREPARATION TIME *15 minutes, plus 2-8 hours marinating* **COOKING TIME** *5-10 minutes* **SERVES 6**

3 small aubergines, cut
    into cubes
salt
6 red onions, quartered
3 tbsp medium sherry
1 tbsp Dijon mustard

salt and freshly ground
    black pepper
chopped fresh coriander,
    to serve

MARINADE
6 tbsp balsamic vinegar

3 tbsp clear honey
4 tbsp sesame oil
juice of 1 lemon
¼ tsp ground cumin
¼ tsp ground cardamom
pinch of cayenne pepper

1 Sprinkle the aubergine cubes with salt and leave to drain in a colander for 30 minutes. Rinse thoroughly and dry on kitchen paper. Put into a non-metallic bowl. Separate each onion quarter into two pieces, and add to the aubergine.

2 Make the marinade by combining the ingredients. Stir into the bowl to coat the pieces of vegetables evenly. Cover and leave in a cool place for 2-8 hours.

3 Lift the vegetables from the marinade (reserve the marinade). Thread the aubergines and onions alternately onto skewers. Cook on an oiled grill rack for about 5 minutes until beginning to caramelise, turning regularly.

4 Meanwhile, put the reserved marinade, sherry and mustard into a small saucepan and boil on the grill rack until syrupy. Season to taste. Serve the kebabs with the sauce poured over and sprinkled with coriander.

227 GREEK VEGETABLE SALAD

PREPARATION TIME *15 minutes, plus 1 hour marinating* **COOKING TIME** *20-30 minutes* **SERVES 4**

225g (8oz) feta cheese, cut
    into 1cm (½in) thick slices
115ml (4fl oz) virgin
    olive oil
grated zest and juice of
    1½ lemons
1 tbsp balsamic vinegar

2 garlic cloves, finely
    chopped
2-3 tbsp fresh thyme
freshly ground black
    pepper

1.3kg (3lb) mixed
    aubergines, courgettes,
    ripe but not soft
    tomatoes, and 1 red
    onion
115g (4oz) pitted kalamata
    olives

1 Put the cheese into a shallow non-metallic dish. Combine 2 tablespoons of the olive oil with the lemon zest and juice, balsamic vinegar, garlic, 1 tablespoon of the thyme, and black pepper. Pour over the cheese and leave in a cool place to marinate for 1 hour.

2 Meanwhile, cut the aubergines and courgettes diagonally into 1cm (½in) thick slices. Halve the tomatoes. Cut the red onion into 1cm (½in) slices from top to bottom. Put the courgettes, aubergines and red onion into a bowl, pour over the remaining oil, add black pepper and stir to coat the vegetables well.

3 Lift the vegetables from the bowl with a slotted spoon and cook on an oiled grill rack for 5-6 minutes on each side until tender and lightly charred.

4 Meanwhile, brush the tomatoes with the oil. Cook on the grill rack for 3 minutes on each side.

5 Transfer the vegetables as they are done to a bowl or platter and cover with clingfilm.

6 Lift the cheese from the marinade and cook on the grill rack for about 3 minutes on each side until golden (feta cheese is easier to turn on the grill rack if it is cooked in an oiled hinged basket).

7 Scatter the olives and remaining thyme over the vegetables and top with the cheese. Serve immediately, while the cheese is still warm.

228 MUSHROOMS WITH AUBERGINE AND RED PEPPER RELISH

PREPARATION TIME *10 minutes* **COOKING TIME** *40–50 minutes* **SERVES 4**

6-8 large cap mushrooms, about 6.25cm (2½in) in diameter, stalks removed
olive oil, for brushing
salt and freshly ground black pepper
cottage cheese or ricotta cheese, to serve

AUBERGINE AND RED PEPPER RELISH
1 aubergine, halved lengthways
1 red pepper, halved lengthways and seeded
1-2 plump garlic cloves, unpeeled

115g (4oz) kalamata olives, pitted
2 tsp capers
6 large fresh basil leaves, chopped
1 tsp lemon juice, or to taste
salt and freshly ground black pepper

1   Preheat the oven to 200ºC/400ºF/Gas 6. Make the relish by brushing the cut surfaces of the aubergine lightly with oil. Put the aubergine, cut-side down, on an oiled baking sheet and cook for 35–45 minutes. Cook the red pepper in the same way for 15–20 minutes, and the garlic cloves for 10–15 minutes.
2   Chop the cooked pepper and aubergine and put into a blender or food processor. Squeeze the garlic from the skin and add it to the pepper and aubergine, along with the olives and capers. Mix until the ingredients are coarsely chopped.
3   Scrape the relish into a saucepan and stir in the basil, lemon juice, salt and plenty of black pepper, to taste. Warm on the side of the grill rack.
4   Brush the mushrooms with olive oil and sprinkle with seasoning. Cook on an oiled grill rack, stalk side down, for 1–2 minutes, then turn them over, fill the cavity with the relish and cook for a further 1–2 minutes.
5   Carefully lift the mushrooms from the grill rack and top with a spoonful of cottage cheese or ricotta cheese.

229 GRILLED BABY VEGETABLES WITH BALSAMIC VINEGAR

PREPARATION TIME *15 minutes* **COOKING TIME** *6 minutes* **SERVES 6**

6 baby sweetcorn
225g (8oz) ripe but not too soft vine-ripened tomatoes, halved
225g (8oz) baby courgettes, lightly scored with a fork
115g (4oz) mini leeks

50g (2oz) mangetout
115ml (4fl oz) chilli oil
2 plump garlic cloves, peeled
50ml (2fl oz) balsamic vinegar
salt and freshly ground

black pepper
115g (4oz) sun-dried tomatoes in oil, drained
leaves from several fresh thyme sprigs
grated zest of 1 small lemon

1   Brush the vegetables with chilli oil and cook on an oiled grill rack, giving the courgettes and leeks about 6 minutes, the baby sweetcorn 4–6 minutes, the tomatoes 3–5 minutes and the mangetout 2–5 minutes, turning so they char and soften evenly. Remove the vegetables that are cooked first as soon as they are ready, put into a bowl and cover with clingfilm.
2   Meanwhile, press the garlic through a garlic press into the balsamic vinegar. Season.
3   Toss the cooked vegetables with the vinegar and sun-dried tomatoes. Scatter over the thyme leaves and lemon zest, and serve.

230 ROAST VEGETABLE SALAD WITH MUSTARD AND CAPER SAUCE

PREPARATION TIME *15 minutes, plus 2 hours marinating* **COOKING TIME** *15-20 minutes* **SERVES 4**

900g (2lb) mixed vegetables, such as baby turnips, baby carrots, baby parsnips, courgettes, aubergines, chicory, fennel bulb, red onion, baby leeks (or small leeks, halved lengthways)	**8 garlic cloves, unpeeled** **4 fresh rosemary sprigs** **5 tbsp virgin olive oil** **½ tbsp balsamic vinegar** **sea salt and freshly ground black pepper**	MUSTARD AND CAPER SAUCE **175ml (6fl oz) mayonnaise (see page 179)** **1½ tsp Dijon mustard** **1½ tsp capers, drained and chopped** **3 tbsp chopped flat-leaf parsley**

1 Blanch the baby turnips, carrots and parsnips separately in boiling water for 5 minutes, then drain and dry well.
2 Slice the courgettes and aubergines diagonally. Quarter the chicory lengthways and remove the core but leave the leaves attached. Cut the fennel lengthways into wedges. Cut the red onion into wedges, leaving them attached at the root end.
3 Place all the vegetables and the garlic in a large dish and add the rosemary, olive oil, balsamic vinegar and seasoning. Stir everything around, then cover and leave to marinate in a cool place for a couple of hours.
4 Meanwhile, make the sauce by stirring the ingredients together. Set aside.
5 Thread the garlic onto soaked wooden cocktail sticks (see page 10) and cook on an oiled grill rack for about 3 minutes until soft, turning occasionally. Cook the other vegetables, turning as necessary for even cooking, until they are tender and lightly charred.
6 As the vegetables are cooked, transfer them to a bowl and cover with clingfilm. When all the vegetables are done, serve them with the sauce.

231 FIRE-COOKED AUBERGINES WITH GARLIC, CORIANDER AND LEMON

PREPARATION TIME *5 minutes* **COOKING TIME** *10 minutes* **SERVES 4**

4 small long, quite thin aubergines **2 plump garlic cloves, chopped**	**leaves from a small bunch of fresh coriander** **2 tbsp lemon juice, or to taste**	**4-6 tbsp virgin olive oil** **salt and freshly ground black pepper**

1 Cook the whole aubergines on an oiled grill rack for about 10 minutes, until evenly charred and softened, turning occasionally.
2 Meanwhile, put the garlic, coriander, lemon juice and olive oil into a small blender and mix together. Season to taste, and adjust the amounts of lemon juice and olive oil, if necessary.
3 Remove the aubergines from the grill rack and cut a deep slash along the centre of each one. Serve with the garlic, coriander and lemon mixture spooned into them.

232 GRILLED VEGETABLES WITH THAI DRESSING

PREPARATION TIME *15 minutes, plus 2 hours marinating* **COOKING TIME** *25–30 minutes* **SERVES 4**

450g (1lb) sweet potatoes	THAI DRESSING	1 tbsp Thai fish sauce
4 mini fennel bulbs	15g (½oz) fresh root ginger,	grated zest and juice
225g (8oz) slim asparagus	coarsely chopped	of 1 lime
spears	2 garlic cloves, crushed	1 tbsp peanut butter
1 bunch spring onions	1–2 red chillies, seeded	1 tsp soft brown sugar
1 lemon grass stalk,	and coarsely chopped	
crushed	400ml (14fl oz) coconut	
fresh coriander, to garnish	milk	

1   Put the whole sweet potatoes into a saucepan of cold water, bring to the boil, then lower the heat and simmer for 15–20 minutes until just tender. Drain, leave until cool enough to handle, then cut into wedges.
2   Blanch the fennel for 2–3 minutes, cool under running cold water, drain and leave until cold. Blanch the asparagus for 1–2 minutes in the same way.
3   Put the sweet potato wedges, fennel, asparagus, spring onions and crushed lemon grass into a large non-metallic dish.
4   Put the dressing ingredients into a blender and mix until smooth. Pour over the vegetables, stir so the vegetables are evenly coated, cover and leave in a cool place for 2 hours.
5   Lift the vegetables from the dressing and discard the lemon grass. Cook the vegetables on an oiled grill rack, giving the asparagus and sweet potatoes 5–6 minutes, the fennel 5 minutes and the spring onions about 3 minutes, turning the vegetables occasionally until tender and marked with brown. Serve garnished with fresh coriander.

233 CHICORY WITH STILTON AND WALNUTS

PREPARATION TIME *10 minutes* **COOKING TIME** *7–12 minutes* **SERVES 4**

2 large or 4 small heads of	2 ripe but firm pears,	175g (6oz) Stilton cheese,
chicory, halved	thickly sliced	crumbled
lengthways, cored	2 tbsp walnut oil	50g (2oz) walnut halves,
1 tbsp mild olive oil,	juice of 1 small lemon	chopped
plus extra for brushing	1½ tsp fresh thyme leaves	

1   Brush the chicory with olive oil and cook on an oiled grill rack, turning and brushing regularly, for 7–9 minutes for smaller heads, 10–12 minutes for larger ones, until softened and charred.
2   Meanwhile, cook the pear slices on the grill rack until softened.
3   Whisk the tablespoon of olive oil with the walnut oil and lemon juice.
4   Transfer the chicory to warmed plates and season. Place the pears on top and immediately scatter over the cheese, then the thyme leaves. Trickle over the walnut oil mixture, sprinkle with the nuts, and serve.

234 VEGETABLE FAJITAS WITH AVOCADO AND TOMATO RELISH

PREPARATION TIME *10 minutes, plus 4 hours marinating* **COOKING TIME** *30 minutes* **SERVES 6**

2 red and 2 yellow peppers, quartered
3 courgettes, sliced diagonally
2 aubergines, sliced diagonally
175g (6oz) baby corn, halved lengthways
3 mild red chillies
6 tbsp olive oil

2 tbsp chopped mixed fresh parsley, oregano and thyme
juice of 1 lime
freshly ground black pepper
18 tortillas, 20cm (8in) in diameter
soured cream, fresh coriander and lime wedges, to serve

AVOCADO AND TOMATO RELISH
1 large avocado, pitted and finely chopped
3 tbsp lime juice
½ red chilli, seeded and finely chopped
1 vine-ripened plum tomato, seeded and diced
½ red onion, finely diced
handful of fresh coriander leaves, chopped

1 Put all the vegetables, including the chillies, into a large bowl. Mix together the olive oil, herbs, lime juice and black pepper. Stir into the vegetables, cover, then leave to marinate for about 4 hours, stirring occasionally.
2 Meanwhile, make the relish by tossing the ingredients together. Cover and chill for 30 minutes.
3 Lift the vegetables from the marinade and cook on an oiled grill rack until softened and lightly charred. Remove the vegetables that are cooked first as soon as they are ready, put into a bowl and cover with clingfilm.
4 Meanwhile, warm the tortillas for 30 seconds on each side on the grill rack.
5 When the chillies are cool enough to handle, cut off the tops. Chop them, discarding the seeds.
6 Divide the vegetables and chillies among the tortillas. Top with avocado relish, spoon on some soured cream and fold over. Serve with coriander and lime wedges.

235 GRILLED MIXED VEGETABLE PLATTER

PREPARATION TIME *15 minutes, plus 2–24 hours marinating* **COOKING TIME** *15 minutes* **SERVES 8**

1 papaya

1 squash, about 500g (1lb 2oz)

8 baby aubergines (leave the stalk ends on)

8 yellow and green patty pan squash

1 red pepper, cut into 6 large strips

2 heads of chicory, quartered

8 baby leeks, trimmed to 12.5cm (7½in)

115g (4oz) oyster mushrooms

8 vine-ripened cherry plum tomatoes

TO SERVE

finely chopped fresh coriander

Greek yogurt flavoured with garlic, chopped fresh herbs and seasoning

MARINADE

150ml (5fl oz) virgin olive oil

juice of 1½ limes

2 garlic cloves, crushed

½ chilli, seeded and finely chopped

4 tbsp dark soy sauce

1 tbsp wholegrain mustard

1 tbsp paprika

1½ tsp ground cumin

1 Make the marinade by combining the ingredients. Set aside for at least 1 hour or up to 24 hours, to allow the flavours to infuse.

2 Cut the papaya and squash into slices 2.5cm (1in) wide and about 10cm (4in) long. Cut shallow slashes in the surface of the aubergines and patty pan squash.

3 Put all the vegetables into a non-metallic dish. Stir in the marinade and leave to marinate in a cool place for 1 hour.

4 Lift the vegetables from the marinade (reserving the marinade) and pack alternately onto skewers. Brush liberally with the reserved marinade.

5 Cook on an oiled grill rack for about 15 minutes, turning occasionally and brushing with marinade, until the vegetables are charred and sizzling all over. Remove from the grill rack, sprinkle with coriander and serve with the yogurt.

236 SPICED LENTIL BURGERS

PREPARATION TIME *15 minutes, plus 1 hour chilling* **COOKING TIME** *45–50 minutes* **SERVES 4**

225g (8oz) green or brown lentils

2 large onions, finely chopped

2 carrots, finely chopped

1 celery stick, finely chopped

olive oil, for frying

2 garlic cloves, finely chopped

1 tsp ground cumin

1 tsp ground coriander

3 tbsp chopped fresh parsley

3 tbsp chopped fresh coriander

1 tbsp lemon juice

salt and freshly ground black pepper

seasoned plain flour, for coating

Avocado, Tomato and Red Pepper Salsa (see page 174)

1 Cook the lentils in boiling unsalted water for about 20–30 minutes until tender. Drain well and leave to cool.

2 Fry the onion, carrot and celery in a little olive oil for 10 minutes until soft and lightly browned. Stir in the lentils, garlic, spices, herbs, lemon juice and seasoning. Mix to a coarse purée in a food processor until the mixture holds together. Alternatively, mash with a potato masher.

3 With floured hands, form into 12 flat burgers about 1–2cm (½–¾in) thick. Coat the burgers in seasoned flour and pat in gently. Cover and chill for at least 1 hour to firm up, or overnight, if possible, to allow the flavours to develop.

4 Cook in an oiled grill basket, on an oiled mesh grill or on an oiled grill rack, turning once, for 6–8 minutes until crisp and browned. Serve with the avocado, tomato and red pepper salsa.

237 FALAFEL BURGERS WITH YOGURT AND MINT RELISH

PREPARATION TIME *10 minutes, plus 2 hours chilling* **COOKING TIME** *10 minutes* **SERVES 4-6**

2 x 400g (14oz) cans
  chickpeas, drained
  and rinsed
1 garlic clove, chopped
2 tbsp tahini
1 tsp ground cumin
1 tsp ground coriander
50g (2oz) fresh
  breadcrumbs

3 tbsp chopped fresh
  coriander
salt and freshly ground
  black pepper
seasoned plain flour,
  for coating
pitta bread and lettuce
  leaves, to serve

YOGURT AND MINT RELISH
1 small garlic clove, peeled
salt and freshly ground
  black pepper
150ml (5fl oz) Greek yogurt
4 tbsp chopped fresh mint
dash of Tabasco sauce
small spring of mint leaves,
  to garnish

1. Put all the burger ingredients except the plain flour into a food processor and mix until the chickpeas are finely chopped, but do not let the mixture turn to a purée.
2. Transfer to a bowl and stir in about 2 tablespoons of water, kneading until the mixture holds together. With well-floured hands, form the mixture into eight burgers about 2.5cm (1in) thick. Chill for at least 2 hours.
3. To make the relish, crush the garlic with a pinch of salt, then mix it with the yogurt. Add the mint, and season with Tabasco and black pepper, to taste. Chill before serving. Garnish with the mint leaves to serve.
4. Cook the burgers in an oiled grill basket, on an oiled mesh grill or on an oiled grill rack for about 5 minutes on each side until crisp and brown on the outside and warmed through.
5. Meanwhile, warm the pitta breads on the side of the grill rack for 30 seconds on each side. Split the pitta breads open, add the falafel and top with the lettuce, and yogurt and mint relish.

238 ASPARAGUS WITH CRISP CRUMB, EGG AND OLIVE GREMOLATA

PREPARATION TIME *10 minutes* **COOKING TIME** *6 minutes* **SERVES 4**

450g (1lb) slim asparagus*
olive oil, for brushing
50g (2oz) unsalted butter,
  diced
25g (1oz) fresh, coarse
  breadcrumbs

grated zest of 1 lemon
2 tbsp chopped fresh
  parsley
50g (2oz) pitted green
  olives, chopped

1 large hard-boiled egg,
  shelled and finely
  chopped
salt and freshly ground
  black pepper
lemon wedges, to serve

1. Trim the tough ends from the asparagus spears. Brush with olive oil and cook on a grill rack, turning halfway through, for about 6 minutes until tender and lightly charred. Take care that the spears do not become over-charred.
2. Meanwhile, to make the gremolata, heat the butter in a heavy-based frying pan, add the breadcrumbs and fry until crisp and golden, stirring frequently. Remove from the heat and stir in the lemon zest, parsley, olives and seasoning.
3. Transfer the asparagus to a plate, or plates and season. Scatter the crumb mixture and chopped egg evenly over the spears, leaving the tips uncovered. Serve with lemon wedges.
* If only fatter asparagus spears are available, pare off the tougher skin from the lower parts of the stalks using a potato peeler. Par-boil the spears in boiling water, drain and dry well before brushing with the oil.

239 SPICED TOFU BURGERS WITH FRESH CORIANDER CHUTNEY

PREPARATION TIME *20 minutes, plus 2–24 hours marinating* **COOKING TIME** *15 minutes* **SERVES 4**

115g (4oz) leeks, cut into 5cm (2in) lengths
1 stick celery (about 125g/4½oz), grated lengthways
olive oil, for frying
2 garlic cloves, finely chopped
¾ tsp cumin seeds, crushed
2 tsp sun-dried tomato paste

1 tsp curry paste
250g (9oz) pack tofu, drained
6 tbsp fresh breadcrumbs
salt and freshly ground black pepper
beaten egg
seasoned plain flour, for coating

FRESH CORIANDER CHUTNEY
40g (1½oz) fresh coriander, coarsely chopped
2 tsp grated fresh root ginger
1 garlic clove, chopped
2 tsp lime juice
1–2 peppadews (bottled mild sweet piquante peppers)*, finely chopped
pinch of sugar

1 Grate the leeks lengthways and mix with the celery. Using kitchen scissors, cut into shorter pieces.

2 Heat the oil in a frying pan, add the leek and celery and fry, stirring, until softened, reduced and lightly coloured, then add the garlic towards the end of cooking. Stir in the cumin, tomato paste and curry paste and cook, stirring, for a couple of minutes. Remove from the heat.

3 Mash the tofu. Using your hands or a fork, mix the tofu with the vegetable mixture, breadcrumbs, seasoning and a little egg until the mixture holds together; be careful of using too much egg – add only enough to bind the mixture. With floured hands, press firmly into eight burgers about 1–2cm (½–¾in) thick. Chill, uncovered, for at least 2 hours, or overnight.

4 Make the coriander chutney by putting the half the coriander, the ginger, garlic, lime juice, peppadews and 2 tablespoons of water in a blender and mixing until smooth. Add the remaining coriander and mix again, leaving some texture in the coriander leaves. Season to taste with sugar, salt and pepper. Transfer to a small serving bowl, cover and chill for up to 30 minutes.

5 Cook the burgers on an oiled grill rack for about 4 minutes on each side, turning carefully once, until browned. Serve with the fresh coriander chutney.

* Alternatively, use ½ fresh red chilli, seeded and finely chopped

240 LEEK AND GOATS' CHEESE BURGERS

PREPARATION TIME *15 minutes, plus 4 hours chilling* **COOKING TIME** *20–25 minutes* **SERVES 4**

300g (10oz) potatoes
80g (3oz) soft goats' cheese
125g (4½oz) leeks, finely chopped
15g (½oz) butter

50g (2oz) feta cheese, crumbled
25g (1oz) fresh breadcrumbs
salt and freshly ground black pepper

olive oil, for brushing
Green Salad with Herbs (see page 167) and/or Mayonnaise (see page 179), to serve

1 Chop the potatoes into small chunks and boil for 10–15 minutes or until tender, then drain well. Return to the pan over a low heat and shake the pan gently to dry the potatoes. Remove from the heat. Mash the potatoes and beat in the goats' cheese.

2 Fry the leeks in the butter until very soft and dry. Beat them into the potato with the feta cheese, breadcrumbs and seasoning, using plenty of black pepper. Transfer to a plate, cover and chill for at least 4 hours.

3 With floured hands, shape into eight burgers about 6.5cm (2½in) in diameter. Brush with oil. Cook on an oiled grill rack for about 3 minutes until browned and crisp, then turn over and cook on the other side. Serve with the green salad with herbs and/or mayonnaise.

241 GRILLED BABY AUBERGINES WITH MOROCCAN TOPPING

PREPARATION TIME *10 minutes* **COOKING TIME** *4–6 minutes* **SERVES 4**

8 baby aubergines
olive oil, for brushing
salt and freshly ground
   black pepper

MOROCCAN TOPPING
about 2 tbsp virgin olive oil
1½ tsp harissa paste
1 plump garlic clove,
   finely chopped
1 tsp cumin seeds,
   toasted and ground
1½ tsp paprika

4 small vine-ripened plum
   tomatoes, finely
   chopped
sea salt and freshly ground
   black pepper
pinch of sugar
1 tbsp chopped fresh
   coriander

1   Make the topping by combining the olive oil and harissa, then mix in the garlic, cumin seeds and paprika. Stir in the tomatoes and salt and pepper, and a pinch of sugar to taste, if necessary. Cover and set aside until required.

2   Halve the aubergines lengthways, leaving the stalk on. Brush with olive oil and sprinkle with seasoning. Cook cut side down on an oiled grill rack over a medium-high heat, until browned in patches. Turn over and cook for a further 2–3 minutes until tender.

3   Pile the topping onto the hot aubergine halves. Sprinkle over the chopped coriander. Transfer to a serving dish and serve warm or cold.

242 TOFU KEBABS

PREPARATION TIME *15 minutes, plus 4 hours marinating* **COOKING TIME** *10–12 minutes* **SERVES 4**

	TOFU MARINADE	KEBAB MARINADE
250g (9oz) firm tofu, drained and cut into 2.5cm (1in) cubes	1 tbsp dark soy sauce	1 tbsp sherry vinegar
8 button onions, peeled	1 tbsp dry sherry	½ tbsp Dijon vinegar
8 cherry tomatoes, preferably plum	1 tbsp sesame oil	1 small garlic clove, finely chopped
1 large yellow pepper, grilled, skinned and cut lengthways into 8 strips	1 tsp Dijon mustard	75ml (3fl oz) olive oil
	1 plump garlic clove, finely chopped	½ tbsp finely chopped mixed fresh herbs
	2 tsp rice wine vinegar	

1 Make the tofu marinade by combining the ingredients. Add the tofu and turn the cubes over to make sure they are evenly coated. Cover and leave in a cool place for at least 4 hours, preferably overnight.
2 Meanwhile, blanch the onions in boiling water for 2–3 minutes, drain and refresh under cold running water. Drain again and leave to drain further on paper towels.
3 Make the kebab marinade by shaking the ingredients together in a screw-topped jar. Season.
4 Lift the tofu from the marinade and thread alternately onto skewers with the vegetables. Brush with the kebab marinade.
5 Cook on an oiled grill rack for about 8 minutes, turning regularly, until browned.

243 SWEET POTATOES WITH FETA AND BLACK OLIVE RELISH

PREPARATION TIME *15 minutes* **COOKING TIME** *14–18 minutes* **SERVES 4**

200g (7oz) feta cheese, crumbled	50g (2oz) pitted oil-cured black olives, chopped	freshly ground black pepper
1 plump garlic clove, crushed	2 tsp herbes de Provence	1 large sweet potato, about 500g (1lb 2oz) in weight
	4 tbsp virgin olive oil, plus extra for brushing	fresh coriander, to garnish

1 Mash the feta cheese with the garlic, olives, herbs, olive oil and black pepper. Set aside.
2 Cut the sweet potato into eight wedges lengthways. Add to a pan of boiling water, return quickly to the boil and boil for 3 minutes. Drain, rinse under running cold water and leave to drain.
3 Dry the sweet potato wedges to remove any remaining moisture, then brush with olive oil. Grind over black pepper and cook on an oiled grill rack for 10–15 minutes until cooked through and well browned on both sides.
4 Garnish the relish with the coriander and serve with the sweet potatoes.

244 COURGETTE BURGERS WITH DILL TZATZIKI

PREPARATION TIME *15 minutes, plus 2 hours chilling* **COOKING TIME** *15-20 minutes* **SERVES 4**

500g (1lb 2oz) small courgettes, grated	6 spring onions, very finely chopped	4 ciabatta rolls, split into halves
salt and freshly ground black pepper	1 heaped tbsp chopped fresh mint	
175g (6oz) fresh breadcrumbs	2 heaped tbsp chopped fresh parsley	DILL TZATZIKI 400ml (10fl oz) sheep's milk yogurt
2 eggs, lightly beaten		2 tbsp chopped fresh dill

1. Layer the courgettes and a good sprinkling of salt in a colander. Leave for 30–60 minutes.
2. Meanwhile, preheat the oven to 190°C/375°F/Gas 5. Reserve 4 tablespoons of the breadcrumbs and spread the remainder on a baking sheet. Bake for 10 minutes, stirring occasionally, until brown and crisp. Spread on a plate and set aside to cool.
3. Rinse the courgettes thoroughly, squeeze firmly to expel as much water as possible, then pat dry between two clean tea towels.
4. Mix the courgettes with the reserved breadcrumbs, the eggs, spring onions, herbs and black pepper. With floured hands, form into 18 burgers about 1–2cm (½–¾in) thick. Coat evenly and thoroughly in the toasted breadcrumbs, and press the breadcrumbs in. Leave uncovered in the fridge for 1 hour or so.
5. Make the tzatziki by beating the yogurt until smooth, then stir in the dill and seasoning.
6. Cook the burgers on an oiled grill rack, preferably using an oiled fine mesh grill or hinged wire basket, for about 3–4 minutes until browned and crisp underneath, then turn carefully and cook on the other side.
7. Meanwhile, lightly toast the rolls on the side of the grill rack. Serve the burgers in the rolls with the tzatziki spooned on top.

245 ASH-BAKED SQUASH

PREPARATION TIME *10 minutes* **COOKING TIME** *20-30 minutes* **SERVES 4**

4 portion-sized small squash, such as acorn, gem or sweet dumpling	TO SERVE Pesto *(see pages 172-174)* or flavoured mayonnaise *(see pages 180-181)* or unsalted butter or cream	freshly grated Parmesan freshly ground black pepper
salt and freshly ground black pepper		

1. Using a sharp knife, slice the cap off each squash and set aside. Scoop out and discard the squash seeds and strings. With a small, sharp knife, cut slashes in the squash flesh. Season inside the squash and replace the lid.
2. Wrap the squash individually in roomy but well-sealed double-thickness foil parcels. Cook in the embers of the fire for 20–30 minutes or until tender, turning occasionally.
3. Remove from the fire and serve with the chosen accompaniment(s).
   VARIATION Halved butternut squash can be cooked in the same way. Allow one half per person.

246 CANNELLINI BEAN AND RED PESTO BURGERS WITH AÏOLI

PREPARATION TIME *10 minutes, plus 1–24 hours chilling* **COOKING TIME** *6–8 minutes* **SERVES 2**

425g (15oz) can cannellini beans, drained
2½ tbsp Red Pesto (see page 173)
2½ tbsp chopped fresh parsley

2 tbsp snipped fresh chives
50g (2oz) fresh breadcrumbs, preferably ciabatta
1 egg yolk

salt and freshly ground black pepper
olive oil, for brushing
aïoli (see page 106), to serve

1 Put the beans, pesto, herbs, breadcrumbs, egg yolk and seasoning into a food processor and mix until evenly combined. Make sure the beans are not reduced to a completely smooth purée (some should remain coarsely chopped).
2 With wet hands, shape the mixture into four burgers about 7.5cm (3in) in diameter, cover and chill for at least 1 hour, to firm up, or overnight, if possible, to allow the flavours to develop.
3 Brush the burgers with olive oil and cook in an oiled grill basket, on an oiled mesh grill or on an oiled grill rack for about 3–4 minutes until browned in ridges. Turn them over and brown on the other side. Serve with the aïoli.

247 ASH-BAKED SWEET POTATO

PREPARATION TIME *5 minutes* **COOKING TIME** *45 minutes* **SERVES 4**

4 sweet potatoes, pricked

TO SERVE
Pesto (see pages 172–174), or flavoured mayonnaise

(see pages 180–181), or flavoured butter (see pages 187–189), or unsalted butter

freshly grated Parmesan and black pepper, or cottage cheese or ricotta and red pesto

1 Wrap the sweet potatoes individually in roomy but well-sealed double-thickness foil parcels.
2 Cook in the embers of the fire for about 45 minutes or until tender, turning occasionally.
3 Remove from the fire and serve with the chosen accompaniment(s).

248 GRILLED CORN WITH SOY SAUCE BUTTER

PREPARATION TIME *10 minutes* **COOKING TIME** *30 minutes* **SERVES 6**

6 fresh corn on the cob
olive oil, for brushing
85g (3oz) unsalted butter, chopped

1½ tbsp dark soy sauce
¾ tsp Sichuan peppercorns, toasted and finely ground

1 tsp fresh red chilli, seeded and finely chopped

1 Strip off any outer husks that are covering the cobs, and pull away the silky brown threads. Brush the cobs with olive oil. Wrap individually in heavy-duty foil.
2 Cook the foil parcels on a grill rack over a medium-high heat for 20 minutes, turning occasionally for even cooking.
3 Meanwhile, heat the butter with the soy sauce, Sichuan peppercorns and chilli in a small pan on the side of the grill rack, until it has melted. Keep warm to allow the flavours to infuse.
4 Unwrap the cobs, brush with some of the butter and cook for about 10 minutes, turning frequently and brushing with the butter, until flecked with brown and tender. Serve with any remaining butter.

249 ASPARAGUS WITH SESAME, GINGER AND LIME MAYONNAISE

PREPARATION TIME *10 minutes* **COOKING TIME** *6 minutes* **SERVES 4–6**

450g (1lb) slim asparagus*
olive oil, for brushing

SESAME, GINGER AND LIME
MAYONNAISE
grated zest and juice of
    2 small limes

2–3 tsp sesame oil
1 heaped tsp sesame seeds,
    lightly toasted and
    crushed
1–2 tsp ginger juice**
300ml (10fl oz) mayonnaise
    (see page 179)

salt and freshly ground
    black pepper

1   Make the mayonnaise by stirring the lime zest and juice, sesame oil, sesame seeds and ginger juice, to taste, into the mayonnaise. Check the seasoning and set aside until required.

2   Trim the tough ends from the asparagus. Brush the asparagus with oil and cook on a grill rack, turning halfway through, for about 6 minutes until tender and lightly charred. Take care that the spears do not become over-charred.

3   Season the spears and serve warm with the mayonnaise.

*   If only fatter asparagus spears are available, pare off the tougher skin from the lower parts of the stalks using a potato peeler. Par-boil the spears in boiling water, drain and dry well before brushing with the oil.

** Ginger juice is made by squeezing grated fresh root ginger through a garlic press.
    VARIATION For a simpler version, omit the mayonnaise. Whisk together 3 tbsp virgin olive oil, 1 tbsp sesame oil, 1 tbsp lime juice and salt and freshly ground black pepper. Pour over the cooked asparagus spears.

250 MUSHROOM KEBABS

PREPARATION TIME *10 minutes* **COOKING TIME** *5 minutes* **SERVES 2–4**

450g (1lb) oyster
    mushrooms
lemon juice
freshly ground black
    pepper
25g (1oz) unsalted butter,
    melted

Basil and Grilled Tomato
    Pesto *(see page 172)* or
    Tomato Tartare Sauce
    (see page 179) or
    Sun-dried Tomato and
    Garlic Mayonnaise *(see
    page 180)*, to serve

1   Sprinkle the mushrooms with a little lemon juice and season them with black pepper.
2   Thread the mushrooms onto oiled skewers and brush with melted butter.
3   Cook on an oiled grill rack, turning frequently, for 5 minutes. Serve with your choice of the suggested accompaniments.

ACCOMPANIMENTS

This chapter covers accompaniments to go with both vegetarian and non-vegetarian dishes. It includes recipes that are cooked on the grill rack as well as some that are prepared in advance. Potatoes cooked in their skins, in the ashes of the barbecue, are probably the first dish that springs to mind when thinking of an accompaniment to barbecued food. Whole small squash and sweet potatoes are also delicious when cooked by this method.

Bread comes next on the accompaniments list, but you don't have to buy the bread or make it beforehand in the kitchen. You can bake it on the grill rack to serve while still warm and fragrant. Yeast breads, such as naan breads, can be baked in this way (see the pizza recipe on page 20 to get an idea of how this is done) but this chapter includes two recipes made in minutes by simply stirring the ingredients together, kneading or shaping, and then baking on the rack. One is Herb Damper Bread and the other is Sun-dried Tomato, Olive and Goats' Cheese Soda Bread.

Strong flavours are the order of the day. Creamy dishes don't sit easily alongside barbecued foods, and delicately-flavoured foods are lost against the robust tastes of food from the grill rack. Sophisticated recipes are also out of place, not only with the food but also the setting and atmosphere. Instead, try Green Salad with Caesar Dressing or Marinated Mushrooms, to complement your meal perfectly.

251 MUSHROOM AND SPINACH SALAD

PREPARATION TIME *10 minutes* **COOKING TIME** *None* **SERVES 4**

4 handfuls baby spinach
  leaves
175g (6oz) button
  mushrooms, thinly sliced
2½ tbsp olive oil

1½ tsp hazelnut or
  walnut oil
2 tsp balsamic vinegar
1½ tsp wholegrain mustard

salt and freshly ground
  black pepper
1–2 tbsp pine nuts, lightly
  toasted

1 Put the spinach into a bowl and add the sliced mushrooms.
2 Just before serving, whisk the oils, vinegar, mustard and seasoning together until emulsified. Pour over the salad and toss lightly. Sprinkle over the pine nuts and serve.

252 FRUITED COUSCOUS

PREPARATION TIME *10 minutes, plus cooling* **COOKING TIME** *None* **SERVES 4**

575ml (1 pint) hot
  vegetable stock
225g (8oz) couscous
75g (3oz) dried apricots,
  chopped
50g (2oz) raisins
75g (3oz) mi-cuit
  plums, chopped*

50g (2oz) pine nuts,
  lightly toasted
50g (2oz) pistachio nuts,
  lightly toasted
4 tbsp chopped fresh
  flat-leaf parsley
2 tbsp chopped fresh
  coriander

1 tbsp chopped fresh mint
4 tbsp olive oil
grated zest and juice of
  1 orange
salt and freshly ground
  black pepper

1 Pour the stock over the couscous, stir with a fork and leave to cool.
2 Fluff up the couscous with a fork, then fork in the fruits, nuts and herbs.
3 Combine the olive oil with the orange zest and juice and salt and black pepper. Whisk until emulsified and stir into the couscous.
* Pitted fresh dates or dried figs can be used instead.

253 COOKED MEDITERRANEAN FENNEL SALAD

PREPARATION TIME *10 minutes* **COOKING TIME** *5 minutes* **SERVES 4**

2 tbsp virgin olive oil
3 small fennel bulbs,
  thinly sliced
75g (3oz) sun-blush
  tomatoes

12 oil-cured black olives,
  halved and pitted
2 tbsp balsamic vinegar
pinch of caster sugar,
  to taste

salt and freshly ground
  black pepper
fresh fennel herb, to
  garnish

1 Heat the oil in a saucepan, add the fennel and 1 tablespoon of water, cover and cook for about 5 minutes until the fennel has softened slightly and the water has evaporated.
2 Stir in the sun-blush tomatoes, olives, vinegar, and sugar and black pepper to taste. Only add salt if necessary. Heat through, then leave to cool.
3 Serve the salad at room temperature, garnished with fennel herb.

254 GREEN SALAD WITH CAESAR DRESSING AND GARLIC AND HERB CROUTONS

PREPARATION TIME *10 minutes* **COOKING TIME** *5 minutes* **SERVES 4-6**

6 handfuls Cos lettuce,
  torn into pieces

CROUTONS
5 tbsp olive oil
2-3 slices of country bread,
  crusts removed, cut into
  1cm (½in) cubes

2 garlic cloves, lightly
  crushed

DRESSING
1 egg yolk
2 tsp wholegrain mustard
75ml (3fl oz) olive oil
3 garlic cloves, finely
  chopped

2 tbsp red wine vinegar
4-6 tbsp freshly grated
  Parmesan cheese
3 anchovy fillets, drained
  and chopped
freshly ground black
  pepper

1 To make the croûtons, heat the oil in a frying pan, add the bread cubes and the garlic and fry until crisp and lightly browned. Transfer to paper towels to drain.

2 Make the dressing by mixing the egg yolk with the mustard, then slowly pour in the oil, whisking. Add the garlic, vinegar, Parmesan cheese, anchovy fillets and plenty of black pepper. Whisk until thoroughly mixed.

3 Just before serving, put the lettuce leaves into a bowl. Pour over the dressing, toss to combine, and then add the croûtons and toss once more.

255 PARMESAN POLENTA

PREPARATION TIME *10 minutes, plus 1 hour chilling* **COOKING TIME** *20 minutes* **SERVES 4**

750ml (1¼ pints) water
salt and freshly ground
  black pepper
225g (8oz) instant polenta

40g (1½oz) unsalted butter,
  diced
115g (4oz) Parmesan
  cheese, freshly grated

2 tbsp finely chopped
  fresh parsley

1 Bring the water and a pinch of salt to the boil in a large saucepan. Add the polenta in a thin, steady stream, stirring constantly and continue to stir until the polenta is thick and comes away from the sides of the pan.

2 Remove the pan from the heat and stir in the butter, Parmesan, parsley and plenty of black pepper. Leave to cool for about 10 minutes.

3 Spread out a large sheet of clingfilm. Spoon the polenta down the centre, fold the clingfilm over it and use to shape the clingfilm into a smooth cylinder 8.25cm (3½in) wide and about 25cm (10in) long. Chill for 1 hour.

4 Remove the clingfilm and using a large, sharp knife, cut the polenta roll into eight even slices. Cook on an oiled grill rack, turning once, for about 3 minutes on each side until crisp and golden.

256 MARINATED COURGETTES WITH LEMON AND MINT

PREPARATION TIME *10 minutes* **COOKING TIME** *3 minutes* **SERVES 4-6**

450g (1lb) mini courgettes
olive oil, for brushing
4 spring onions, white parts
only, finely chopped

small fresh mint leaves,
to garnish

DRESSING
5 tbsp extra virgin olive oil
2 tbsp lemon juice

1 garlic clove, chopped
1 tbsp chopped fresh mint
pinch of caster sugar
salt and freshly ground
black pepper

1   Using the point of a small, sharp knife, cut a slash along the length of each courgette. Brush with olive oil and cook the courgettes on an oiled grill rack for about 3 minutes or until lightly charred and softened, turning once.
2   Meanwhile, make the dressing by whisking the ingredients together.
3   Transfer the courgettes to a bowl, stir in the dressing, cover with clingfilm and leave until cold.
4   To serve, add the spring onions, adjust the seasoning and scatter over the small mint leaves.

257 COURGETTE SLICES WITH CHIVES AND TOMATOES

PREPARATION TIME *10 minutes* **COOKING TIME** *10 minutes* **SERVES 4**

15g (½oz) chives, snipped
100ml (3½fl oz) virgin olive
oil, plus extra for
brushing
finely grated zest and juice
of 1 lime

450g (1lb) vine-ripened
tomatoes, peeled,
seeded and finely
chopped
salt and freshly ground
black pepper

4 small courgettes, about
115g (4oz) each

1   Put the chives into a blender with the oil and lime juice. Mix to a purée, then pour into a bowl and stir in the lime zest, tomatoes and seasoning.
2   Using a vegetable peeler, cut the courgettes lengthwise into long, thin strips. Arrange them in pairs and thread onto skewers. Brush the courgettes generously with olive oil and season them.
3   Cook on an oiled barbecue rack over a fairly high heat, turning frequently and brushing with oil, for about 10 minutes until cooked and lightly charred.
4   Remove from the rack and spoon over some of the dressing. Serve with the remaining dressing.

258 SUN-DRIED TOMATO, OLIVE AND GOATS' CHEESE SODA BREAD

PREPARATION TIME *15 minutes* **COOKING TIME** *20–25 minutes* **SERVES 4-6**

450g (1lb) plain white flour
1½ tsp bicarbonate of soda
salt and freshly ground
    black pepper
50-75g (2-3oz) unsalted
    butter, diced

50g (2oz) sun-dried
    tomatoes in oil, drained
    and chopped
12 oil-cured black olives,
    pitted and coarsely
    chopped

75g (3oz) goats' cheese,
    cut into small cubes
about 300ml (½ pint)
    buttermilk or
    soured milk*

1   Sift the flour, bicarbonate of soda and seasoning into a bowl. Toss in the butter and rub in with fingertips. Stir in the sun-dried tomatoes, olives and cheese, followed by the buttermilk or soured milk to form a medium-firm, soft but not sticky dough. If necessary, add a little more liquid.

2   Knead lightly on a floured surface until the dough just begins to come together and form a ball; do not over-handle or the bread will be heavy. Place on a lightly floured baking sheet and pat to a circle no more than 2.5cm (1in) thick.

3   Put the bread in the centre of a large, oiled, double-thickness of heavy-duty foil. Fold the sides of the foil over the bread and pleat them firmly together to seal.

4   Cook on the grill rack over a medium-hot heat for 10–12 minutes on each side until browned and cooked through (it should sound hollow when tapped). Serve warm, cut into thick wedges.

*   To sour milk, add 1 tablespoon of lemon juice to 300ml (½ pint) milk.

259 TOMATOES WITH TAPENADE AND PARSLEY TOPPING

PREPARATION TIME *10 minutes* **COOKING TIME** *6–8 minutes* **SERVES 4**

8 large ripe but firm plum tomatoes, halved
olive oil, for brushing

TOPPING
50g (2oz) dry breadcrumbs
2 tbsp extra virgin olive oil
2 tbsp tapenade

1 pack fresh flat-leaf parsley, chopped
salt and freshly ground black pepper

1   Brush the outside of the tomatoes with oil.
2   Make the topping by combining the breadcrumbs with the oil, tapenade and parsley. Season, taking care over the amount of salt you add. Divide the topping among the cut side of the tomato halves, pressing it down lightly.
3   Cook, skin-side down only, on an oiled grill rack for 6–8 minutes.

260 PITTA CRISPS WITH GARLIC AND HERBS

PREPARATION TIME *10 minutes* **COOKING TIME** *2–4 minutes* **SERVES 4**

4 pitta breads
3 garlic cloves
sea salt and freshly ground black pepper

6 tbsp virgin olive oil
1 tsp dried oregano
1 tsp dried thyme

pinch of fennel seeds, finely crushed

1   Split the pitta breads open into two halves.
2   Crush the garlic with a pinch of salt, then mix with the olive oil, herbs, seeds and black pepper. Brush over the inner surfaces of the pitta breads.
3   Cook on an oiled grill rack for 1–2 minutes on each side until golden. Remove and leave to cool. Break the pitta breads into pieces to serve.

261 GRILLED VEGETABLE PARCELS

PREPARATION TIME *10 minutes* **COOKING TIME** *8–10 minutes* **SERVES 4**

225g (8oz) mixed mushrooms such as shiitake, oyster and chestnut, thickly sliced
150g (5oz) broccoli, broken into small florets
2 courgettes, cut into slim lengthways batons

8 spring onions, cut into 2.5cm (1in) lengths
1½ tbsp groundnut oil
2 tsp sesame oil
2 tbsp rice wine
4 tbsp soy sauce
5cm (2in) piece of fresh root ginger, finely chopped

2 garlic cloves, finely chopped
1 tsp cardamom seeds, finely crushed
freshly ground black pepper

1   Pile the vegetables into the centre of four 30cm (12in) double-thickness squares of heavy-duty foil, making sure each parcel has a good mix of vegetables. Fold up the sides.
2   Combine all the remaining ingredients. Divide among the vegetables, then twist the foil edges together to seal tightly.
3   Cook the packages on the side of a grill rack for 8–10 minutes until the vegetables are tender.

262 MASALA POTATO WEDGES

PREPARATION TIME *10 minutes* **COOKING TIME** *25 minutes* **SERVES 4**

2 large potatoes, unpeeled	1½ tsp ground coriander	2 tbsp sun-dried tomato
salt	pinch of chilli powder	paste
1 tsp ground cumin	2 tbsp olive oil	2 tbsp lemon juice

1 Cook the whole potatoes in a pan of boiling, salted water for 15–20 minutes until just tender. Drain, leave until cool enough to handle, then remove the skins. Cut each potato into eight lengthways wedges.
2 Mix together the spices, oil, sun-dried tomato paste, lemon juice and 1 tablespoon of water.
3 Put the potatoes into a shallow dish, spoon the spice mixture evenly over and stir to ensure all the wedges are coated.
4 Cook the wedges on an oiled grill rack for 5–6 minutes until tender and marked with brown.

263 GARLICKY POTATO SLICES

PREPARATION TIME *10 minutes* **COOKING TIME** *20-25 minutes* **SERVES 4**

550g (1¼lb) unpeeled	2 garlic cloves	handful of thyme or
potatoes	4 tbsp virgin olive oil	rosemary twigs, for
sea salt and freshly ground		cooking (optional)
black pepper		

1 Cook the potatoes in their skins in boiling water until just tender. Drain and when cool enough to handle, cut into 1cm (½in) thick slices. Season the potatoes with plenty of black pepper.
2 Crush the garlic with a pinch of salt, then mix with the oil. Brush over the potato slices.
3 Put the herb twigs on the fire, if using. Cook the potato slices on an oiled grill rack for 5 minutes on each side until the outsides are crisp and lightly charred, turning the slices halfway through.

264 HERB DAMPER BREADS

PREPARATION TIME *10 minutes* **COOKING TIME** *6-8 minutes* **SERVES 4-6**

450g (1lb) plain white flour	chopped fresh mixed herbs	25-50g (1-2oz) butter,
4 tsp baking powder	such as chives, parsley,	melted
salt and freshly ground	thyme, tarragon,	about 350ml (12 fl oz) milk
black pepper	oregano, rosemary	

1 Sift the flour, baking powder and seasoning into a bowl. Stir in the herbs, then quickly stir in the butter and enough milk to make a soft but not sticky dough that comes together. Divide into eight evenly sized pieces.
2 With floured hands, pat each piece into a circle about 1cm (½in) thick.
3 Cook the breads on an oiled grill rack for 3–4 minutes on each side until they are crisp, brown and puffy. Serve warm.

265 ASH-BAKED POTATOES WITH OLIVE, BASIL AND SUN-DRIED TOMATO BUTTER

PREPARATION TIME *5 minutes* **COOKING TIME** *1¼–1½ hours* **SERVES 4**

4 large potatoes, 300g (10oz) each	OLIVE, BASIL AND SUN-DRIED TOMATO BUTTER	4 sun-dried tomatoes, very finely chopped
2 tbsp olive oil	115g (4oz) unsalted butter, softened	1 tbsp chopped fresh basil
sea salt and freshly ground black pepper	25g (1oz) pitted oil-cured black olives, finely chopped	salt and freshly ground black pepper

1   Preheat the oven to 200°C/400°F/Gas 6. Prick the potatoes and bake in the oven for about 40–50 minutes until almost tender.

2   Meanwhile, make the flavoured butter by beating the butter until softened, then add the remaining ingredients and mix everything together until evenly blended.

3   Spoon the flavoured butter onto a sheet of clingfilm or non-stick baking parchment. Using the clingfilm or parchment, shape the butter into a roll about 4cm (1½in) in diameter. Wrap tightly and chill until required. Cut into slices to serve. Alternatively, pack the butter into ramekin dishes.

4   Remove the potatoes from the oven and leave until cool enough to handle. Rub the skins liberally with olive oil and sprinkle with salt and pepper. Wrap individually in three layers of heavy-duty foil.

5   Push the packages into the ashes and cook for a further 30–40 minutes until cooked and the skins are crisp. Turn frequently so the potatoes cook evenly and do not burn. Serve the potatoes with the butter (only about half should be needed). Warn diners that the potatoes inside the packages will be very hot.

*   Alternatively, serve with Rocket and Goats' Cheese Pesto (see page 173).

266 POTATO SALAD

PREPARATION TIME *10 minutes* **COOKING TIME** *15 minutes* **SERVES 4**

450g (1lb) new potatoes, or other small waxy potatoes	2 shallots, finely chopped	1½ tbsp finely chopped fresh flat-leaf parsley or chives
salt and freshly ground black pepper	115ml (4fl oz) virgin olive oil	
	2½ tbsp tarragon vinegar	

1   Bring the potatoes to the boil in a saucepan of salted water. Lower the heat and simmer until the potatoes are tender through to the centre, but still firm.

2   Meanwhile, put the shallots, oil, vinegar and seasoning in a screw-topped jar and shake vigorously until the dressing has emulsified.

3   Drain the potatoes and slice them thickly into a salad bowl. Pour over the dressing, sprinkle over some parsley or chives and toss everything together. Leave to cool.

267 PEPPER AND ASPARAGUS NOODLE SALAD

PREPARATION TIME *15 minutes* **COOKING TIME** *15 minutes* **SERVES 4**

350g (12oz) noodles
225g (8oz) slim asparagus
8 tbsp virgin olive oil,
    plus extra for brushing
2 large red peppers, grilled
    (see page 20), peeled
    and sliced

4 sun-dried tomato halves
    in oil, drained and sliced
2 tbsp salted capers, well
    rinsed and dried
10 kalamata olives, pitted
    and sliced
1½ tbsp balsamic vinegar

salt and freshly ground
    black pepper
3 tbsp chopped fresh basil

1   Cook the noodles in a large saucepan of boiling salted water according to the packet instructions, until tender. Drain well.
2   Meanwhile, blanch the asparagus in boiling water for 3 minutes, drain well and pat dry.
3   Heat a heavy, ridged cast-iron grill pan. Brush the asparagus with olive oil and cook in the pan for 3–4 minutes until charred and tender. Remove and chop into short lengths.
4   Toss the noodles with the asparagus, red peppers, sun-dried tomatoes, capers and olives.
5   Whisk together the oil, vinegar and seasoning. Trickle over the salad, add the basil and gently toss everything together.

268 NEW POTATO BROCHETTES WITH BASIL AÏOLI

PREPARATION TIME *10 minutes* **COOKING TIME** *15-20 minutes* **SERVES 4**

450g (1lb) small new
  potatoes, or other small
  waxy potatoes, halved or
  quartered, if necessary
salt and freshly ground
  black pepper

3 tbsp olive oil

BASIL AÏOLI
1 garlic clove
115g (4oz) fresh basil
1 egg yolk

1 tbsp lemon juice
150-175ml (5-6fl oz)
  olive oil

1 Put the garlic, basil, egg yolk and lemon juice into a blender or food processor. Add a little oil and mix until blended. Add the remaining oil, mix to a smooth paste, season and transfer to a bowl.
2 Bring the potatoes to the boil in a saucepan of salted water. Lower the heat and simmer until the potatoes are almost tender. Drain well, then return to the pan and add the oil and seasoning. Toss and shake the potatoes around to coat in oil.
3 Thread the potatoes onto skewers and cook on an oiled grill rack for 7-8 minutes, turning regularly, until tender. Serve the potatoes accompanied by the basil aïoli.

269 MARINATED MUSHROOMS

PREPARATION TIME *5 minutes, plus 12 hours marinating* **COOKING TIME** *15-20 minutes* **SERVES 4**

450g (1lb) small
  mushrooms
2 tbsp olive oil
75ml (3fl oz) white wine
200ml (7fl oz) fresh
  vegetable stock (not
  from a cube) or water

2 tsp black peppercorns
1 bay leaf, torn across
2 thyme sprigs
2 tbsp tomato purée
4 tomatoes, chopped
1 tbsp lemon juice, or
  to taste

salt and freshly ground
  black pepper
shredded fresh basil or flat-
  leaf parsley, to garnish

1 Put the mushrooms, oil, wine, stock, peppercorns, herbs and tomato purée into a saucepan. Bring to the boil, cover and simmer for 10-15 minutes until the mushrooms are tender.
2 Using a slotted spoon, transfer the mushrooms from the liquid to a bowl. Boil the liquid hard until reduced to a light sauce. Taste, season and add lemon juice to taste, if necessary. Pour over the mushrooms, add the tomatoes and leave to cool. Cover and store in a cool place for 12 hours.
3 To serve, stir the mushrooms and scatter over the herbs.

270 GRILLED ONION SLICES

PREPARATION TIME *10 minutes* **COOKING TIME** *8 minutes* **SERVES 4**

2 large red onions, cut into
  1cm (½in) thick rounds
olive oil, for brushing

sea salt and freshly ground
  black pepper

pecorino or Parmesan
  cheese, finely grated,
  for sprinkling

1 Push skewers through each onion round, from side to side. Brush with olive oil.
2 Cook on an oiled grill rack for 2 minutes. Turn the slices 90 degrees to create a criss-cross pattern of brown lines. Grill for another 2 minutes, then turn them over and repeat once more.
3 Transfer to a dish, season and sprinkle with pecorino or Parmesan cheese. Serve straightaway.

271 CARAMELISED SHALLOTS

PREPARATION TIME *5 minutes* **COOKING TIME** *40 minutes* **SERVES 4**

450g (1lb) shallots, peeled	**few dashes balsamic**	**salt and freshly ground**
3 fresh thyme sprigs	**vinegar, to taste**	**black pepper**
1 bay leaf, torn across	**25g (1oz) unsalted butter,**	
2 tbsp brown sugar	**diced**	

1 Put the shallots in the centre of a large sheet of double-thickness, heavy-duty foil, nestling the thyme sprigs and bay leaf amongst them. Fold the foil loosely over the shallots and twist the edges together to seal them firmly.

2 Put the parcel on the side of the grill rack and cook for 30 minutes.

3 Open the foil (the shallots should be soft), carefully stir in the sugar, sprinkle over a little balsamic vinegar and dot with the butter. Season, and re-seal the edges. Return to the grill rack and cook for a further 10 minutes, by which time the shallots should be a rich golden brown.

272 MIXED TOMATO SALAD

PREPARATION TIME *10 minutes* **COOKING TIME** *None* **SERVES 4**

50g (2oz) watercress	**50ml (2fl oz) oil from the**	**175g (6oz) vine-ripened**
2 tbsp pine nuts	**sun-dried tomatoes**	**tomatoes, quartered**
1 small garlic clove,	**2 tbsp freshly grated**	**175g (6oz) ripe cherry**
crushed	**Parmesan cheese**	**tomatoes, halved**
45g (1½oz) sun-dried	**salt and freshly ground**	**3 ripe large ridged**
tomatoes in oil, drained	**black pepper**	**tomatoes, chopped**
and shredded		

1 Put the watercress, pine nuts, garlic and 2 tablespoons of the oil in a food processor or small blender and mix until almost smooth.

2 With the motor still running, slowly trickle in the remaining oil. Add the cheese, mix briefly, then add the seasoning.

3 Toss the tomatoes with the dressing and serve as soon as possible.

273 ORIENTAL PANZANELLA

PREPARATION TIME *10 minutes* **COOKING TIME** *None* **SERVES 3-4**

1 naan bread, cut into	**5-6 spring onions,**	**1 small garlic clove,**
1cm (½in) pieces	**including a little green,**	**chopped**
flesh from 1 ripe mango,	**finely chopped**	**salt and freshly ground**
cut into 1cm (½in) pieces	**1 red chilli, seeded and**	**black pepper**
1 red pepper, seeded	**finely chopped (optional)**	**2 tbsp lime juice**
and diced	**3 tbsp chopped fresh**	**75ml (3fl oz) yogurt**
	coriander leaves	**1 tbsp mint jelly**

1 Toss the naan, mango, red pepper, spring onions, chilli (if using) and coriander together.

2 Crush the garlic to a paste with a pinch of salt and mix with the lime juice, yogurt, mint jelly and black pepper. Stir into the salad. Serve as soon as possible.

274 RATATOUILLE SALAD

PREPARATION TIME *10 minutes, plus 1 hour draining* **COOKING TIME** *50 minutes* **SERVES 4–6**

2 aubergines, sliced
salt and freshly ground
  black pepper
olive oil, for cooking
2 red peppers, sliced

6 small courgettes, quite
  thickly sliced
1 large onion, thinly sliced
3 garlic cloves, crushed
  and chopped

2 large, ripe tomatoes,
  chopped
a few sprigs of thyme,
  marjoram and parsley
leaves from a few sprigs
  of fresh basil, shredded

1   Sprinkle the aubergines with salt and leave in a colander to drain for 1 hour. Rinse them
    thoroughly, then dry well.
2   Heat a little oil in a large frying pan, add the aubergines, in batches if necessary, and fry until
    lightly browned. Remove with a fish slice and drain on kitchen paper.
3   Add the peppers to the pan and fry for a few minutes until softened, but take care not to
    overcook them. Remove to kitchen paper.
4   Fry the courgettes (add a little more oil if necessary) and cook until just beginning to soften,
    stirring occasionally. Remove to kitchen paper.
5   Fry the onion (add a little more oil if necessary) and cook until softened, stirring frequently. Stir in
    the garlic and tomatoes for few minutes, then return the other vegetables to the pan and add the
    thyme, marjoram and parsley. Season lightly, and add 2 tablespoons of oil, if liked. Cover and
    cook gently for about 30–35 minutes, stirring occasionally.
6   Stir in the basil, remove from the heat and leave to cool, uncovered. Serve at room temperature.

275 CORIANDER NOODLE SALAD

PREPARATION TIME *10 minutes* **COOKING TIME** *5 minutes* **SERVES 4**

225g (8oz) dried Chinese egg noodles	2 tbsp Thai fish sauce	3 tbsp chopped fresh coriander
1 garlic clove, finely crushed	1½ tbsp sesame oil grated zest and juice of 1 lime	2 tbsp Japanese pickled ginger*, shredded
6 spring onions, thinly sliced on the diagonal	2 tbsp groundnut oil	few drops of chilli oil
1 tbsp soy sauce	2 tbsp sesame seeds, lightly toasted	freshly ground black pepper

1 Cook the noodles in a saucepan of boiling water according to the packet instructions.
2 Meanwhile, combine the remaining ingredients.
3 Drain the noodles into a colander, then tip into a serving bowl. Toss with the dressing.
* Japanese pickled ginger can be bought from specialist food shops and some supermarkets, but it is very easy to make. Bring 6 tablespoons of rice vinegar to the boil in a small saucepan, with 1 tablespoon of caster sugar, 1 teaspoon of salt and a 50g (2oz) piece fresh root ginger, very thinly sliced. Simmer for 1–2 minutes, then leave to cool. The pickled ginger can be stored in a closed jar in the fridge for up to one month.

276 GREEN SALAD WITH HERBS

PREPARATION TIME *10 minutes* **COOKING TIME** *None* **SERVES 4-6**

4 handfuls mixed salad leaves, such as lamb's lettuce, frisée, rocket and radicchio, torn into bite-sized pieces	4 tbsp chopped mixed fresh herbs, such as chervil, marjoram, flat-leaf parsley, dill, tarragon and mint	4 tbsp extra virgin olive oil 1½ tbsp balsamic vinegar salt and freshly ground black pepper

1 Toss the salad leaves and herbs together.
2 Whisk the oil with the vinegar and seasoning until emulsified. Pour over the salad and toss so the leaves are evenly coated. Serve within 30 minutes.

277 ORIENTAL COLESLAW

PREPARATION TIME *10 minutes* **COOKING TIME** *None* **SERVES 4-6**

½ small head white cabbage (about 150g/5oz)	1 carrot, finely shredded 50g (2oz) water chestnuts, chopped	3 tbsp orange juice 1½ tbsp rice wine vinegar 2 tsp grated fresh root ginger
½ head Chinese leaves, thinly shredded (about 200g/7oz)	DRESSING	
2 small fennel bulbs, thinly sliced	1 tbsp soy sauce ½ tbsp sesame oil	

1 Discard the outer leaves of the cabbage, and cut away the core and any large ribs. Finely shred the cabbage. Put into a large bowl with the Chinese leaves, fennel, carrot and water chestnuts.
2 Make the dressing by whisking all the ingredients together until emulsified. Pour over the salad and toss so the leaves are evenly coated. Serve within 30 minutes.

278 WILTED TOMATOES

PREPARATION TIME *10 minutes* **COOKING TIME** *15 minutes* **SERVES 4**

100ml (3½fl oz) virgin olive oil
2 shallots, finely chopped
2 garlic cloves, finely chopped

2 anchovy fillets, chopped
1 tsp chilli oil
450g (1lb) plum tomatoes, peeled, seeded and quite finely chopped

1 tbsp sun-dried tomato paste
salt and freshly ground black pepper

1   Warm the olive oil in a saucepan. Add the shallots, garlic and anchovy and sweat very slowly until the shallots have softened and the flavours have mellowed.

2   Add the chilli oil, tomatoes and tomato paste to the pan. Continue to cook slowly for 3–4 minutes until the tomatoes wilt and soften. Taste for seasoning and add salt and pepper if necessary. Serve while still warm.

279 SUMMER TABOULEH

PREPARATION TIME *10 minutes* **COOKING TIME** *None* **SERVES 4**

225g (8oz) bulgur
2–3 garlic cloves, crushed
115g (4oz) black olives, pitted
3 well-flavoured sun-ripened tomatoes, chopped

6 spring onions, finely chopped
2 tbsp chopped fresh coriander
1 tbsp chopped fresh mint
1 tbsp chopped fresh flat-leaf parsley

6 sun-dried tomatoes in oil, drained and sliced
3 tbsp virgin olive oil
juice of 1 lemon
salt and freshly ground black pepper

1   Put the bulgur into a heatproof bowl. Pour over boiling water to cover. Leave for 30 minutes.

2   Drain off any remaining water.

3   Fold all the remaining ingredients into the bulgur, using plenty of seasoning.

280 BEETROOT SALAD

PREPARATION TIME *10 minutes, plus 30 minutes chilling* **COOKING TIME** *None* **SERVES 4**

225ml (8fl oz) yogurt
freshly ground black pepper
500g (1lb 2oz) cooked beetroot (not in brine), cut into 1cm (½in) cubes

leaves from a small bunch of fresh coriander, chopped
50g (2oz) wild rocket
150–175g (5–6oz) feta cheese, cubed

chopped walnut halves, to garnish (optional)

1   Season the yogurt with black pepper, then stir in the beetroot cubes and chopped coriander. Chill for 30 minutes.

2   Make a ring of rocket on a deep serving plate. Pile the beetroot mixture in the centre and scatter over the feta cheese. Sprinkle over the walnuts, if liked, and serve.

281 WATERCRESS, CHICORY AND ORANGE SALAD

PREPARATION TIME *15 minutes* **COOKING TIME** *None* **SERVES 4**

1 large bunch watercress, coarse stems removed

1 fennel bulb, cored and thinly sliced across

1 red onion, very thinly sliced

2 heads of chicory, leaves separated, and torn into pieces, if liked

2-3 juicy oranges

3 tbsp virgin olive oil

salt and freshly ground black pepper

1   Combine the watercress, fennel, red onion and chicory in a salad bowl.

2   Working over a bowl to catch the juice and using a small, sharp knife, carefully cut off the orange peel and pith. Put the oranges on a plate (again to catch the juice) and cut across into slices. Add the slices to the salad and the orange juice from the plate into the bowl of orange juice.

3   Whisk the oil with the orange juice and season to taste. Pour over the salad and toss to mix. Serve within 30 minutes.

SALSAS, MARINADES, SAUCES AND BUTTERS

The recipes in this chapter can all be used to turn plain food into barbecued treats. Most marinades are mixtures of oil (which moistens the food), an acid ingredient (which tenderises), and flavourings. Marinades are best made in advance (especially if the food will not be marinated for long) to allow the flavours to develop. Don't overdo the oil as this can cause a flare-up.

Leave foods to marinate or absorb a rub or paste in a cool place rather than the fridge, to avoid dulling the flavour. If foods are refrigerated, return them to room temperature 30–60 minutes before cooking. The more tender a food, the shorter the time it should be marinated, otherwise the acid in a marinade will make it soft. Use non-metallic dishes for marinating because acids do not react with them. Allow about 75–115ml (3–4fl oz) of marinade per 450g (1lb) food. Cutting slashes in food will allow the marinade or rub to penetrate. Drain and pat dry marinated food before cooking (moisture prevents it browning), and scrape off any particles such as herbs.

Honey, sugar or maple syrup-based mixtures give a sweet, rich coating to the food. However, they can burn, so are best brushed on the food halfway through cooking or just before the end. Herb and spice rubs, which give a deliciously crisp finish, can be either rubbed into the food or combined with a little oil first.

CHAPTER 7

282 PESTO

PREPARATION TIME *10 minutes* **COOKING TIME** *None* **SERVES 4**

2 garlic cloves, chopped
2 handfuls of fresh basil
   leaves
50g (2oz) pine nuts

150ml (5fl oz) olive oil
50g (2oz) Parmesan cheese,
   freshly grated

salt and freshly ground
   black pepper

1   Put the garlic, basil and pine nuts into a small blender or food processor. Mix to a paste. With the motor running, slowly pour in the oil to make a creamy paste.
2   Add the cheese, season to taste and mix briefly.

283 FRESH COCONUT, LEMON GRASS AND CHILLI PESTO

PREPARATION TIME *10 minutes* **COOKING TIME** *None* **SERVES 4**

50g (2oz) freshly grated
   coconut
3-4 lemon grass stems,
   outer layers discarded,
   chopped

1 plump garlic clove,
   chopped
1 mild red chilli, seeded
   and chopped

juice of 1 lime or small
   lemon
50-75ml (2-3fl oz)
   groundnut oil
salt

1   Put the coconut, lemon grass, garlic, chilli and juice into a small blender or food processor.
2   With the motor running, slowly pour in the oil to make a thick sauce. Season with salt.

284 BASIL AND GRILLED TOMATO PESTO

PREPARATION TIME *10 minutes* **COOKING TIME** *5-10 minutes* **SERVES 4-6**

350g (12oz) vine-ripened
   tomatoes
40g (1½oz) basil leaves
2 garlic cloves, chopped
50g (2oz) blanched
   almonds, chopped

50g (2oz) walnut halves,
   chopped
115ml (4fl oz) fruity olive oil
50g (2oz) pecorino cheese,
   freshly grated

salt and freshly ground
   black pepper
sun-dried tomato paste
   or a pinch of sugar
   (optional)

1   Preheat the grill and line the grill pan with foil. Grill the tomatoes, turning them frequently, until they are blistered and lightly charred. Leave until cool enough to handle, then remove the blackened patches.
2   Put the grilled tomatoes, basil leaves, garlic, nuts and a little of the oil into a small blender or food processor. Pulse until chopped together.
3   With the motor running, slowly pour in the oil to make a paste. Add the cheese. Season and add a little tomato paste or sugar, if necessary.

285 ROCKET AND GOATS' CHEESE PESTO

PREPARATION TIME *10 minutes* **COOKING TIME** *None* **SERVES 6**

1 garlic clove, coarsely
chopped
25g (1oz) shelled pistachio
nuts

115g (4oz) soft goats'
cheese
75g (3oz) wild rocket
2 tbsp freshly grated
Parmesan cheese

200ml (7fl oz) olive oil
salt and freshly ground
black pepper

1 Put the garlic, nuts, goats' cheese, rocket and Parmesan into a small blender or food processor with a little of the oil. Mix briefly until blended.
2 With the motor running, pour in the remaining oil. Season.

286 RED PESTO

PREPARATION TIME *5 minutes* **COOKING TIME** *20 minutes* **SERVES 4**

1 large red pepper
3 pieces of sun-dried
tomato in oil, drained
and chopped

1 plump garlic clove,
chopped
50g (2oz) pine nuts
about 5 tbsp virgin olive oil

50g (2oz) pecorino or
Parmesan cheese,
freshly grated
salt

1 Preheat the oven to 200ºC/400ºF/Gas 6. Roast the pepper for about 20 minutes until it starts to soften and the skin begins to blister. Remove from the oven and leave until cool enough to handle.
2 Peel off the skin and discard, along with the seeds. Chop the flesh and put into a small blender or food processor with the sun-dried tomatoes, garlic and pine nuts.
3 With the motor running, slowly pour in the oil to make a paste. Add the cheese. Season with salt.

287 CORIANDER, GINGER AND CASHEW NUT PESTO

PREPARATION TIME *10 minutes* **COOKING TIME** *None* **SERVES 4**

50g (2oz) coriander leaves
2 tbsp grated fresh root
   ginger
50g (2oz) cashew nuts,
   chopped

2 garlic cloves, chopped
juice of 1 lime or small
   lemon
125–175ml (4–6 fl oz) olive
   oil

salt and freshly ground
   black pepper

1   Put the coriander, ginger, cashew nuts, garlic and lime or lemon juice into a small blender or food processor. Mix to a paste.
2   With the motor running, slowly pour in the oil to make a creamy paste. Season to taste.

288 DILL PESTO

PREPARATION TIME *10 minutes* **COOKING TIME** *None* **SERVES 4**

2 garlic cloves, chopped
large handful of fresh dill
50g (2oz) blanched
   almonds

150ml (5fl oz) olive oil
25g (1oz) Parmesan cheese,
   freshly grated

salt and freshly ground
   black pepper

1   Put the garlic, dill and almonds in a small blender or food processor. Mix to a paste. With the motor running, slowly pour in the oil to make a creamy paste.
2   Add the cheese, season to taste and mix briefly.

289 AVOCADO, TOMATO AND RED PEPPER SALSA

PREPARATION TIME *10 minutes, plus 30 minutes chilling* **COOKING TIME** *20 minutes* **SERVES 4**

1 red pepper
2 large, ripe avocados
1 garlic clove, finely
   chopped
1 plum tomato, finely
   chopped

1 small red onion, very
   finely chopped
1 red chilli, seeded and
   finely chopped
juice of 1 small lime

4 tbsp chopped fresh
   coriander
salt and freshly ground
   black pepper

1   Cook the red pepper on an oiled grill rack on a barbecue, or under a preheated hot grill, turning occasionally, until well charred and soft. Leave until cool enough to handle, then remove the skin and discard the seeds. Chop the flesh very finely. Put into a bowl.
2   Peel the avocados, remove the stones and chop the flesh finely. Add to the bowl with the remaining ingredients. Toss gently to combine. Cover and chill for 30 minutes.

290 ROASTED TOMATO SALSA

PREPARATION TIME *10 minutes* **COOKING TIME** *6–7* **SERVES 4-6**

6 ripe tomatoes, halved
2–3 tbsp lime juice
2 tbsp olive oil
3 tbsp chopped fresh
   coriander

5 spring onions, finely
   chopped
2 garlic cloves, finely
   chopped

1 small red chilli, seeded
   and chopped
1 tsp ground cumin
salt

1   Put the tomatoes, skin side down, on an oiled grill rack and cook for about 6–7 minutes until
    slightly softened and the skin is charred in patches.
2   Remove from the grill rack, leave until cool enough to handle, then peel off the skins. Coarsely
    chop the flesh and mix with the remaining ingredients. Serve warm.

291 NUTTY BANANA SALSA

PREPARATION TIME *10 minutes* **COOKING TIME** *None* **SERVES 4**

½ small red onion, finely
   chopped, rinsed and
   dried
1 small garlic clove, finely
   chopped

zest and juice of 1 lime
dash of sweet chilli sauce
25g (1oz) unsweetened
   coconut flakes or
   shredded coconut

salt and freshly ground
   black pepper
3 bananas

1   Put the red onion, garlic, lime zest and juice, chilli sauce and coconut into a bowl. Stir together
    and season to taste.
2   Just before serving, dice the bananas and add to the bowl. After mixing, check the seasoning.
    Serve within 30 minutes.

292 FRESH PINEAPPLE AND MANGO SALSA

PREPARATION TIME *15 minutes, plus 1 hour chilling* **COOKING TIME** *None* **SERVES 6-8**

1 miniature pineapple,
   or ½ a large one
1 small, ripe but firm
   mango, peeled, pitted
   and finely chopped
1 red chilli, seeded and
   very finely chopped

2.5cm (1in) piece of fresh
   root ginger, finely grated
5 spring onions, finely
   chopped
1 tbsp chopped fresh mint
2½ tbsp lime juice
salt and freshly ground
   black pepper

1   Using a large, sharp knife, cut the top and bottom from the pineapple. Stand the pineapple on a
    board and, cut off the peel. Make sure all the "eyes" are removed. Cut the pineapple into quarters
    from top to bottom, then cut out the core. Chop the flesh finely and put into a bowl.
2   Add the remaining ingredients to the bowl and stir to combine. Chill for 1 hour before serving.

293 SPICED PEAR SALSA

PREPARATION TIME *15 minutes, plus 1 hour chilling* **COOKING TIME** *None* **SERVES 8**

grated zest and juice
 of 1 lime
1 tbsp ginger syrup
1 piece stem ginger in
 syrup, drained and finely
 chopped

2 large, ripe pears, about
 225g (8oz) each, cored
 and cut into 1cm (½in)
 cubes
2 dried pear halves,
 chopped
3 spring onions, chopped

1 red chilli, seeded and
 finely chopped
2.5cm (1in) piece fresh root
 ginger, grated
½ cucumber, peeled, seeded
 and chopped
2 tbsp chopped fresh mint

1   Stir together the lime zest and juice and the ginger syrup.
2   Put the remaining ingredients into a bowl. Pour over the lime mixture and stir all the ingredients
    together. Cover and chill for up to 1 hour.

294 SALSA VERDE

PREPARATION TIME *10 minutes* **COOKING TIME** *None* **SERVES 4-6**

2 garlic cloves, chopped
3 anchovy fillets, drained
 and chopped
leaves from a bunch of
 fresh flat-leaf parsley

15 fresh basil leaves
10 fresh mint leaves
1 tbsp capers, drained
2 tsp Dijon mustard

150ml (5fl oz) fruity olive oil
freshly ground black
 pepper

1   Put the garlic, anchovies, herbs, capers, mustard and a few tablespoons of the oil into a small
    blender or food processor.
2   Mix briefly to a smooth paste, then, with the motor running, slowly pour in the remaining oil
    to produce a consistency like a coarse, green mayonnaise. Season with black pepper.

295 MEXICAN TOMATO SALSA FRESCA

PREPARATION TIME *10 minutes* **COOKING TIME** *None* **SERVES 6-8**

6 vine-ripened tomatoes,
 seeded and finely
 chopped
1 green chilli, seeded and
 very finely chopped

2 garlic cloves, finely
 chopped
1 small red onion, finely
 chopped
1 tbsp lime juice

leaves from a small bunch
 of fresh coriander
2 tbsp olive oil
salt and freshly ground
 black pepper

1   Put the tomatoes, chilli, garlic, red onion, lime juice, coriander and olive oil into a bowl. Stir
    together and season to taste.
2   Cover and leave at room temperature for 30 minutes. Chill, if liked, before serving, or serve within
    30-60 minutes.

296 MANGO AND MINT SALSA

PREPARATION TIME *10 minutes* **COOKING TIME** *None* **SERVES 4**

175ml (6fl oz) yogurt
1 tsp curry paste
flesh from 1 mango, cubed

2 tbsp chopped fresh mint
 leaves

1 red chilli, seeded and
 finely chopped
salt

1 Beat the yogurt and curry paste together until the paste is evenly mixed, then stir in the
   remaining ingredients.

297 LYCHEE, GRAPE AND FRESH COCONUT SALSA

PREPARATION TIME *20 minutes, plus 1 hour chilling* **COOKING TIME** *None* **SERVES 4**

½ small coconut
115g (4oz) fresh lychees,
 peeled and pitted
175g (6oz) seedless green
 grapes, halved

1 tbsp shredded fresh basil
2.5cm (1in) piece fresh root
 ginger, grated
grated zest and juice of
 1 lime

½ tsp Thai fish sauce
1 tsp clear honey
dash of chilli sauce, to taste

1 Using a skewer or screwdriver, pierce the three coconut "eyes". Drain off the water and reserve
   for use in another recipe.
2 Put the coconut into a plastic bag, seal the end and put onto a firm floor or worktop. Using a
   hammer, hit the coconut firmly and hard to crack it open. Use a small, sturdy sharp knife to
   prise the flesh from the shell. If necessary, break the flesh into smaller pieces. Grate the flesh
   into a bowl. Use half the flesh in this recipe and save the rest for another use.
3 Add the lychees, grapes and basil and toss together.
4 Stir the ginger, lime zest and juice, fish sauce, honey and chilli sauce together. Pour over the
   salsa and toss to combine evenly. Cover and chill for 1 hour.

298 PROVENCAL SALSA

PREPARATION TIME *10 minutes* **COOKING TIME** *None* **SERVES 4**

25g (1oz) pitted oil-cured
  black olives, coarsely
  chopped
3 garlic cloves, crushed
  and chopped

50g (2oz) sun-dried
  tomatoes, sliced
50g (2oz) anchovy fillets,
  drained and chopped
juice of 2 lemons

75ml (3fl oz) virgin olive oil
4 tbsp chopped fresh basil
salt and freshly ground
  black pepper

1 Put all the ingredients into a bowl, being careful with additional salt, and stir together.

299 PINEAPPLE AND MACADAMIA NUT SALSA

PREPARATION TIME *15 minutes* **COOKING TIME** *None* **SERVES 4**

1 small pineapple
25g (1oz) macadamia nuts,
  chopped

1 red onion, finely chopped
1 garlic clove, finely
  chopped
1 tbsp light soy sauce

3 tbsp lime juice
freshly ground black
  pepper

1 Using a large, sharp knife, cut the top and bottom from the pineapple. Stand the pineapple on a
   board and, cut off the peel. Make sure all the "eyes" are removed. Cut the pineapple into quarters
   from top to bottom, then cut out the core. Chop the flesh finely and put into a bowl.
2 Add all the remaining ingredients to the bowl and toss together.

300 CORIANDER, LEMON GRASS AND COCONUT SAUCE

PREPARATION TIME *10 minutes* **COOKING TIME** *1 minute* **SERVES 4**

150g (5oz) creamed
  coconut, crumbled
300ml (½ pint) boiling water
2 tsp cumin seeds
1 red chilli, seeded
  and coarsely chopped

3 garlic cloves, coarsely
  chopped
½ tsp sea salt
1 stem lemon grass, outer
  layer removed, thinly
  sliced

2 tbsp lime juice
3 tbsp chopped fresh
  coriander
3 tbsp chopped fresh
  flat-leaf parsley

1 Put the creamed coconut in a bowl, pour on the boiling water and stir until smooth.
2 Heat a small, dry, heavy-based frying pan, add the cumin seeds and heat for about 10 seconds
   until fragrant. Tip into a small blender or food processor. Add the chilli, garlic, sea salt and lemon
   grass. Mix together, then add the creamed coconut liquid, lime juice, coriander and parsley.
   Process to a smooth paste.
3 Pour the sauce into a small saucepan and put on the side of the barbecue to warm through
   while the food is cooking.

301 TOMATO TARTARE SAUCE

PREPARATION TIME *15 minutes* **COOKING TIME** *5 minutes* **SERVES 4**

3 tbsp white wine vinegar
½ shallot, finely chopped
4 black peppercorns, lightly
  crushed
a few tarragon stalks,
  coarsely chopped

115ml (4fl oz) mayonnaise
  (see below)
1 tsp Dijon mustard
2 plum tomatoes, seeded
  and finely chopped

2 tbsp finely chopped
  pitted green olives
2 tbsp gherkins, finely
  chopped

1 Boil the vinegar in a small saucepan with the shallot, peppercorns and tarragon until the liquid has reduced to 1 teaspoon. Leave to cool.

2 Mix the mayonnaise and mustard together and strain the vinegar into the mustard mayonnaise. Stir in the remaining ingredients. Taste for seasoning.

302 BARBECUE SAUCE

PREPARATION TIME *10 minutes* **COOKING TIME** *5 minutes* **SERVES 4**

275ml (9½fl oz) Tomato
  Ketchup *(see page 184)*
175ml (6fl oz) cider vinegar
  or red wine vinegar
3 tbsp soy sauce
3 tbsp Worcestershire
  sauce

1 tbsp chilli powder
1 garlic clove, finely
  chopped
100g (3½oz) light brown
  sugar
1½ tbsp English mustard
  powder

¾ tbsp grated fresh root
  ginger
squeeze of lemon juice
salt and freshly ground
  black pepper

1 Put all the ingredients into a saucepan and bringing to the boil, stirring.

2 Simmer for 5 minutes, stirring frequently. Leave to cool.

303 MAYONNAISE

PREPARATION TIME *10 minutes* **COOKING TIME** *None* **SERVES 4-6**

2 egg yolks, at room
  temperature
1 tsp Dijon mustard, or
  to taste

2-3 tsp white wine vinegar
  or lemon juice
salt and freshly ground
  black pepper·

300ml (10fl oz) mild olive
  oil, at room temperature

1 Put the egg yolks, mustard, vinegar or lemon juice and a pinch of salt into a blender. Mix for about 10 seconds until blended, then, with the motor running, pour in the oil in a slow, steady stream until the mixture is thick and creamy.

2 Adjust the seasoning, levels of mustard and vinegar or lemon juice, if necessary. Store in a closed jar in the fridge for up to three days.

* **NOTE** Pregnant women, young children, the elderly and those with impaired immune systems should avoid eating raw eggs because of the potential risk of salmonella food poisoning.

304 SUN-DRIED TOMATO AND GARLIC MAYONNAISE

PREPARATION TIME *10 minutes* **COOKING TIME** *None* **SERVES 4**

2 egg yolks
4 garlic cloves, crushed
juice of ½ lemon, or to taste
250ml (8fl oz) olive oil

50ml (2fl oz) oil from the
   sun-dried tomatoes
8 sun-dried tomato halves
   in oil, drained and finely
   chopped

salt and freshly ground
   black pepper

1 Put the egg yolks, garlic and lemon juice into a blender or food processor. Mix briefly. With the
  motor running, slowly pour in the oils until the mixture forms a thick cream.
2 Transfer to a bowl, stir in the chopped sun-dried tomatoes and season to taste, adding a little
  more lemon juice, if necessary.

305 SALSA VERDE MAYONNAISE

PREPARATION TIME *10 minutes* **COOKING TIME** *None* **SERVES 4**

3 heaped tbsp flat-leaf
   parsley
1 heaped tbsp mint leaves
3 tbsp capers, drained and
   rinsed

6 anchovy fillets in oil,
   drained
1 garlic clove, peeled
6 tbsp mayonnaise
   (see page 179)

1 tsp Dijon mustard
1 tbsp lemon juice
salt

1 Coarsely chop the parsley, mint, capers, anchovies and garlic together.
2 Stir together with the mayonnaise, mustard, lemon juice and salt.

306 CORIANDER AND GINGER MAYONNAISE

PREPARATION TIME *10 minutes* **COOKING TIME** *None* **SERVES 4**

2 egg yolks
1 garlic clove, crushed
⅛ tsp Dijon mustard
1 tsp grated fresh root
 ginger

300ml (10fl oz) mixed
 groundnut oil and
 sunflower oil
2–3 tbsp rice wine vinegar

3 tbsp chopped fresh
 coriander
salt and freshly ground
 black pepper

1 Put the egg yolks, garlic, mustard and ginger into a blender or food processor. Mix briefly. With the motor running, slowly pour in the oils until the mixture forms a thick cream; slowly pour in the vinegar towards the end.

2 Transfer to a bowl, stir in the coriander and season, adding more rice vinegar if necessary.

307 CAJUN REMOULADE

PREPARATION TIME *5 minutes* **COOKING TIME** *None* **SERVES 6-8**

6 spring onions, chopped
2 anchovy fillets, chopped
2 tbsp fresh flat-leaf
 parsley
2 tbsp snipped fresh chives

1 red chilli, seeded and
 finely chopped
1 tbsp capers, chopped
3 tbsp tomato ketchup
 (see page 184)

1 tbsp Worcestershire
 sauce
1 tbsp Dijon mustard
juice of 1 lemon
550ml (1 pint) mayonnaise
 (see page 179)

1 Beat all the ingredients into the mayonnaise.

308 MEXICAN MARINADE

PREPARATION TIME *10 minutes* **COOKING TIME** *None* **SERVES 4**

2 garlic cloves, crushed
salt and freshly ground
 black pepper
2 tbsp tequila

2 tbsp olive oil
2 tsp paprika
1–2 tsp chilli powder
¾ tsp ground cumin

¾ tsp dried oregano
juice of 1½ limes

1 Mash the garlic to a paste with a pinch of salt. Combine with the remaining ingredients.

309 THAI-STYLE MARINADE

PREPARATION TIME *5 minutes* **COOKING TIME** *None* **SERVES 4**

2 garlic cloves, chopped
2.5cm (1in) piece of fresh
 root ginger, chopped
2 lemon grass stalks, outer
 leaves removed,
 chopped

juice of 2 small limes
1 red chilli, seeded and
 chopped
150ml (5fl oz) coconut milk
1–2 tbsp soft brown sugar

2 tbsp chopped fresh
 coriander

1 Put all the ingredients into a blender or food processor and mix to a purée.

310 NORTH AFRICAN MARINADE

PREPARATION TIME *5 minutes* **COOKING TIME** *None* **SERVES 4**

1 tsp ground cumin
1 tsp ground coriander

1 tsp ground ginger
1 tsp paprika

pinch of chilli powder
sunflower oil

1   Combine the spices, then mix with enough oil to make a paste.

311 HARISSA MARINADE

PREPARATION TIME *5 minutes* **COOKING TIME** *None* **SERVES 4**

3 tbsp olive oil
2 tbsp lemon juice
1 tsp harissa paste

1 garlic clove, finely
    chopped
1½ tsp pimenton (smoked
    paprika)

1 tsp ground cardamom
1 tsp ground cumin

1   Put all the ingredients into a bowl and stir together until evenly blended.

312 TANDOORI MARINADE

PREPARATION TIME *5 minutes* **COOKING TIME** *None* **SERVES 6**

1 onion, coarsely chopped
4 large garlic cloves,
    chopped
25g (1oz) fresh root ginger,
    chopped
4 tbsp groundnut oil

4 tbsp lemon juice
225ml (8fl oz) yogurt
1 tbsp ground turmeric
1 tbsp ground coriander
1 tsp ground cumin
½ tsp ground cinnamon

½ tsp nutmeg
½ tsp freshly ground black
    pepper
¼ tsp ground cloves
¼ tsp ground chillies

1   Put the onion, garlic and ginger into a blender and process until reduced to a paste.
2   Add the remaining ingredients and mix until smooth.

313 COCONUT, LIME AND PINEAPPLE MARINADE

PREPARATION TIME *10 minutes* **COOKING TIME** *None* **SERVES 4**

200ml (7fl oz) coconut milk
flesh from ½ lime, chopped

¼ pineapple, peeled and
    chopped

1 tbsp Tabasco sauce
salt

1   Pour the coconut milk into a small blender. Add the remaining ingredients and mix together until evenly blended.

314 LEMON AND DILL MARINADE

PREPARATION TIME *10 minutes* **COOKING TIME** *None* **SERVES 4**

175ml (6fl oz) grapeseed oil
grated zest and juice of
   1 small lemon

2 tbsp chopped fresh dill
salt and freshly ground
   black pepper

1   Put all the ingredients into a bowl and whisk together.

315 GINGER AND CORIANDER MARINADE

PREPARATION TIME *5 minutes* **COOKING TIME** *None* **SERVES 4**

1cm (½in) piece of fresh root
   ginger, grated
2 tbsp chopped fresh
   coriander

1 garlic clove, crushed
1 tbsp groundnut oil
1 tbsp rice wine vinegar
½ tsp turmeric

½ tsp sweet chilli sauce

1   Put all the ingredients into bowl. Add 1 tablespoon of water and stir everything together.

316 TAMARIND MARINADE

PREPARATION TIME *10 minutes* **COOKING TIME** *10 minutes* **SERVES 4**

2 walnut-sized lumps of
   tamarind, soaked and
   squeezed
3 garlic cloves, crushed
2.5cm (1in) piece of fresh
   root ginger, chopped

2 lemon grass stalks, outer
   leaves removed,
   chopped
4 lime leaves, sliced
2 shallots, chopped

2 chillies, seeded and
   chopped
2 tbsp groundnut oil
salt and freshly ground
   black pepper

1   Put all the ingredients into a blender or food processor and mix to a purée.
2   Transfer to a small frying pan and cook, stirring frequently, for about 10 minutes. Spoon into a bowl and leave to cool.

317 ROUILLE

PREPARATION TIME *10 minutes* **COOKING TIME** *None* **MAKES** *about 550ml (1 pint)*

2 large egg yolks
5 garlic cloves, crushed
2 tbsp chopped red pepper
1 tbsp lemon juice
1 tsp Dijon mustard

1 tsp tomato purée
1 tsp paprika
pinch of cayenne pepper
375ml (13fl oz) virgin
   olive oil

85ml (3fl oz) extra virgin
   olive oil
salt

1   Put the egg yolks, garlic, red pepper, lemon juice, mustard, tomato purée, paprika and cayenne into a blender. Mix together, then, with the motor running, add 1 tablespoon of oil. When this is incorporated, slowly pour in the remaining oils.
2   Add salt to taste, and any other flavourings you feel need boosting. Store, covered, in the fridge for up to 1 week.

318 HOME-MADE TOMATO KETCHUP

PREPARATION TIME *10 minutes* **COOKING TIME** *20-30 minutes* **MAKES** *700ml (1¼ pints)*

1.5kg (3lb) tomatoes, chopped
1 fleshy red pepper, sliced
2 red onions, chopped
½ tsp paprika
175ml (6fl oz) spiced red wine vinegar*

1 Put the tomatoes, red pepper, red onion and paprika into a saucepan with the vinegar. Simmer until thick, stirring occasionally.
2 Press through a nylon or plastic sieve, return the juice to the rinsed pan and boil vigorously until thick. Pour into warmed, very clean jars, cover and leave to cool. Store in the fridge or other cold, dark place for up to 3 months.
* To make the spiced red wine vinegar, bring 1 teaspoon celery seeds, 1 small mace blade and 1 teaspoon black peppercorns to the boil in the vinegar, then cover and leave to marinate for a day before straining and using.

319 MANGO DRESSING

PREPARATION TIME *10 minutes* **COOKING TIME** *None* **SERVES 4**

1 very ripe mango
1 tbsp white wine vinegar
1 tbsp Dijon mustard
1 tbsp clear honey
125ml (4fl oz) virgin olive oil
Tabasco sauce
salt and freshly ground black pepper

1 Put the mango flesh into a blender or food processor. Add the vinegar, mustard and honey. Mix briefly then, with the motor running, slowly pour in the olive oil until evenly mixed.
2 Add a few drops of Tabasco, season to taste, then cover and chill until required.

320 SMOKY BARBECUE RELISH

PREPARATION TIME *10 minutes* **COOKING TIME** *35 minutes* **SERVES 4**

3 tbsp olive oil
2 large onions, finely chopped
1 red chilli, seeded and finely chopped
600g (1lb 5oz) ripe tomatoes, coarsely chopped
4 tbsp maple syrup
3 tbsp smoky barbecue sauce, or to taste
2 tbsp sherry vinegar
2 corn on the cob
salt and freshly ground black pepper

1 Heat the oil in a heavy-based pan and fry the onions and chilli gently until soft and pale brown, stirring occasionally.
2 Increase the heat and add the tomatoes, maple syrup, barbecue sauce and vinegar. Heat until bubbling, then adjust the heat so the sauce simmers, and cook for about 25 minutes until thick, stirring occasionally.
3 Meanwhile, cut the kernels from the corn and dry-fry in a large heavy-based frying pan for about 5 minutes until speckled with brown. Stir into the relish and season to taste.

321 TOASTED CORN AND ROASTED RED PEPPER RELISH

PREPARATION TIME *10 minutes* **COOKING TIME** *10 minutes* **SERVES 4**

1 corn on the cob	1 small red onion, finely	3–4 tsp finely chopped
1 red pepper, roasted,	diced	fresh sage
peeled and diced *(see*	2 tbsp lime juice	salt and freshly ground
page 173)	2 tbsp olive oil	black pepper

1 Preheat a heavy, dry ridged cast-iron grill pan and toast the corn on the cob for about 10 minutes until nicely charred, turning frequently. Leave to cool.

2 Using a large, heavy knife, slice off the sweetcorn kernels and put into a bowl. Stir in the red pepper, red onion, lime juice, olive oil and sage, and season to taste. Cover and chill until required.

322 RED PEPPER, BLACK OLIVE AND CAPER RELISH

PREPARATION TIME *10 minutes* **COOKING TIME** *10 minutes* **SERVES 4**

3 red peppers	60g (2½oz) capers (in	2½ tbsp coarsely chopped
150g (5oz) pitted oil-cured	balsamic vinegar),	fresh flat-leaf parsley
kalamata olives,	coarsely chopped	2 tbsp olive oil
chopped	2½ tbsp coarsely chopped	salt and freshly ground
	fresh basil	black pepper

1 Preheat the grill. Grill the peppers, turning frequently, until the skins char and blister. Leave until cool enough to handle, then peel off and discard the skins, seeds and core. Chop the flesh.

2 Mix the pepper flesh with the olives, capers, herbs and oil. Season to taste, then cover and chill until required.

323 SPICED SWEET MUSTARD RUB

PREPARATION TIME *10 minutes* **COOKING TIME** *None* **SERVES 4**

2 tbsp wholegrain mustard	1 tsp Sichuan peppercorns,	2 tbsp chopped fresh
2 garlic cloves, finely	toasted and finely	coriander
chopped	crushed	2 tbsp pomegranate
grated zest and juice of	1 tsp dried oregano	molasses
½ lemon		

1 Put all the ingredients into a bowl. Stir everything together to make a light paste.

324 PAPRIKA SPICE RUB
PREPARATION TIME *5 minutes* **COOKING TIME** *2 minutes* **SERVES 5–6**

20g (½oz) paprika	2 tsp chilli powder	¼ tsp ground cinnamon
1 tbsp ground cumin	¼ tsp ground red pepper	small pinch of salt

1 Place a heavy non-stick frying pan over a medium heat.
2 Add all the ingredients and stir together for 2 minutes.

325 TEXAN SPICE RUB
PREPARATION TIME *5 minutes* **COOKING TIME** *None* **SERVES 6**

1 tsp black mustard seeds	1 tsp paprika	½ tsp ground cumin
1 garlic clove, peeled	2 tsp chilli powder	
2 tsp salt	½ tsp ground coriander	

1 Crush the mustard seeds, garlic and salt to a paste with a pestle and mortar, or put into a small bowl and use the end of a rolling pin.
2 Add the remaining ingredients and combine thoroughly.

326 LEMON AND HERB RUB
PREPARATION TIME *5 minutes* **COOKING TIME** *None* **SERVES 6**

grated zest of 1 lemon	1 tsp dried basil	freshly ground black
3 garlic cloves, peeled	½ tsp dried thyme	pepper
small pinch of salt	2 tsp dried rosemary	

1 Crush the lemon zest, garlic and salt together with a pestle and mortar, or put into a small bowl and use the end of a rolling pin.
2 Finely chop the basil, thyme and rosemary together. Combine with the lemon zest mixture and season with pepper.

327 SWEET SPICED RUB
PREPARATION TIME *5 minutes* **COOKING TIME** *None* **SERVES 6**

1 tbsp soft brown sugar	2 tsp freshly ground black	1 tsp mustard powder
2 tsp chilli powder	pepper	1 tsp ground cumin
	1 tsp cayenne pepper	1 tsp garlic salt

1 Put all the ingredients into a bowl and stir them together thoroughly.

328 GINGER AND ORANGE BUTTER

PREPARATION TIME *10 minutes* **COOKING TIME** *None* **SERVES 8**

115g (4oz) unsalted butter,
  softened
1 tbsp grated fresh root
  ginger

1 tbsp orange juice
1 tbsp orange zest
salt and freshly ground
  black pepper

1 Beat the butter until softened, then add the remaining ingredients and mix everything together
   until evenly blended.
2 Spoon the flavoured butter onto a sheet of clingfilm or non-stick baking parchment. Using the
   clingfilm or parchment, shape the butter into a roll about 4cm (1½in) in diameter. Wrap tightly
   and chill until required. Cut into slices to serve. Alternatively, pack the butter into ramekin dishes.

329 BLACK OLIVE, CAPER AND ANCHOVY BUTTER

PREPARATION TIME *10 minutes* **COOKING TIME** *None* **SERVES 8**

100g (3½oz) unsalted
  butter
10 oil-cured black olives,
  finely chopped

6 capers, drained and
  finely chopped
3 anchovy fillets,
  finely chopped

freshly ground black
  pepper

1 Beat the butter until softened, then add the remaining ingredients and mix everything together
   until evenly blended.
2 Spoon the flavoured butter onto a sheet of clingfilm or non-stick baking parchment. Using the
   clingfilm or parchment, shape the butter into a roll about 4cm (1½in) in diameter. Wrap tightly
   and chill until required. Cut into slices to serve. Alternatively, pack the butter into ramekin dishes.

330 ROASTED CHILLI BUTTER

PREPARATION TIME *10 minutes* **COOKING TIME** *10–15 minutes* **SERVES 8**

2 large red chillies
1 tbsp olive oil
115g (4oz) unsalted butter

½ tbsp chopped fresh
  parsley
salt

1 Preheat the oven to 230ºC/450ºF/Gas 8. Brush the chillies with the oil and lay in a single
   layer in a small roasting tin. Roast for 10–15 minutes until the skin is charred and blistered,
   turning halfway. Leave to cool, then scrape out and discard the seeds and finely chop the flesh.
2 Beat the butter until softened, then add the remaining ingredients and the chilli, and mix
   everything together until evenly blended.
3 Spoon the flavoured butter onto a sheet of clingfilm or non-stick baking parchment. Using the
   clingfilm or parchment, shape the butter into a roll about 4cm (1½in) in diameter. Wrap tightly
   and chill until required. Cut into slices to serve. Alternatively, pack the butter into ramekin dishes.

331 PARSLEY AND CHIVE BUTTER

PREPARATION TIME *10 minutes* **COOKING TIME** *None* **SERVES 8**

115g (4oz) unsalted butter
2 tbsp chopped fresh
  parsley

2 tbsp snipped fresh chives
2 tbsp lemon juice
zest of 1 lemon

salt and freshly ground
  black pepper

1   Beat the butter until softened, then add the remaining ingredients and mix everything together until evenly blended.
2   Spoon the flavoured butter onto a sheet of clingfilm or non-stick baking parchment. Using the clingfilm or parchment, shape the butter into a roll about 4cm (1½in) in diameter. Wrap tightly and chill until required. Cut into slices to serve. Alternatively, pack the butter into ramekin dishes.

332 BASIL AND SUN-DRIED TOMATO BUTTER

PREPARATION TIME *10 minutes* **COOKING TIME** *None* **SERVES 8**

115g (4oz) unsalted butter
3 tbsp coarsely chopped
  fresh basil

3 sun-dried tomatoes in oil,
  drained and chopped

salt and freshly ground
  black pepper

1   Beat the butter until softened, then add the remaining ingredients and mix everything together until evenly blended.
2   Spoon the flavoured butter onto a sheet of clingfilm or non-stick baking parchment. Using the clingfilm or parchment, shape the butter into a roll about 4cm (1½in) in diameter. Wrap tightly and chill until required. Cut into slices to serve. Alternatively, pack the butter into ramekin dishes.

333 GINGER AND MINT BUTTER

PREPARATION TIME *10 minutes* **COOKING TIME** *None* **SERVES 8**

115g (4oz) unsalted butter
2 tbsp chopped fresh mint

1 tbsp grated fresh root
  ginger

salt and freshly ground
  black pepper

1 Beat the butter until softened, then add the remaining ingredients and mix everything together until evenly blended.
2 Spoon the flavoured butter onto a sheet of clingfilm or non-stick baking parchment. Using the clingfilm or parchment, shape the butter into a roll about 4cm (1½in) in diameter. Wrap tightly and chill until required. Cut into slices to serve. Alternatively, pack the butter into ramekin dishes.

334 JAMAICAN SPICED BASTE

PREPARATION TIME *10 minutes* **COOKING TIME** *none* **SERVES 4**

2 garlic cloves, chopped
salt and freshly ground
  black pepper

1 tsp ground allspice
2 small red chillies, seeded
  and finely chopped

2 tbsp dark rum
2 tbsp tomato ketchup *(see page 184)*

1 Combine the ingredients together thoroughly.

335 JAMAICAN JERK SEASONING

PREPARATION TIME *5 minutes* **COOKING TIME** *None* **SERVES 4**

5 red chillies, seeded and
  chopped
2 spring onions, chopped
1 tbsp dried thyme
1 tbsp dried basil

2 tbsp orange juice
2 tbsp white wine vinegar
1 tbsp yellow mustard
  seeds
1 tsp ground allspice

1 tsp ground cloves
salt and freshly ground
  black pepper

1 Put all the ingredients into a blender and mix to a thick sauce. If necessary, add a little more orange juice or vinegar to obtain the right consistency.

336 CHIMICHURRI

PREPARATION TIME *10 minutes, plus 3 hours marinating* **COOKING TIME** *None* **SERVES 4**

115ml (4fl oz) olive oil
50ml (2fl oz) red wine
  vinegar
1 small red onion, finely
  chopped

3 garlic cloves, finely
  chopped
1 tsp dried oregano
10g (¼oz) chopped mixed
  fresh parsley and
  coriander

dash of Tabasco sauce
salt and freshly ground
  black pepper

1 Whisk the oil with the vinegar until emulsified. Stir in the remaining ingredients. Cover and leave the marinade for at least 3 hours before using, or cover and refrigerate for up to 2 days.

DESSERTS

Barbecued desserts are the most appropriate and delicious way to end your meal. Some people might be surprised at the variety of desserts that can be cooked on a grill rack and if the grill rack is covered, the range is even greater.

Choose fruits that are ripe but not too soft, and remove them from the grill rack before they overcook. Tropical fruits such as pineapple and mango are always popular, but there are many others that work equally well: pears, peaches, bananas cooked in their skins – all become wonderful treats when served sizzling and lightly caramelised from a grill rack. Add some spices, either simply sprinkled on or in a marinade, baste or butter, and they become exotic.

Individual fruits or combinations can be enclosed in foil parcels and cooked on the grill rack. This is particularly good for fragile items such as strawberries and raspberries and for fruits that are too ripe and soft to be cooked directly on the grill rack. Slices of sweet breads and cakes also grill well, and provide bases for the fruit, making more substantial desserts.

Clean any particles of savoury food off the grill rack before cooking desserts on it. If possible, cook the fruit on an oiled fine mesh grill rack or in an oiled hinged grill basket, for ease of turning and lifting.

CHAPTER 8

337 BAKED APPLES

PREPARATION TIME *10 minutes* **COOKING TIME** *30-40 minutes* **SERVES 4**

4 large dessert apples, such
  as Braeburn
40g (1½oz) caster sugar
1 tsp ground cinnamon
50g (2oz) marzipan,
  chopped

25g (1oz) blanched
  almonds, chopped
50g (2oz) dried mango,
  chopped
knob unsalted butter,
  chopped

Greek yogurt or vanilla ice
  cream, to serve

1 Keeping the apples intact, remove the cores.
2 Using the point of a small sharp knife, cut an incision about 2cm (¾in) deep around the
   circumference of each apple. Place each one on a piece of double-thickness foil large enough to
   enclose it.
3 Mix the sugar with the cinnamon, then add the marzipan, almonds and mango and use to fill the
   centres of the apples. Add a small piece of butter to the top and fold the foil loosely around the
   apples. Twist the edges together firmly to seal tightly.
4 Place on the very edge of the barbecue for 30-40 minutes. Serve with Greek yogurt or vanilla
   ice cream.

338 STUFFED PEACHES

PREPARATION TIME *10 minutes* **COOKING TIME** *8-10 minutes* **SERVES 4**

25g (1oz) amaretti biscuits,
  fairly finely crushed
50g (2oz) Madeira cake,
  crumbed

4 tbsp amaretto liqueur
4 ripe but firm large
  peaches, halved and
  pitted

8 tbsp orange juice
25g (1oz) flaked almonds,
  toasted

1 Mix together the amaretti biscuits, cake crumbs and 2 tablespoons of amaretto. Divide among
   the hollows in the peaches.
2 Combine the remaining amaretto with the orange juice.
3 Put two peach halves on a piece of foil that is large enough to enclose them. Fold up the sides
   of the foil. Sprinkle one quarter of the nuts over the filling. Pour one quarter of the orange juice
   mixture over. Fold the foil loosely over the peaches and pleat the sides together to make a secure
   parcel. Repeat with the remaining peach halves.
4 Cook on a grill rack for 8-10 minutes until the peaches have softened and warmed through.

339 HONEYED APRICOT KEBABS WITH LEMON TZATZIKI

PREPARATION TIME *10 minutes* **COOKING TIME** *5–7 minutes* **SERVES 4**

2 lemons
8 ripe but not too soft
  apricots, quartered and
  chilled

12 small bay leaves
200ml (7fl oz) Greek yogurt,
  chilled
4 tbsp clear honey

1 Grate the zest and squeeze the juice from one lemon. Cut the other lemon into about 12 pieces and thread the pieces alternately with the apricot quarters and bay leaves onto skewers, beginning and ending with an apricot quarter.
2 To make the tzatziki, combine the lemon zest with the yogurt and chill until required.
3 Melt the honey with the lemon juice in a small pan, and bubble for 3–4 minutes until reduced by about half. Brush the kebabs with some of the hot honey mixture and cook on an oiled grill rack for 2–3 minutes, turning once, until the edges of the apricots begin to caramelise.
4 Serve with the remaining honey mixture trickled over and accompanied by the lemon tzatziki.

340 CARAMELISED APPLES WITH BRIOCHE TOASTS

PREPARATION TIME *10 minutes* **COOKING TIME** *4–5 minutes* **SERVES 4**

4 dessert apples, cored
  and thickly sliced
juice of 1 lime
2 tbsp caster sugar

1 tsp ground cinnamon
4 tbsp unsalted butter,
  melted
4 thick slices brioche

Greek yogurt, to serve

1 Sprinkle the cut surfaces of apple with lime juice.
2 Stir the sugar and cinnamon together and stir half of the mixture into the warm butter until the sugar has dissolved. Brush over the brioche and apple slices.
3 Cook the apples on an oiled grill rack for 4–5 minutes, turning once, until browned. Add the brioche slices to the side of the grill rack a couple of minutes later and keep an eye on them as they can burn easily.
4 Remove the brioche slices to plates. Cut the apples into halves or quarters and put onto the brioche slices. Sprinkle with the remaining sugar and cinnamon. Serve with Greek yogurt.

341 FRUIT KEBABS WITH HONEY, ORANGE AND PECAN SAUCE

PREPARATION TIME *10 minutes* **COOKING TIME** *6-8 minutes* **SERVES 4**

2 apples, cored and cut into wedges

2 pears, cored and cut into wedges

6 plums, pitted and cut into wedges

single cream, to serve

HONEY, ORANGE AND PECAN SAUCE

1 orange

2 tbsp clear honey

50g (2oz) unsalted butter

1 tbsp icing sugar

5cm (2in) rosemary sprig

50g (2oz) shelled pecans

1 Make the sauce by paring the zest from the orange and cutting it into fine shreds. Blanch the shreds in boiling water for 1 minute. Drain and repeat once more. Set aside.

2 Squeeze the juice from the orange and pour into a small saucepan with the honey, butter and icing sugar. Add the rosemary and heat gently for 5 minutes, stirring until evenly mixed.

3 Thread the fruits alternately onto skewers. Brush the fruit with the honey mixture and cook on an oiled grill rack until sizzling and lightly browned.

4 Meanwhile, discard the rosemary from the sauce, add the pecans and reheat.

5 Transfer the kebabs to plates, pour some of the sauce around them and sprinkle over the blanched orange zest shreds. Serve with single cream.

342 PAPAYA, PEAR, ORANGE AND GINGER BROCHETTES

PREPARATION TIME *15 minutes* **COOKING TIME** *15 minutes* **SERVES 4**

3 small oranges

flesh from 1 ripe but firm papaya, cut into 2.5cm (1in) cubes

flesh from 1 ripe but firm (unpeeled) pear, cut into 2.5cm (1in) cubes

18 slices of crystallised ginger

25g (1oz) unsalted butter, chopped

1 tbsp soft brown sugar

4 tbsp ginger wine, or syrup from the ginger jar

1 Cut a slice from each end of the oranges. Stand each orange in turn upright on a plate (to catch any juice) and slice off all the skin and pith. Cut across each orange to make six slices, then cut each slice in half.

2 Thread the papaya, pear, orange and ginger alternately onto eight parallel pairs of soaked bamboo skewers (see page 10) that are spaced slightly apart.

3 Heat the butter, sugar and ginger wine or syrup in a small saucepan over a low heat, stirring occasionally, until smooth. Remove from the heat, cool slightly then brush over the fruits.

4 Cook the brochettes on an oiled grill rack for about 10 minutes, turning once and brushing with any remaining butter mixture.

343 PAPAYA WITH CHILLI LIME SYRUP

PREPARATION TIME *5 minutes* **COOKING TIME** *10 minutes* **SERVES 4**

8 tbsp light soft brown sugar	**zest of 2 limes, cut into fine strips**	**2 papayas**
1 red chilli, seeded and cut into thin strips	**juice of 2 limes**	

1 Make the syrup by putting the sugar, chilli, and 200ml (7fl oz) water in a saucepan and bringing to the boil. Reduce the heat and simmer for 5 minutes to make a syrup. Add the lime zest and juice and pour into a jug.

2 Cut the papayas into thin wedges, brush with some of the syrup and cook on an oiled grill rack for about 4 minutes until lightly caramelised. Serve with the remaining syrup.

344 SEARED CINNAMON-GLAZED PEACHES

PREPARATION TIME *5 minutes* **COOKING TIME** *8 minutes* **SERVES 4**

2 tbsp soft light brown
    sugar
2 tsp ground cinnamon

4 large ripe but firm
    peaches, halved and
    pitted

vanilla ice cream, to serve

1 Combine the brown sugar and cinnamon and sprinkle over the peaches.
2 Cook, cut side down, on an oiled grill rack for about 8 minutes until lightly charred but still firm.
   Serve with vanilla ice cream

345 KIWI, PINEAPPLE AND BANANA WITH VANILLA MASCARPONE DIP

PREPARATION TIME *10 minutes* **COOKING TIME** *10 minutes* **SERVES 6**

1 small pineapple, cut into
    even wedges, skin and
    leafy tops left intact
3 bananas, halved, skin
    left intact

6 kiwi fruit, quartered
    lengthwise, skin left on
icing sugar, for sprinkling

VANILLA MASCARPONE DIP
1 vanilla pod, split
    lengthwise
225g (8oz) mascarpone,
    chilled
icing sugar, to taste

1 Make the dip by scraping the seeds from the vanilla pod into the mascarpone. Stir well, then add
   icing sugar to taste. Chill until required.
2 Remove the fibrous core from the pineapple wedges. Sprinkle all the fruit lightly with icing sugar.
3 Place the fruit on an oiled grill and cook for about 10 minutes, turning a couple of times, until
   lightly caramelised. Remove the bananas from their skins and serve the warm fruits with the dip.

346 GRILLED FIGS WITH BITTER CHOCOLATE AND PISTACHIOS

PREPARATION TIME *10 minutes* **COOKING TIME** *5–8 minutes* **SERVES 3–6**

6 ripe but not too soft, large
    black figs
100g (3½oz) plain chocolate
    with at least 70% cocoa
    solids, chopped

1 tsp unsalted butter
115–150ml (4–5fl oz) vanilla
    cream *(see page 200)*
1 tbsp pistachio nuts,
    coarsely chopped

1 Cut the figs into quarters from top to bottom without going all the way through.
2 Grill the figs on the barbecue for 5–8 minutes until heated through but not too soft.
3 Meanwhile, melt the chocolate and butter with 2 tablespoons of hot water in a small bowl placed
   over a small pan of hot water, beating to make a smooth sauce.
4 Remove the figs from the grill rack. Put a spoonful of the vanilla cream into the centre. Trickle
   over some of the sauce. Sprinkle with pistachio nuts and serve.

347 PEARS WITH CHOCOLATE SAUCE

PREPARATION TIME *5 minutes* **COOKING TIME** *12–15 minutes* **SERVES 4**

4 ripe but firm pears	CHOCOLATE SAUCE	**50g (2oz) cocoa powder**
	75g (3oz) good-quality	**25g (1oz) caster sugar,**
	plain chocolate (at least	**or to taste**
	70% cocoa solids),	**150ml (5fl oz) boiling water**
	chopped	

1 Make the sauce by melting the chocolate in 115ml (4fl oz) of the boiling water in a small bowl placed over a saucepan of hot water. Stir regularly until smooth.

2 Dissolve the cocoa powder and sugar in the remaining boiling water, then pour into the melted chocolate, stirring. Set aside.

3 Cut the pears into quarters lengthways and remove the cores. Cook on an oiled grill rack (in an oiled hinged grilling basket for ease of turning) for about 4 minutes on each side until warmed, slightly softened and lightly charred.

4 Meanwhile, warm the bowl of sauce over a saucepan of hot water on the side of the grill rack. Serve the pears with the warm sauce poured over.

348 NECTARINES WITH CARAMEL ORANGE SAUCE

PREPARATION TIME *10 minutes* **COOKING TIME** *15 minutes* **SERVES 4**

4 ripe but firm nectarines,	CARAMEL ORANGE SAUCE	**zest and juice of 1 orange**
halved and pitted	**115g (4oz) granulated**	**50ml (2fl oz) single cream**
icing sugar, for sprinkling	**sugar**	

1 Make the sauce by putting the sugar and orange zest into a heavy-bottomed saucepan. Add 2 tablespoons of water and heat gently, stirring until the sugar has dissolved. Increase the heat and boil for 4–5 minutes until the sauce becomes a golden caramel colour. Immediately remove from the heat and whisk in the cream and orange juice; take care because it might splutter. Return the pan to a low heat and cook, stirring until the sauce is smooth.

2 Sprinkle icing sugar over the cut side of the nectarines, then place them cut-side down towards the side of the grill rack for 5 minutes until warm and lightly charred but still firm.

3 Meanwhile, warm the sauce on the side of the grill rack. Serve the nectarines with the sauce.

349 CARAMEL ORANGES

PREPARATION TIME *15 minutes* **COOKING TIME** *12–14 minutes* **SERVES 4**

4 large oranges	2 tbsp Orange Nassau,	vanilla ice cream, to serve
melted unsalted butter,	Cointreau, Grand Marnier	
for brushing	or other orange liqueur	
1–2 tbsp brown sugar		

1 Working over a bowl to catch any juice, carefully cut away all the orange skin and white pith. Reserve some of the skin. Cut across each orange to make six slices.

2 Remove the pith from the peel, then cut the peel into very fine shreds. Blanch these in boiling water for 2–3 minutes. Drain and dry.

3 Cut four double-thickness squares of foil that are large enough to wrap loosely around an orange. Butter the centre of each square thoroughly with unsalted butter.

4 Divide the slices among well-buttered foil. Fold up the sides of the foil. Divide the orange juice from the bowl, the sugar and liqueur among the oranges, then twist the edges of the foil firmly together to make roomy but tightly sealed parcels.

5 Cook the parcels of oranges on the side of the barbecue for about 10 minutes.

6 Carefully transfer the cooked parcels to serving plates and open up the foil. Add a scoop of vanilla ice cream.

350 GRILLED MANGO WITH LIME SYRUP

PREPARATION TIME *10 minutes* **COOKING TIME** *5 minutes* **SERVES 4**

2 mangoes, peeled, pitted and thickly sliced	**2 tbsp caster sugar**	**chilled crème fraîche, to serve**
2 tbsp lime cordial	**pinch of ground ginger**	

1 Cook the mango slices on an oiled grill rack for 3–4 minutes on each side.
2 Meanwhile, put the lime cordial, sugar and ginger into a small pan and heat gently on the side of the grill rack, stirring until the sugar has dissolved.
3 Remove the mango from the grill rack, trickle over the syrup and serve with chilled crème frâiche.

351 SEARED PEARS WITH CARDAMOM BUTTER

PREPARATION TIME *15 minutes* **COOKING TIME** *8–12 minutes* **SERVES 4**

4 ripe but firm pears, cored and thickly sliced	CARDAMOM BUTTER:	**seeds from 3 cardamom pods, crushed**
caster sugar or brown sugar, for sprinkling	**75g (3oz) unsalted butter, diced**	
	1½ tsp lemon juice	

1 Make the cardamom butter by melting the butter with the lemon juice and cardamom seeds in a small saucepan.
2 Brush the pears with some of the butter and sprinkle with sugar.
3 Cook the slices on an oiled fine mesh grill, in an oiled hinged grill basket, or on an oiled grill rack, turning occasionally and brushing with the butter, for 4–6 minutes on each side until softening and beginning to caramelise. Serve the pears with any remaining butter spooned over.

352 PLUMS WITH CINNAMON CREAM

PREPARATION TIME *10 minutes* **COOKING TIME** *5 minutes* **SERVES 4**

8 large, ripe but not too soft plums, halved and pitted	CINNAMON CREAM
1 tbsp clear honey, warmed slightly	**225ml (8fl oz) double cream**
	½ tsp ground cinnamon
	1 tbsp icing sugar

1 Make the cinnamon cream by whipping the cream to the soft peak stage. Combine the cinnamon with the sugar and fold into the cream. Cover and chill until required.
2 Thread the plum halves onto bamboo skewers that have been soaked in water for 30 minutes. Brush the plums with the honey and cook on an oiled grill rack for about 5 minutes, turning once, until warmed and just softened.
3 Remove from the grill rack and serve with the cinnamon cream.

353 STRAWBERRY AND BROWNIE KEBABS WITH VANILLA CREAM

PREPARATION TIME *10 minutes* **COOKING TIME** *3 minutes* **SERVES 4**

1-2 tbsp vanilla sugar,
  or to taste*
150ml (5fl oz) whipping
  cream

8 large ripe but still firm
  strawberries, hulled
8 chocolate brownies,
  3cm (1¼in) square

1 Whip the vanilla sugar into the cream until soft peaks form. Chill.
2 Thread the strawberries and brownie squares alternately onto skewers. Cook on an oiled grill rack for about 3 minutes, turning once or twice. Serve with the vanilla whipped cream.
* To make vanilla sugar, simply insert a vanilla pod into a jar of caster sugar and leave for 2 weeks before using. The jar can be topped up with more sugar as it empties.

354 FIGS WITH GOATS' CHEESE, HONEY AND THYME

PREPARATION TIME *10 minutes* **COOKING TIME** *5-6 minutes* **SERVES 4**

12 ripe but not too soft figs,
  halved lengthwise

8 tbsp soft mild goats'
  cheese

fresh thyme, for sprinkling
4 tbsp clear honey

1 Spread each fig half with goats' cheese. Sprinkle lightly with thyme and trickle over the honey.
2 Cook the figs on an oiled grill rack over low heat for about 5-6 minutes until soft.

355 GRILLED PLUM BRUSCHETTAS

PREPARATION TIME *10 minutes* **COOKING TIME** *10 minutes* **SERVES 4**

8-10 ripe but firm plums,
  quartered and pitted
1 vanilla pod, split

2 tbsp kirsch
2 tbsp sugar
4 slices brioche

chilled mascarpone,
  to serve

1 Put the plums on a large square of buttered foil. Add the vanilla pod, kirsch and sugar. Fold up the foil to make a parcel and twist the edges together to seal. Put the parcel on the grill rack for 10 minutes.
2 Meanwhile, cook the brioche slices on the grill rack until nicely browned on both sides.
3 Spread the mascarpone thickly over the toasted brioche. Pile the fruit on top and trickle over the juices from the foil parcel. Serve immediately.

356 FRUIT BROCHETTES WITH PEAR SAUCE

PREPARATION TIME *15 minutes, plus 30 minutes soaking* **COOKING TIME** *5 minutes* **SERVES 6**

6 large ripe lychees, peeled, pitted and halved
flesh from 1 baby pineapple, or 2 thick slices, cubed
3 large figs, quartered

1 tbsp dark clear honey, warmed slightly

PEAR SAUCE
150g (5oz) ready-to-eat dried pears
1 tsp grated fresh root ginger

½ tsp ground cinnamon, plus extra for dusting
juice of 1 orange
½ tsp vanilla extract
50ml (2fl oz) yogurt
1 tsp dark clear honey

1   Make the sauce by just covering the pears with hot water and leaving to soak for 30 minutes.
2   Drain the pears, reserving 50ml (2fl oz) of the liquid. Put the liquid and pears into a food processor or blender. Add the ginger, cinnamon, orange juice, vanilla extract and yogurt, and mix until smooth. Pour into a bowl and chill until required.
3   Thread the fruit alternately onto skewers and trickle over the warmed honey. Cook on an oiled grill rack for about 5 minutes, turning once, until the fruit is lightly charred.
4   Finish the sauce by trickling the honey over the top and sprinkling with cinnamon. Serve with the hot brochettes.

357 PINEAPPLE WEDGES WITH HONEYED RUM

PREPARATION TIME *10 minutes* **COOKING TIME** *5-6 minutes* **SERVES 4**

1 ripe pineapple, peeled and quartered lengthways

2 tbsp dark rum
2 tbsp clear honey
1 tbsp lime juice

1   Cut the core and eyes from the pineapple wedges, then cut the pineapple into 2.5cm (1in) thick triangular slices.
2   Stir the rum, honey and lime juice together until smooth.
3   Brush the pineapple with the honeyed rum and cook on an oiled grill rack, turning once and brushing with the glaze, for 5-6 minutes until lightly caramelised and hot. Serve immediately with any remaining glaze spooned over.

358 FUDGY BANANAS WITH RUM

PREPARATION TIME *5 minutes* **COOKING TIME** *4-5 minutes* **SERVES 4**

4 bananas, peeled

75g (3oz) vanilla fudge, coarsely chopped

4 tbsp rum
vanilla ice cream, to serve

1   Cut a slit along the length of each banana, but don't cut right through.
2   Place each banana on a large square of buttered foil and fill the slits with fudge. Fold up the edges of the foil and pour the rum over the bananas. Twist the edges of the foil together to seal.
3   Grill for 4-5 minutes until heated through. Serve with vanilla ice cream.

359 SLICED COCONUT CAKE WITH CHERRY COMPOTE

PREPARATION TIME *5 minutes* **COOKING TIME** *20 minutes* **SERVES 4**

4 thick slices coconut cake	CHERRY COMPOTE	**1½ tsp caster sugar,**
Greek yogurt, to serve	**450g (1lb) ripe but not**	**or to taste**
	too soft cherries, pitted	**2 tbsp kirsch or brandy**
		1-2 tbsp redcurrant jelly

1 Make the compote by putting the cherries into a saucepan with the caster sugar. Cover the pan and shake over a low heat until the juices begin to run. Add the kirsch or brandy and cook for a further 10 minutes or so until the cherries are soft. Stir in redcurrant jelly, to taste, remove from the heat and leave to cool.

2 Grill the slices of cake until lightly charred. Serve with the compote and Greek yogurt.

360 CHOCOLATE BRIOCHE SANDWICHES

PREPARATION TIME *10 minutes* **COOKING TIME** *5 minutes* **SERVES 4**

8 slices brioche	**150-175g (5-6oz) good-**	**vanilla ice cream, to serve**
good-quality apricot	**quality plain chocolate,**	
conserve, for spreading	**grated**	

1 Spread one side of each brioche slice with conserve. Divide the chocolate among half the apricot-covered slices and cover with the other slices, apricot side down. Press each sandwich together.

2 Cook on an oiled grill rack until the underside is beginning to colour. Turn carefully and repeat on the other side until the chocolate has melted; press gently with a fish slice two or three times.

3 Serve straight away, either on their own or accompanied by vanilla ice cream.

361 TROPICAL FRUIT PARCELS

PREPARATION TIME *15 minutes* **COOKING TIME** *4-5 minutes* **SERVES 4**

4 passion fruit	**2 bananas, thickly sliced**
115g (4oz) lychees, peeled	**5 tbsp elderflower cordial**
and stoned	**2 tbsp white rum (optional)**
flesh from 1 large mango,	**2 sprigs small fresh mint**
sliced, or 1 small to	**leaves**
medium ripe pineapple,	
peeled, cored and sliced	

1 Scoop the seeds and flesh from the passion fruits. Mix with the other fruits. Divide the fruits among four squares of heavy-duty foil large enough to enclose the fruits.

2 Sprinkle with elderflower cordial, and white rum, if using. Reserve a few of the smallest mint leaves and chop the remainder. Add the chopped mint to the fruits. Fold the foil loosely over the fruits and twist the edges together firmly to secure.

3 Put the parcels on the side of a grill rack and cook for 4-5 minutes until heated through. Decorate the fruits with the reserved mint leaves before serving.

362 SUMMER BERRY PARCELS WITH CARDAMOM CREAM

PREPARATION TIME *15 minutes, plus 30 minutes infusion* **COOKING TIME** *4–5 minutes* **SERVES 4**

450g (1lb) prepared mixed red summer fruits, such as ripe but firm strawberries (halved if large), pitted cherries, raspberries, blackberries and blueberries

4 tbsp raspberry eau-de-vie, white rum or peach schnapps
3–4 tbsp golden caster sugar
5 tbsp orange juice
1 tbsp lemon juice

CARDAMOM CREAM
2–3 cardamom pods, split
about 1½ tsp caster sugar, or to taste
300ml (10fl oz) single or whipping cream

1 Make the cream by heating the cardamom and sugar in the cream until it boils. Remove from the heat, cover the pan and leave to infuse for 30 minutes. Strain, cool completely and then chill.

2 Divide the fruits among four squares of heavy-duty foil large enough to enclose the fruits.

3 Warm the eau-de-vie, caster sugar and fruit juices in a small saucepan until the sugar has dissolved. Pour the syrup over the fruits.

4 Fold the foil loosely over the fruits and twist the edges together firmly to secure. Put the parcels on the side of a grill rack and cook for 4–5 minutes until heated through.

5 Taste the cardamom cream for sweetness and serve with the fruit parcels.

363 PINEAPPLE, MANGO, PEAR AND APRICOT KEBABS WITH MAPLE YOGURT SAUCE

PREPARATION TIME *15 minutes* **COOKING TIME** *5 minutes* **SERVES 4**

1 small pineapple, peeled
1 mango, peeled, pitted
   and cut into 2.5cm (1in)
   chunks
1 large ripe but firm pear,
   cored and cut into 2.5cm
   (1in) chunks

4 ripe but firm apricots,
   pitted and quartered
2 tbsp maple syrup
1 tbsp brandy or lemon
   juice

MAPLE YOGURT SAUCE
3-4 tbsp maple syrup
1 tbsp brandy
150ml (5fl oz) yogurt

1   Make the maple yogurt sauce by stirring the maple syrup and brandy into the yogurt. Cover
   and chill until required.
2   Quarter the pineapple lengthways, cut away the core, then cut the flesh into 2.5cm (1in) chunks.
3   Thread all the fruits alternately onto skewers.
4   Combine the maple syrup with the brandy or lemon juice and brush over the fruits. Cook on an
   oiled grill rack for 5 minutes until piping hot and flecked with gold, turning regularly.
5   Serve the kebabs with some of the maple yogurt sauce trickled over. Serve the remaining
   sauce separately.

364 SUMMER FRUIT BRUSCHETTAS

PREPARATION TIME *10 minutes* **COOKING TIME** *3–5 minutes* **SERVES 4**

1 ripe but still firm large peach, pitted and cut into wedges	icing sugar, for sprinkling	unsweetened flaked or shredded coconut, to serve
8 large strawberries	75g (3oz) raspberries	
	4–6 slices brioche	
	115g (4oz) clotted cream*	

1 Halve the peach wedges crossways. Thread onto bamboo skewers that have been soaked in water for 30 minutes. Thread the strawberries onto separate skewers. Sprinkle the peaches and strawberries with icing sugar. Cook on an oiled grill rack for about 3–5 minutes.

2 Meanwhile, put the raspberries onto a piece of foil. Form into a parcel, if liked, and warm on the side of the grill rack. Toast the brioche on the side of the grill rack.

3 Divide the clotted cream among the brioche slices. Slip the strawberries off the skewers onto the clotted cream.

4 Slip the peaches off the skewers onto a plate and cut each wedge into two slices (use a fork to hold the fruit steady if too hot to handle). Divide among the toasts. Scatter over the raspberries. Sprinkle over the coconut and serve.

* If clotted cream is not available, mascarpone can be substituted. Or, for a lighter alternative, use Greek yogurt, regular or low-fat.

365 FRUIT AND NUT BROCHETTES

PREPARATION TIME *15 minutes* **COOKING TIME** *8 minutes* **SERVES 4**

200g (7oz) unsalted butter, chopped	100g (3½oz) shelled pistachios, finely chopped	2 large kiwi fruit, cut into bite-sized cubes
100g (3½oz) soft brown sugar	flesh from 1 pineapple, cored and cut into bite-sized cubes	flesh from 1 papaya, cut into bite-sized cubes
2 tsp cinnamon		100g (3½oz) physalis, husks removed
100g (3½oz) shredded coconut	flesh from 1 mango, cut into bite-sized cubes	

1 Gently heat the butter with the sugar and cinnamon, stirring until the sugar has dissolved. Boil for 1 minute until slightly syrupy.

2 Spread the coconut and pistachios on separate deep plates.

3 Turn the pineapple and the mango separately in the butter, remove with a slotted spoon and allow to drain. Roll the pineapple in the coconut so the cubes are well coated. Roll the mango in the pistachios.

4 Stir the remaining fruit into the rest of the butter.

5 Alternate the fruits on eight skewers. Cook on an oiled grill rack for about 5 minutes, turning frequently, until the nuts are toasted.

INDEX